LONDON DOCKLANDS STREET ATLAS & GUIDE

CONTENTS

A Nicholson Guide

First published 1988

Text by Judy Allen and Jane Carroll
Street Maps by Thames Cartographic Services, Maidenhead
Design by Bob Vickers
Illustrations by Jeremy Ford
Transport Map by Perrott Cartographics

Robert Nicholson Publications
16 Golden Square
London W1R 4BN

Typeset by The Word Shop, Rossendale, Lancs

Printed in Great Britain by Jolly & Barber Ltd, Rugby

ISBN 0 948576 170

88/1/115

KEY TO MAP PAGES 1-12

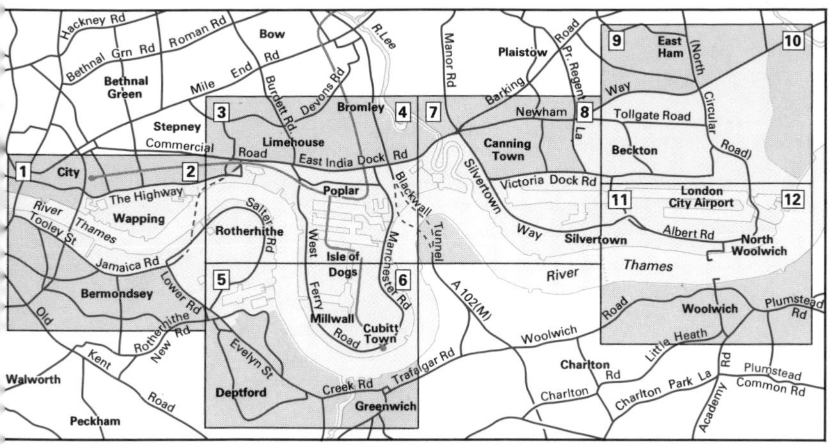

KEY TO MAP SYMBOLS

lain Through Road

ther Roads

/alkway

ne Way Street

estricted Entry

ritish Rail / Station

ocklands Light Railway / Station

ondon Underground / Station

ospital / Health Centre

chool — Sch

hurch

olice Station — Pol

ost Office — PO

ublic Telephone

iblic Convenience — WC

arden/Trees

Land Use Areas

Residential

Industrial / Commercial

Offices

Retail

Media

Sport / Leisure

Parkland / Gardens

Education

Health

Building

Docklands Area Boundary

Borough Boundary

Adjoining Page Number — 4

Page Overlap Area

Non-Docklands Area

½ mile

½ kilometre

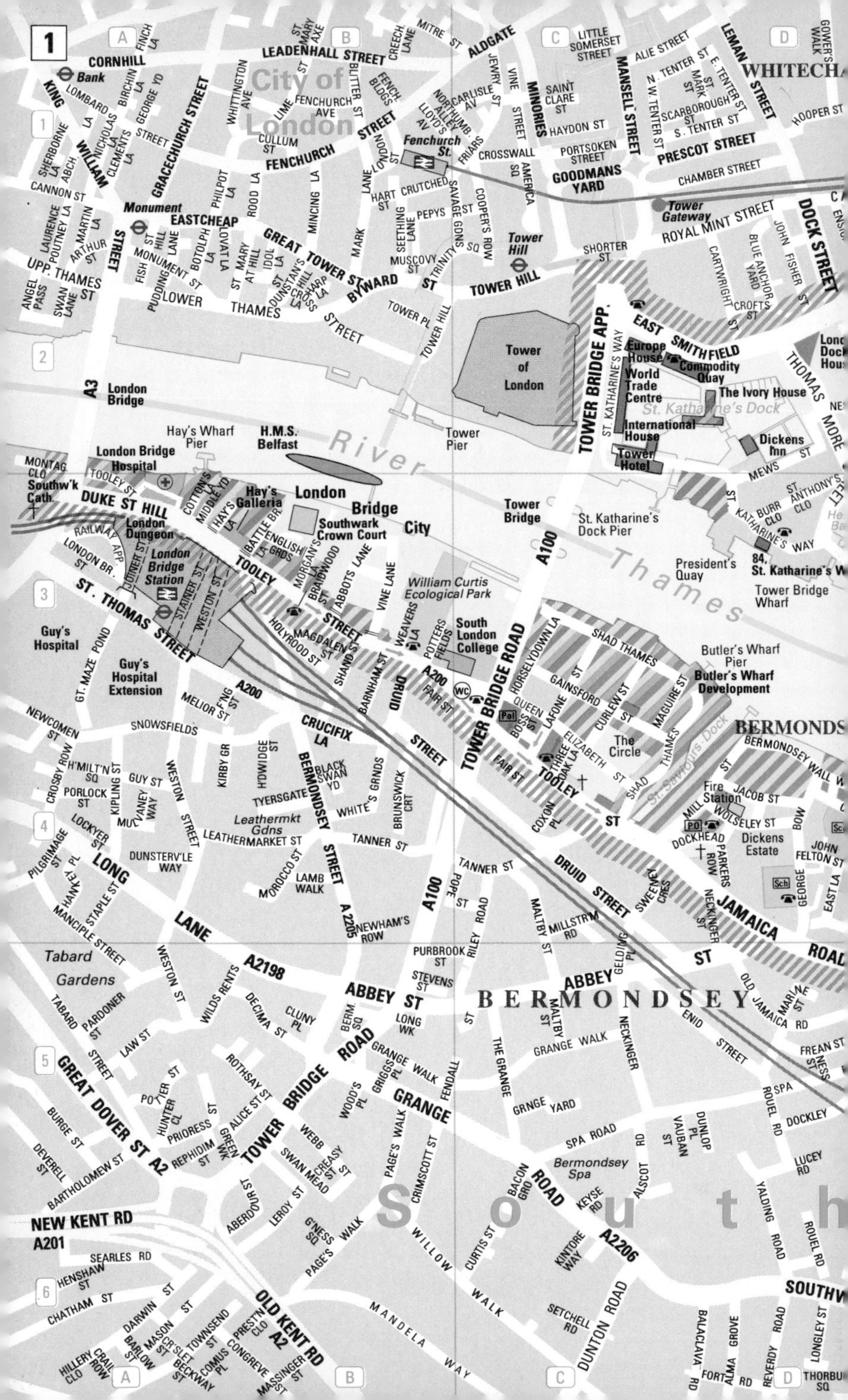
1
A
B
C
D
1
2
3
4
5
6
City of London
LEADENHALL STREET
CORNHILL
Bank
KING WILLIAM
LOMBARD
GRACECHURCH STREET
FENCHURCH STREET
Fenchurch St.
ALDGATE
MITRE ST
LITTLE SOMERSET STREET
ALIE STREET
LEMAN STREET
WHITECHA
MINORIES
MANSELL STREET
PRESCOT STREET
HAYDON ST
CROSSWALL
GOODMANS YARD
CHAMBER STREET
Tower Gateway
ROYAL MINT STREET
DOCK STREET
CANNON ST
Monument
EASTCHEAP
GREAT TOWER ST
BYWARD ST
LOWER THAMES STREET
Tower Hill
TOWER HILL
SHORTER ST
EAST SMITHFIELD
CARTWRIGHT ST
UPP. THAMES ST
Tower of London
TOWER BRIDGE APP.
Europe House
Commodity Quay
World Trade Centre
The Ivory House
St. Katharine's Dock
International House
Tower Hotel
Dickens Inn
THOMAS MORE ST
A3
London Bridge
Hay's Wharf Pier
H.M.S. Belfast
River Thames
Tower Pier
London Bridge Hospital
MONTAG. CLO
Southw'k Cath.
TOOLEY ST
DUKE ST HILL
Hay's Galleria
London Bridge City
Southwark Crown Court
Tower Bridge
St. Katharine's Dock Pier
London Dungeon
London Bridge Station
A100
President's Quay
84, St. Katharine's Way
Tower Bridge Wharf
ST. THOMAS STREET
William Curtis Ecological Park
South London College
Guy's Hospital
Guy's Hospital Extension
TOWER BRIDGE ROAD
SHAD THAMES
Butler's Wharf Pier
Butler's Wharf Development
BERMONDS
A200
SNOWSFIELDS
CRUCIFIX LA
DRUID STREET
The Circle
St. Saviour's Dock
BERMONDSEY WALL W
Fire Station
JACOB ST
WOLSELEY ST
Dickens Estate
BERMONDSEY STREET
Leathermkt Gdns
LEATHERMARKET ST
TANNER ST
LONG LANE
JAMAICA ROAD
A2205
A2198
Tabard Gardens
ABBEY ST
BERMONDSEY
GRANGE WALK
GRANGE ROAD
GREAT DOVER ST A2
TOWER BRIDGE ROAD
SPA ROAD
Bermondsey Spa
NEW KENT RD A201
OLD KENT RD A2
A2206
South
MANDELA WAY
WILLOW WALK
DUNTON ROAD
SOUTHW

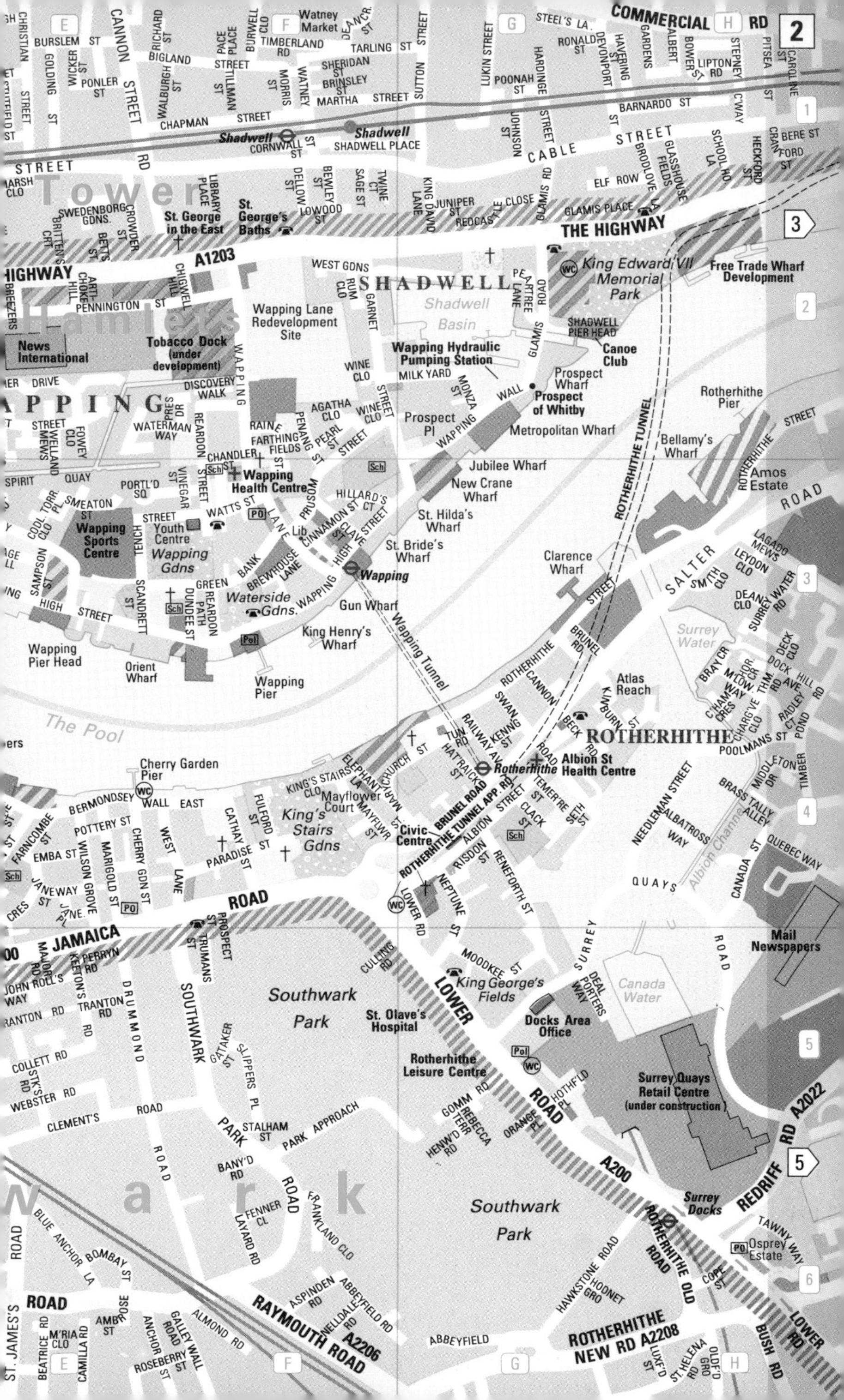
2
COMMERCIAL RD
CANNON STREET
Watney Market
TIMBERLAND RD
TARLING ST
SHERIDAN ST
BRINSLEY ST
MARTHA STREET
SUTTON STREET
BURSLEM ST
BIGLAND ST
PONLER ST
CHAPMAN STREET
Shadwell
Shadwell
CORNWALL ST
SHADWELL PLACE
LUKIN STREET
POONAH ST
JOHNSON ST
HARDINGE STREET
BARNARDO ST
CABLE STREET
ELF ROW
GLASSHOUSE FIELDS
SCHOOL HO LA
HECKFORD ST
BERE ST
Tower
Hamlets
St. George in the East
St. George's Baths
THE HIGHWAY
HIGHWAY
A1203
SWEDENBORG GDNS.
GLAMIS PLACE
GLAMIS RD
JUNIPER ST
REDCASTLE CLOSE
WEST GDNS
SHADWELL
Shadwell Basin
King Edward VII Memorial Park
Free Trade Wharf Development
SHADWELL PIER HEAD
Canoe Club
PENNINGTON ST
News International
Tobacco Dock (under development)
Wapping Lane Redevelopment Site
Wapping Hydraulic Pumping Station
MILK YARD
WAPPING WALL
Prospect Wharf
Prospect of Whitby
Metropolitan Wharf
Rotherhithe Pier
Bellamy's Wharf
ROTHERHITHE TUNNEL
Amos Estate
ROTHERHITHE STREET
WAPPING
DISCOVERY WALK
WATERMAN WAY
AGATHA CLO
PROSPECT PL
Jubilee Wharf
New Crane Wharf
St. Hilda's Wharf
St. Bride's Wharf
Wapping Health Centre
SPIRIT QUAY
Wapping Sports Centre
Youth Centre
Wapping Gdns
WATTS ST
CINNAMON ST
Wapping
Clarence Wharf
SALTER ROAD
Waterside Gdns.
Gun Wharf
King Henry's Wharf
Wapping Tunnel
WAPPING HIGH STREET
Surrey Water
Wapping Pier Head
Orient Wharf
Wapping Pier
The Pool
Atlas Reach
ROTHERHITHE
Cherry Garden Pier
BERMONDSEY WALL EAST
King's Stairs Gdns
Mayflower Court
Rotherhithe
Albion St Health Centre
BRUNEL ROAD
ROTHERHITHE TUNNEL APP. RD
Civic Centre
NEEDLEMAN STREET
Albion Channel
QUAYS
QUEBEC WAY
CANADA ST
JAMAICA ROAD
LOWER ROAD
SOUTHWARK PARK ROAD
Southwark Park
St. Olave's Hospital
King George's Fields
Docks Area Office
Canada Water
Mail Newspapers
Rotherhithe Leisure Centre
Surrey Quays Retail Centre (under construction)
REDRIFF RD A2022
5
A200
Surrey Docks
Southwark Park
Osprey Estate
ROTHERHITHE OLD ROAD
HAWKSTONE ROAD
RAYMOUTH ROAD A2206
ROTHERHITHE NEW RD A2208
LOWER RD
BUSH RD
ABBEYFIELD
BLUE ANCHOR LA
ST. JAMES'S ROAD
wark

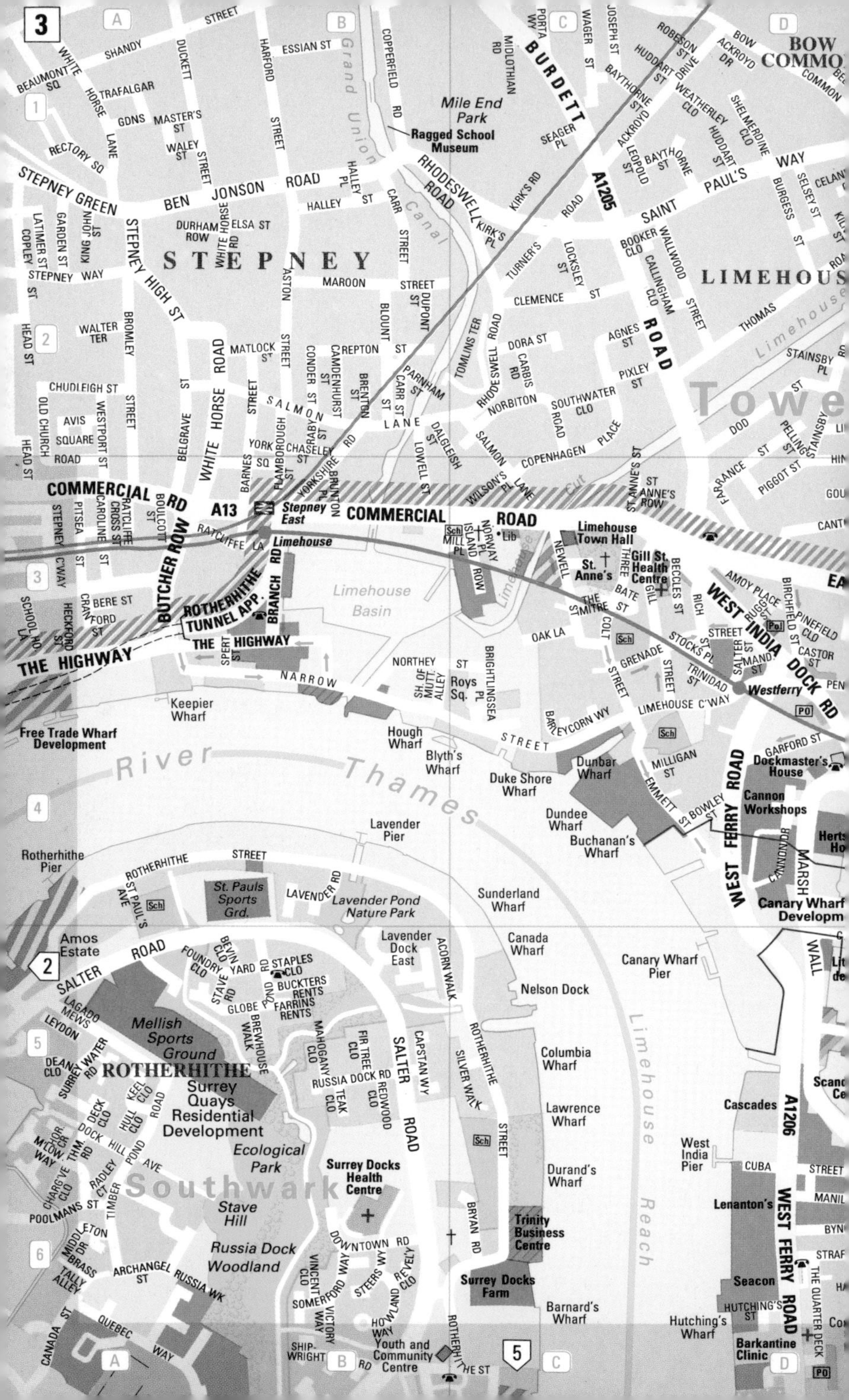
A
B
C
D
1
2
3
4
5
6
BOW COMMON
STEPNEY
LIMEHOUSE
Tower
Southwark
ROTHERHITHE
River Thames
Grand Union Canal
Limehouse Cut
Limehouse Basin
Limehouse Reach
Mile End Park
Ragged School Museum
BEAUMONT SQ
WHITE HORSE LANE
SHANDY STREET
TRAFALGAR GDNS
MASTER'S ST
WALEY ST
DUCKETT STREET
HARFORD STREET
ESSIAN ST
COPPERFIELD RD
RECTORY SQ
STEPNEY GREEN
BEN JONSON ROAD
HALLEY PL
HALLEY ST
CARR STREET
RHODESWELL ROAD
DURHAM ROW
ELSA ST
WHITE HORSE RD
KING JOHN ST
GARDEN ST
LATIMER ST
COPLEY ST
STEPNEY WAY
STEPNEY HIGH ST
ASTON STREET
MAROON STREET
DUPONT ST
BLOUNT ST
HEAD ST
WALTER TER
BROMLEY STREET
MATLOCK ST
CONDER ST
CAMDENHURST ST
REPTON ST
BRENTON ST
PARNHAM ST
CHUDLEIGH ST
OLD CHURCH ROAD
WESTPORT ST
AVIS SQUARE
BELGRAVE ST
WHITE HORSE ROAD
SALMON LANE
YORK SQ
CHASELEY ST
RABY ST
FLAMBOROUGH ST
BARNES ST
YORKSHIRE RD
BRUNTON PL
LOWELL ST
DALGLEISH ST
COMMERCIAL RD
A13
Stepney East
COMMERCIAL ROAD
BOULCOTT ST
RATCLIFFE CROSS ST
CAROLINE ST
PITSEA ST
STEPNEY C'WAY
BUTCHER ROW
RATCLIFFE LA
Limehouse
BRANCH RD
ROTHERHITHE TUNNEL APP.
BERE ST
CRANFORD ST
HECKFORD ST
SCHOOL HO LA
THE HIGHWAY
SPERT ST
NARROW STREET
Keepier Wharf
Free Trade Wharf Development
MIDLOTHIAN RD
PORTA WY
BURDETT ROAD
A1205
WAGER ST
JOSEPH ST
ROBESON ST
HUDDART ST
BAYTHORNE ST
ACKROYD DR
BOW COMMON
HUDDART DRIVE
WEATHERLEY CLO
SHELMERDINE CLO
SEAGER PL
ACKROYD ST
LEOPOLD ST
BAYTHORNE ST
HUDDART ST
SAINT PAUL'S WAY
BURGESS ST
SELSEY ST
KIRK'S RD
KIRK'S PL
TURNER'S RD
LOCKSLEY ST
BOOKER CLO
WALLWOOD STREET
CALLINGHAM CLO
CLEMENCE ST
THOMAS
TOMLINS TER
RHODESWELL ROAD
DORA ST
CARBIS RD
AGNES ST
PIXLEY ST
STAINSBY PL
NORBITON
SOUTHWATER CLO
ROAD
COPENHAGEN PLACE
SALMON LANE
WILSON'S PL
ST ANNE'S ST
ST ANNE'S ROW
DOD ST
PELLING ST
STAINSBY
FARRANCE ST
PIGGOT ST
MILL PL
NORWAY PL
ISLAND ROW
Lib
Limehouse Town Hall
St. Anne's
Gill St. Health Centre
THREE COLT STREET
NEWELL ST
BATE ST
GILL ST
BECCLES ST
RICH ST
THE MITRE
AMOY PLACE
BIRCHFIELD ST
PINEFIELD CLO
RUGG ST
WEST INDIA DOCK RD
CASTOR ST
MAND. ST
SALTER ST
STOCKS PL
TRINIDAD ST
OAK LA
GRENADE STREET
NORTHEY ST
SH. OF MUTT. ALLEY
Roys Sq.
BRIGHTLINGSEA PL
LIMEHOUSE C'WAY
Westferry
BARLEYCORN WY
Hough Wharf
Blyth's Wharf
Duke Shore Wharf
Dunbar Wharf
MILLIGAN ST
EMMETT ST
BOWLEY ST
GARFORD ST
Dockmaster's House
Cannon Workshops
WEST FERRY ROAD
Dundee Wharf
Buchanan's Wharf
CANNON DR
MARSH WALL
Canary Wharf Developm
Lavender Pier
Rotherhithe Pier
ROTHERHITHE STREET
ST PAUL'S AVE
St. Pauls Sports Grd.
LAVENDER RD
Lavender Pond Nature Park
Sunderland Wharf
Canada Wharf
Canary Wharf Pier
Amos Estate
SALTER ROAD
BEVIN CLO
FOUNDRY CLO
YARD
STAPLES CLO
STAVE RD
POND RD
BUCKTERS RENTS
FARRINS RENTS
GLOBE
Lavender Dock East
ACORN WALK
Nelson Dock
LAGADO MEWS
LEYDON
Mellish Sports Ground
BREWHOUSE WALK
MAHOGANY CLO
FIR TREE CLO
SALTER ROAD
CAPSTAN WY
SILVER WALK
ROTHERHITHE STREET
Columbia Wharf
DEANEY CLO
SURREY WATER RD
KEEL CLO
Surrey Quays Residential Development
RUSSIA DOCK RD
TEAK CLO
REDWOOD CLO
Lawrence Wharf
Cascades
A1206
DECK CLO
HULL CLO
DOCK HILL AVE
ECOLOGICAL Park
Durand's Wharf
West India Pier
CUBA STREET
M'LOW. WAY
HORNBEAM RD
THM. RD
RADLEY CT
POND
Surrey Docks Health Centre
Lenanton's
WEST FERRY ROAD
CHARG'VE CLO
TIMBER
POOLMANS ST
Stave Hill
BRYAN RD
Trinity Business Centre
MIDDLETON DR
BRASS TALLY ALLEY
ARCHANGEL ST
RUSSIA WK
Russia Dock Woodland
DOWNTOWN RD
VINCENT CLO
STEERS WAY
REVELY CLO
SOMERFORD WAY
VICTORY WAY
HOWLAND WAY
Surrey Docks Farm
Barnard's Wharf
Seacon
HUTCHING'S ST
Hutching's Wharf
THE QUARTER DECK
Barkantine Clinic
CANADA ST
QUEBEC WAY
SHIP-WRIGHT RD
Youth and Community Centre
ROTHERHITHE ST
Sch
PO
Pol
2
5

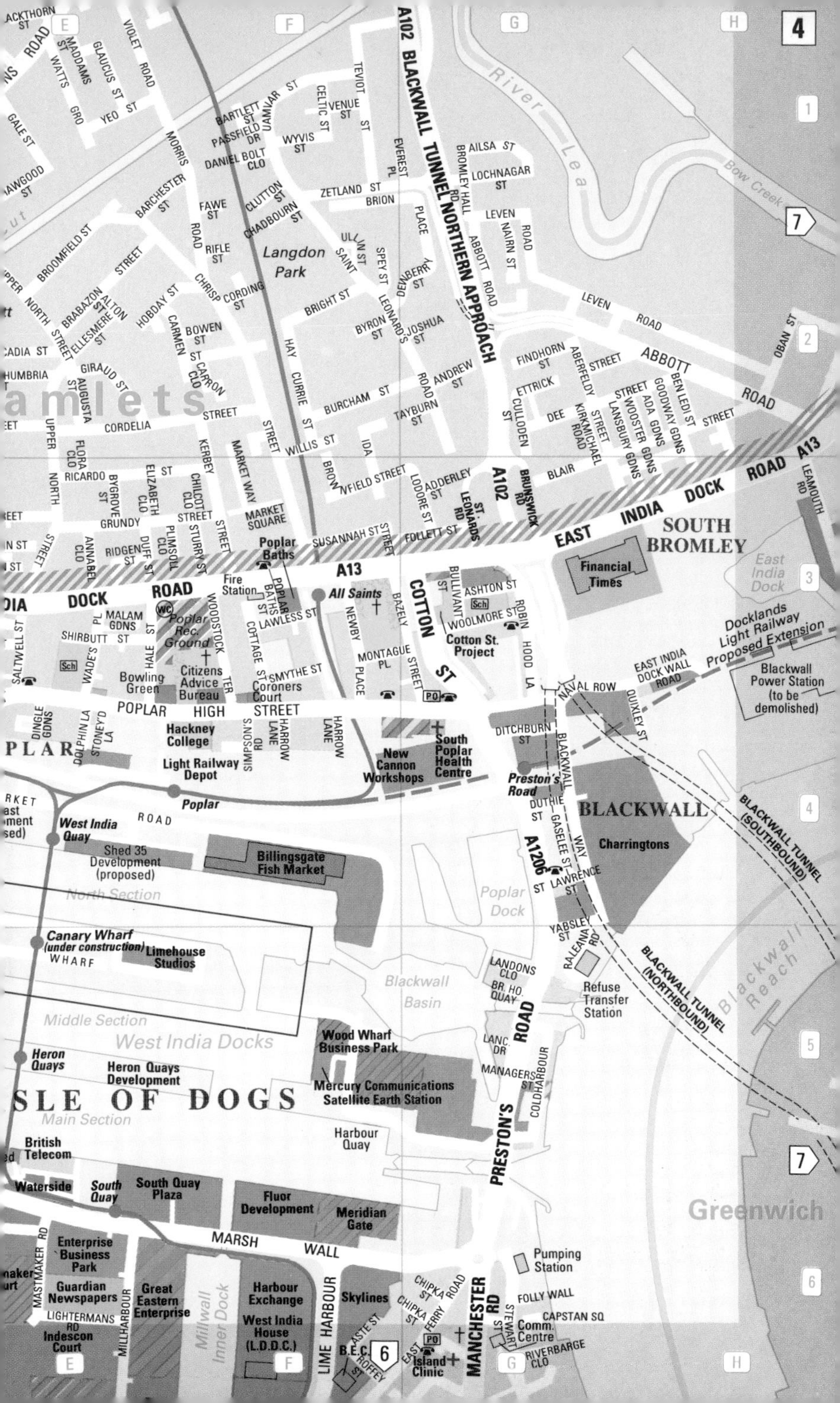
E
F
G
H
A102 BLACKWALL TUNNEL NORTHERN APPROACH
River Lea
Bow Creek
Langdon Park
LEVEN ROAD
ABBOTT ROAD
EAST INDIA DOCK ROAD
A13
SOUTH BROMLEY
Financial Times
East India Dock
Docklands Light Railway Proposed Extension
Blackwall Power Station (to be demolished)
POPLAR HIGH STREET
All Saints
Poplar Baths
Fire Station
Poplar Rec. Ground
Citizens Advice Bureau
Coroners Court
Bowling Green
COTTON ST
Cotton St. Project
Hackney College
Light Railway Depot
New Cannon Workshops
South Poplar Health Centre
Preston's Road
Poplar
West India Quay
BLACKWALL
Charringtons
BLACKWALL TUNNEL (SOUTHBOUND)
BLACKWALL TUNNEL (NORTHBOUND)
A1206
Shed 35 Development (proposed)
Billingsgate Fish Market
North Section
Canary Wharf (under construction)
Limehouse Studios
Poplar Dock
Blackwall Basin
Refuse Transfer Station
Blackwall Reach
Middle Section
West India Docks
Heron Quays
Heron Quays Development
Wood Wharf Business Park
Mercury Communications Satellite Earth Station
ISLE OF DOGS
Main Section
Harbour Quay
PRESTON'S ROAD
British Telecom
Waterside
South Quay
South Quay Plaza
Fluor Development
Meridian Gate
MARSH WALL
Greenwich
Enterprise Business Park
Guardian Newspapers
Great Eastern Enterprise
Millwall Inner Dock
Harbour Exchange
West India House (L.D.D.C.)
Skylines
LIME HARBOUR
MANCHESTER RD
Pumping Station
Island Clinic
Comm. Centre
Indescon Court
B.E.C.
1
2
3
4
5
6
7
6

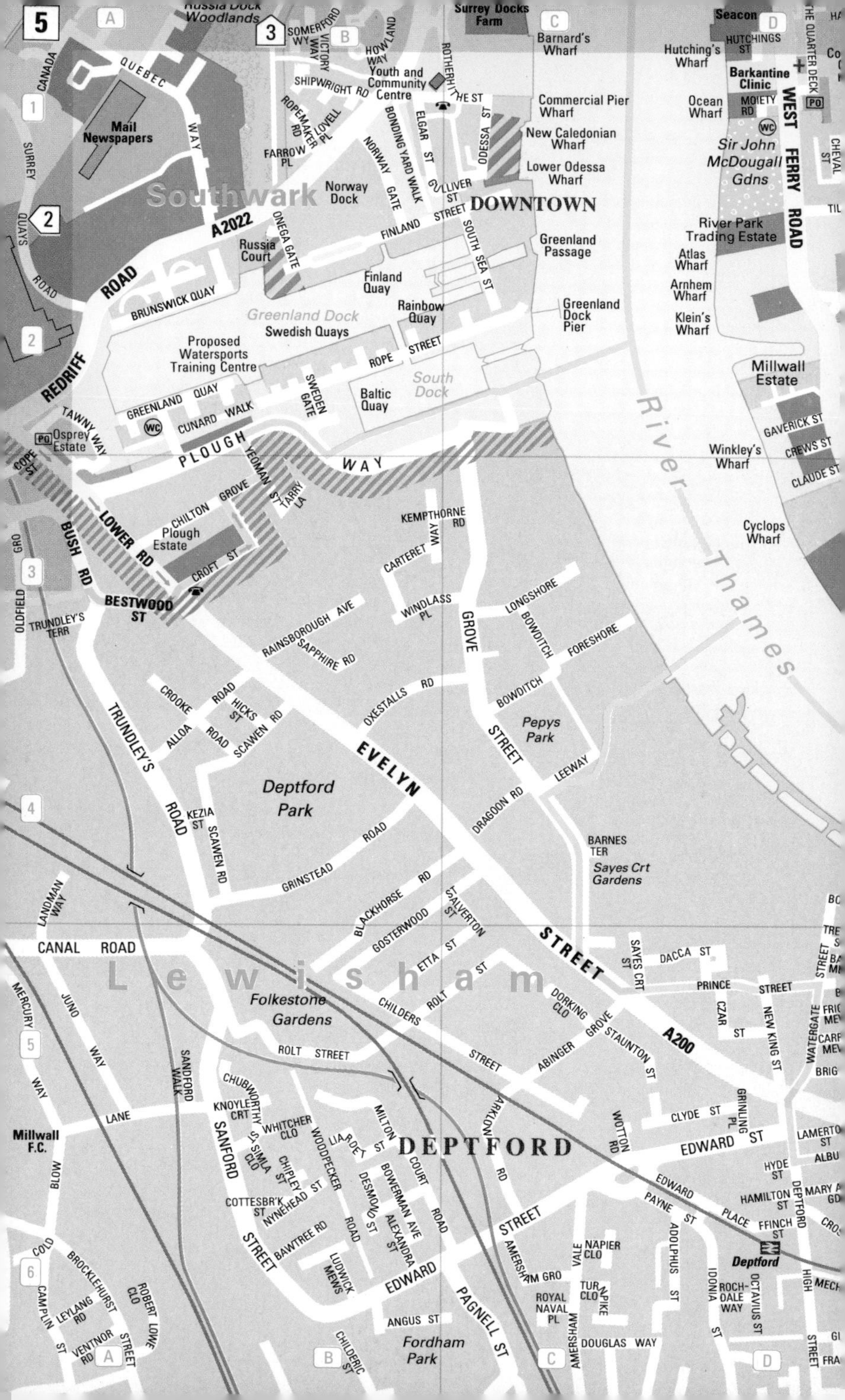
Russia Dock Woodlands
Surrey Docks Farm
Seacon
Barnard's Wharf
Hutching's Wharf
HUTCHINGS ST
Youth and Community Centre
Barkantine Clinic
Commercial Pier Wharf
Ocean Wharf
MOIETY RD
WEST FERRY ROAD
Mail Newspapers
New Caledonian Wharf
Sir John McDougall Gdns
Lower Odessa Wharf
Southwark
Norway Dock
DOWNTOWN
A2022
Russia Court
River Park Trading Estate
Greenland Passage
Atlas Wharf
Finland Quay
Arnhem Wharf
BRUNSWICK QUAY
Rainbow Quay
Greenland Dock Pier
Greenland Dock
Klein's Wharf
Swedish Quays
REDRIFF
Proposed Watersports Training Centre
Millwall Estate
South Dock
Baltic Quay
GREENLAND QUAY
CUNARD WALK
Osprey Estate
PLOUGH WAY
River Thames
Winkley's Wharf
LOWER RD
Plough Estate
Cyclops Wharf
BUSH RD
BESTWOOD ST
EVELYN STREET
Pepys Park
Deptford Park
TRUNDLEY'S ROAD
Sayes Crt Gardens
CANAL ROAD
Lewisham
Folkestone Gardens
A200
DEPTFORD
Millwall F.C.
Deptford
Fordham Park

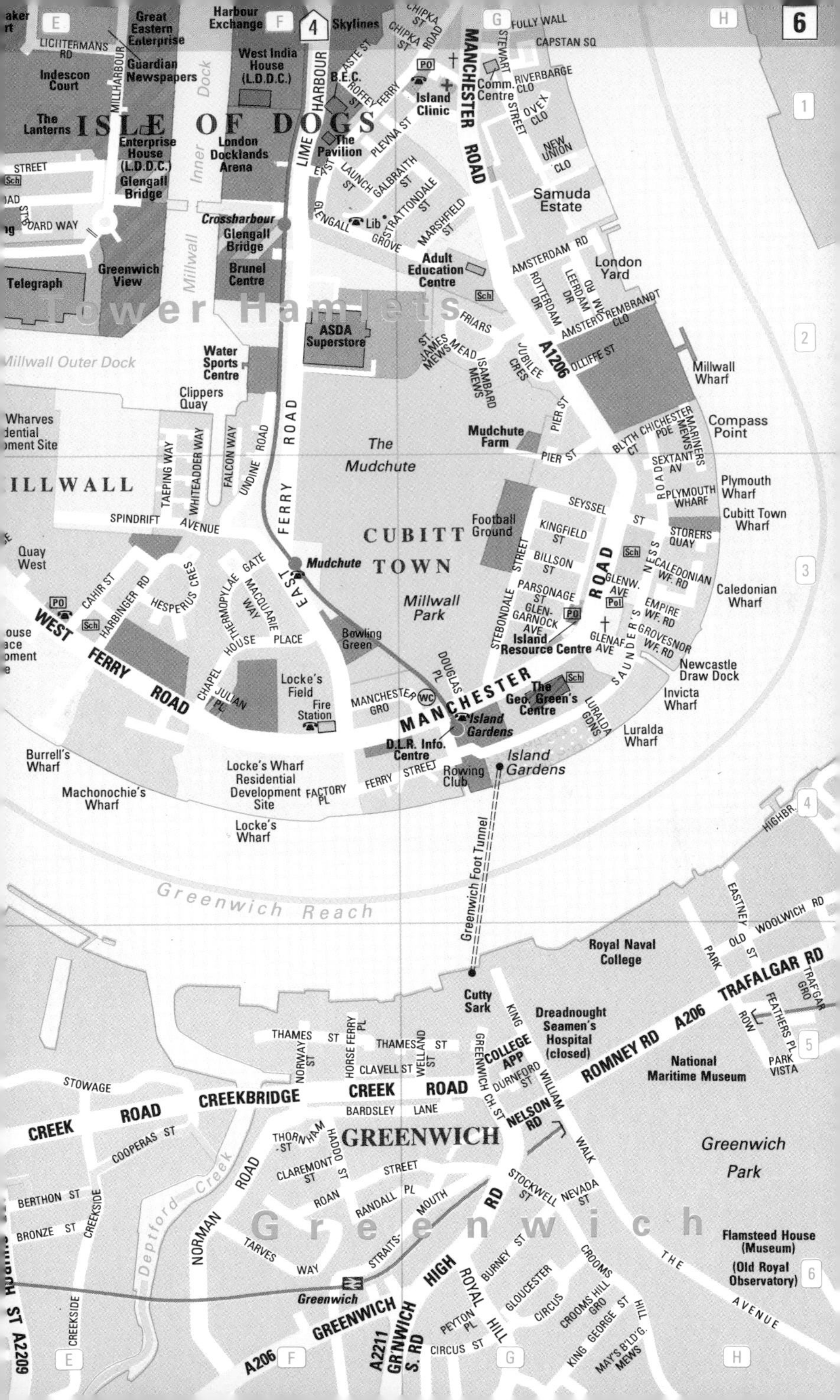
ISLE OF DOGS
Harbour Exchange
Great Eastern Enterprise
Guardian Newspapers
Skylines
Indescon Court
West India House (L.D.D.C.)
Island Clinic
Comm. Centre
The Lanterns
Enterprise House (L.D.D.C.)
London Docklands Arena
The Pavilion
Glengall Bridge
Crossharbour
Samuda Estate
Greenwich View
Brunel Centre
Adult Education Centre
London Yard
Telegraph
Tower Hamlets
ASDA Superstore
Millwall Outer Dock
Water Sports Centre
Clippers Quay
Millwall Wharf
Compass Point
The Mudchute
Mudchute Farm
MILLWALL
Plymouth Wharf
Cubitt Town Wharf
Football Ground
CUBITT TOWN
Mudchute
Quay West
Millwall Park
Caledonian Wharf
Bowling Green
Island Resource Centre
Newcastle Draw Dock
Locke's Field
Fire Station
The Geo. Green's Centre
Invicta Wharf
Island Gardens
D.L.R. Info. Centre
Luralda Wharf
Burrell's Wharf
Locke's Wharf Residential Development Site
Rowing Club
Machonochie's Wharf
Locke's Wharf
Greenwich Foot Tunnel
Greenwich Reach
Royal Naval College
Cutty Sark
Dreadnought Seamen's Hospital (closed)
National Maritime Museum
GREENWICH
Greenwich Park
Greenwich
Flamsteed House (Museum)
(Old Royal Observatory)
WEST FERRY ROAD
EAST FERRY ROAD
MANCHESTER ROAD
A1206
CREEK ROAD
CREEKBRIDGE
ROMNEY RD
A206
TRAFALGAR RD
NELSON RD
GREENWICH HIGH RD
A2211
ROYAL HILL
NORMAN ROAD
THE AVENUE
Deptford Creek

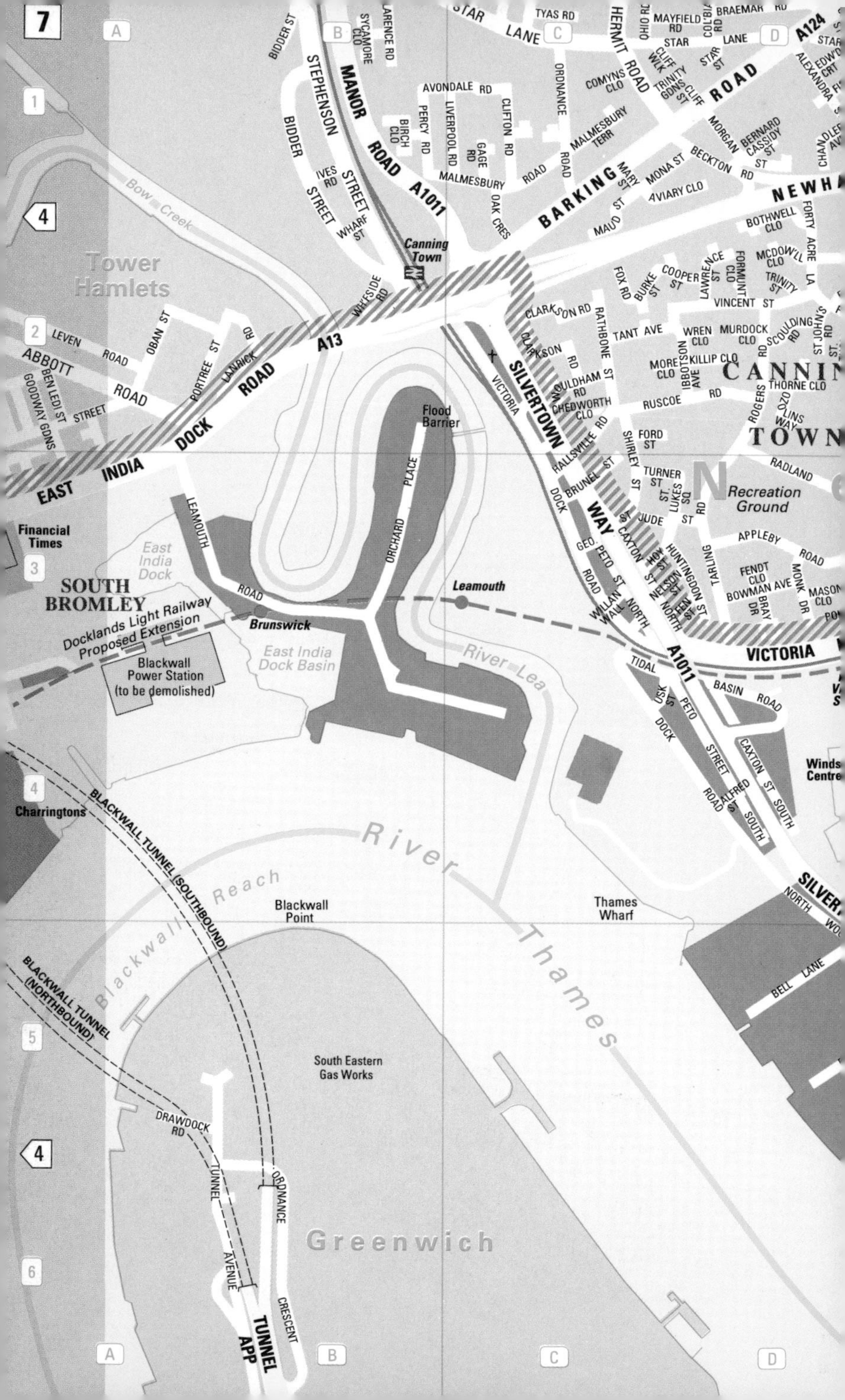

Tower Hamlets
Bow Creek
Canning Town
SOUTH BROMLEY
Financial Times
East India Dock
Docklands Light Railway Proposed Extension
Brunswick
Leamouth
Blackwall Power Station (to be demolished)
East India Dock Basin
Flood Barrier
River Lea
River Thames
Blackwall Reach
Blackwall Point
Thames Wharf
Charringtons
BLACKWALL TUNNEL (SOUTHBOUND)
BLACKWALL TUNNEL (NORTHBOUND)
South Eastern Gas Works
Greenwich
CANNING TOWN
Recreation Ground
Windsor Centre
EAST INDIA DOCK ROAD
A13
BARKING ROAD
A124
NEWHAM
MANOR ROAD
A1011
STAR LANE
HERMIT ROAD
STEPHENSON STREET
BIDDER STREET
BIDDER ST
IVES RD
WHARF ST
WHARFSIDE RD
SYCAMORE CLO
AVONDALE RD
LIVERPOOL RD
PERCY RD
BIRCH CLO
GAGE RD
CLIFTON RD
MALMESBURY ROAD
MALMESBURY TERR
OAK CRES
ORDNANCE ROAD
COMYNS CLO
TYAS RD
OHIO RD
MAYFIELD RD
COLBIA RD
BRAEMAR RD
CLIFF WLK
TRINITY GDNS
CLIFF ST
STAR ST
MORGAN ST
BERNARD CASSIDY ST
BECKTON RD
MARY ST
MONA ST
AVIARY CLO
MAUD ST
BOTHWELL CLO
FORTY ACRE LA
FOX RD
BURKE ST
COOPER ST
LAWRENCE ST
FORMUNT CLO
MCDOWALL CLO
TRINITY ST
VINCENT ST
CLARKSON RD
CLARKSON
RATHBONE ST
TANT AVE
WREN CLO
MURDOCK CLO
SCOULDING RD
ST JOHN'S RD
MORETON CLO
IBBOTSON AVE
KILLIP CLO
THORNE CLO
WOULDHAM RD
CHEDWORTH CLO
RUSCOE RD
ROGERS RD
LINS WAY
HALLSVILLE RD
SHIRLEY ST
FORD ST
TURNER ST
ST. LUKES SQ
RADLAND RD
SILVERTOWN WAY
VICTORIA DOCK ROAD
BRUNEL ST
JUDE ST
CAXTON ST
HOY ST
NELSON ST
HUNTINGDON ST
FEN ST
TARLING ST
APPLEBY ROAD
FENDT CLO
BOWMAN AVE
BRAY DR
MONK DR
MASON CLO
GEO. PETO ST
WILLAN WALL
NORTH ST
TIDAL BASIN ROAD
USK ST
PETO STREET
DOCK ROAD
ALFRED ST
CAXTON ST SOUTH
SOUTH
BELL LANE
LEVEN ROAD
ABBOTT ROAD
OBAN ST
PORTREE ST
LANRICK RD
BEN LEDI ST
GOODWAY GDNS
STREET
LEAMOUTH ROAD
ORCHARD PLACE
DRAWDOCK RD
TUNNEL AVENUE
ORDNANCE CRESCENT
TUNNEL APP

8
E
F
G
H
TINTO RD
CARSON ROAD
CAMBUS RD
DOUGLAS RD
RAVENSCROFT RD
NEW BARN STREET
DENM'K
ECLIPSE RD
CUMBERLAND ST
WESTP RD
PALMER ROAD
HOLBORN
JONES RD
ROAD
CRANLEY RD
BROCK RD
SELBY RD
CHADWIN ROAD
EGHAM RD
BOTHA RD
ALLIANCE RD
CHALK RD
A112 PR. REGENT LA
BENNETT RD
McMillan Stadium
NEWHAM WAY
RIDGWELL ROAD
MACGREGOR RD
TRIANGLE CRT
SULLIVAN AVE
HEATHFIELD CLO
HOGARTH CLO
The Chestnuts
FIRBANK CLO
SHEERWATER ROAD
FLEETWOOD CLO
GOLDCR. CLO
Sch
TOLLGATE ROAD
WAY
A13
WATFORD RD
LOWE AVE
CHARFORD RD
BEEBY RD
Canning Town Recreation Ground
FREEMASONS ROAD
COLMAN ROAD
GIRALDA CLO
HICKMAN CLO
9
FULMER
P'TRIDGE CLO
STANSFIELD RD
West Beckton Health Centre
VANB. CLO
ST MICHAEL'S CLO
TEAL CLO
LONG MARK RD
LAWSON CLO
PRINCE REGENT LANE
ILKLEY RD
BURLEY RD
OTLEY RD
NOTTINGHAM AVENUE
CROOMBS RD
YOUNG RD
BECKTON
HIGHM'DS RD
BROADGATE RD
2
CLINCH CRT
S. MOLTON RD
BRENT RD
ROAD
SOPHIA RD
SARK WALK
JERSEY RD
MORTLAKE ROAD
VARLEY ROAD
BINGLEY RD
RIPLEY RD
WILKINSON RD
HOSKINS CLO
King George V Park
Newham City Farm
RUSSELL RD
HAND'S WALK
BURRARD RD
BUTCHER'S ROAD
MAPLIN RD
LAMBERT ROAD
DEVONSHIRE RD
GARVARY RD
ARGYLE RD
TREE RD
CHURCHILL ROAD
RANDOLPH APP
BAXTER RD
KING GEORGE AVENUE
Albert Dock Hospital
CASPIAN WK
KERRY CLO
HARTINGTON RD
HOOPER RD
VANDOME CLO
GRESHAM RD
THROCKMORTEN ROAD
SHIPMAN RD
FORTIS CLO
ALNWICK ROAD
PRINCE OF WALES RD
FELSTED RD
TASMAN WK
S'GASSO CLO
BERING WLK
Sch
DAMSON RD
BRIDGELAND ROAD
COOLFIN ROAD
LESLIE RD
BERWICK ROAD
CUNDY RD
A112
ROYAL ROAD
3
ELBURY DR
NORMANDY TERR
ETHEL RD
WOOD ST
BETTS RD
LEYES ROAD
MURRAY SQ
Allotments
A1010
VICTORIA DOCK ROAD
CONNAUGHT ROAD
Custom House
Custom House
Prince Regent Lane
Connaught
Royal Docks Area Office
A112
4
CONNAUGHT RD
Royal Victoria Dock
Millenium Quay
Barnwood Court Estate
EVELYN RD
WESTWOOD RD
Sch
HANAMEEL ST
BOXLEY ST
PO
PIRIE ST
FORT ST
MILL RD
Pontoon Dock
Charles St Trading Estate
BURT RD
CHARLES ST
SILVERTOWN BY-PASS
St. Marks Industrial Estate
NORTH WOOLWICH ROAD
A1011
5
Fire Station
THAMES ROAD
Green Shield Industrial Estate
KNIGHT'S ROAD
BRADFIELD ROAD
SILVERTOWN
11
Lyle Park
6
Thames Flood Barrier
E
F
G
H

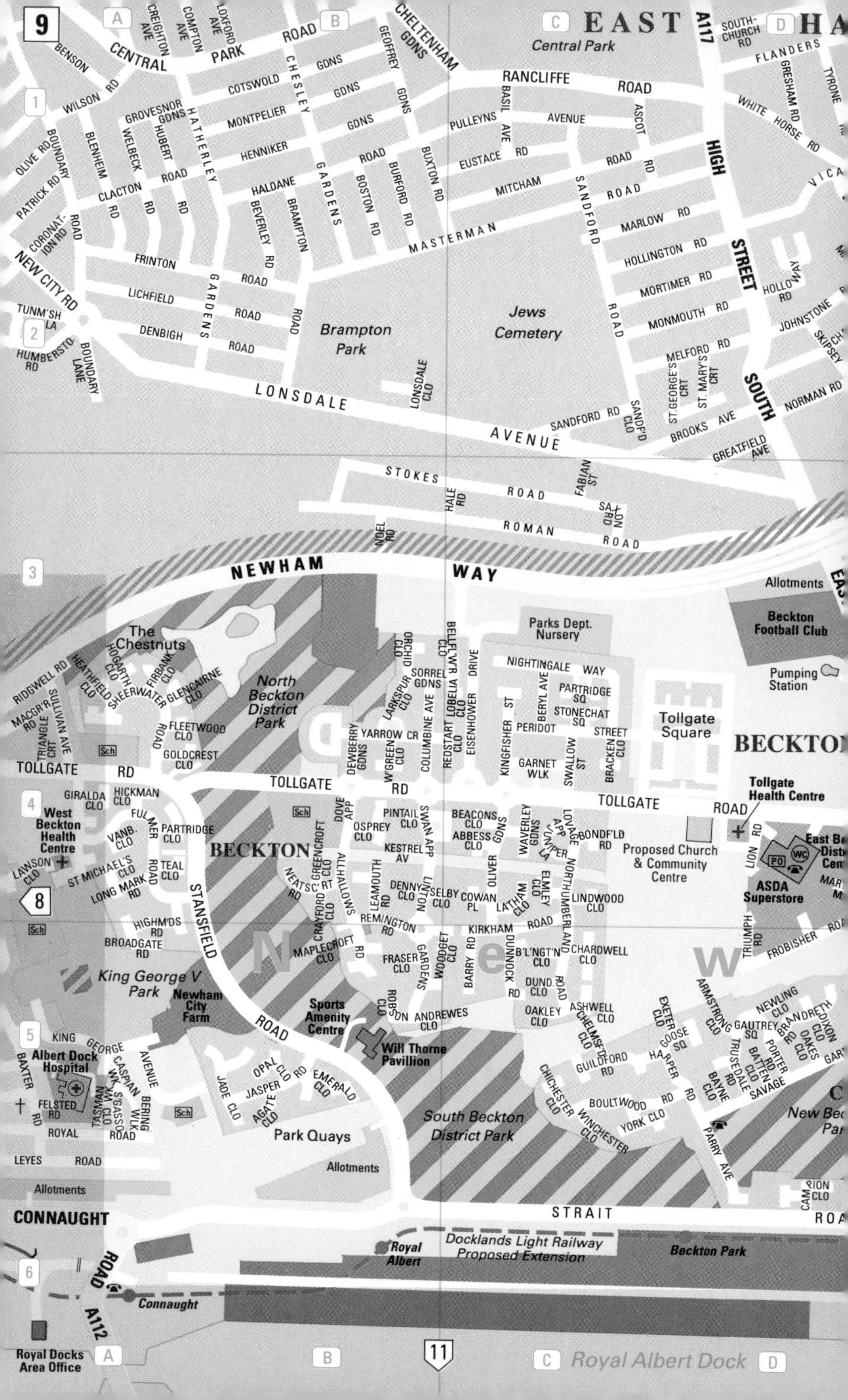
9
EAST HA
Central Park
A117
SOUTH-CHURCH RD
FLANDERS
TYRONE
GRESHAM RD
WHITE HORSE RD
BENSON
CENTRAL PARK ROAD
CREIGHTON AVE
COMPTON AVE
LOXFORD AVE
CHELTENHAM GDNS
GEOFFREY GDNS
RANCLIFFE ROAD
WILSON RD
COTSWOLD GDNS
CHESLEY
MONTPELIER GDNS
GROVESNOR GDNS
HATHERLEY
HENNIKER GDNS
BASIL AVE
PULLEYNS AVENUE
ASCOT RD
EUSTACE RD
ROAD
HIGH STREET
OLIVE RD
BOUNDARY ROAD
BLENHEIM RD
WELBECK RD
HUBERT RD
CLACTON ROAD
HALDANE
GARDENS
BOSTON RD
BURFORD RD
BUXTON RD
MITCHAM ROAD
SANDFORD ROAD
VICA
PATRICK RD
CORONATION RD
BEVERLEY RD
BRAMPTON
MASTERMAN
MARLOW RD
HOLLINGTON RD
MORTIMER RD
HOLLOWAY RD
NEW CITY RD
FRINTON ROAD
LICHFIELD ROAD
GARDENS
ROAD
Brampton Park
Jews Cemetery
MONMOUTH RD
JOHNSTONE
SKIPSEY
TUNM'SH LA
DENBIGH ROAD
MELFORD RD
HUMBERSTO. RD
BOUNDARY LANE
LONSDALE CLO
ST. GEORGE'S CRT
ST. MARY'S CRT
LONSDALE AVENUE
SANDFORD RD
SANDF'D CLO
BROOKS AVE
SOUTH
NORMAN RD
GREATFIELD AVE
STOKES ROAD
HALE RD
FABIAN ST
SAXON RD
NOEL RD
ROMAN ROAD
NEWHAM WAY
Allotments
Beckton Football Club
Pumping Station
The Chestnuts
North Beckton District Park
Parks Dept. Nursery
ORCHID CLO
BELLFLOW'R CLO
SORREL GDNS
LARKSPUR CLO
LOBELIA CLO
EISENHOWER DRIVE
NIGHTINGALE WAY
BERYL AVE
PARTRIDGE SQ
STONECHAT SQ
Tollgate Square
BECKTON
RIDGWELL RD
HEATHFIELD CLO
HOGARTH CLO
FIRBANK CLO
SHEERWATER
GLENCAIRNE CLO
MACGR'R CLO
SULLIVAN AVE
TRIANGLE CRT
FLEETWOOD CLO
GOLDCREST CLO
ROAD
Sch
DEWBERRY GDNS
YARROW CR
W'GREEN CLO
COLUMBINE AVE
REDSTART CLO
KINGFISHER ST
PERIDOT
STREET
BRACKEN CLO
GARNET WLK
SWALLOW ST
TOLLGATE RD
TOLLGATE RD
TOLLGATE ROAD
Tollgate Health Centre
GIRALDA CLO
HICKMAN CLO
West Beckton Health Centre
FULMER ROAD
PARTRIDGE CLO
VANB. CLO
TEAL CLO
DOVE APP
PINTAIL CLO
SWAN APP
BEACONS CLO
ABBESS CLO
GDNS
WAVERLEY GDNS
JUNIPER LA
LOVAGE APP
BONDF'LD RD
Proposed Church & Community Centre
LION RD
PO
WC
East Be Distr Cen
ASDA Superstore
BECKTON
OSPREY CLO
KESTREL AV
LAWSON CLO
ST MICHAEL'S CLO
LONG MARK RD
GREENCROFT CLO
NEATSC'RT RD
ALLHALLOWS
LEAMOUTH RD
DENNY CLO
LINTON
SELBY CLO
COWAN PL
OLIVER
LATHAM CLO
ELMLEY CLO
NORTHUMBERLAND
LINDWOOD CLO
8
STANSFIELD
HIGHM'DS RD
CRAYFORD CLO
REMINGTON RD
KIRKHAM ROAD
TRIUMPH
FROBISHER
BROADGATE RD
MAPLECROFT CLO
FRASER CLO
GARDENS
WOODGET CLO
BARRY RD
DUNNOCK RD
B'L'NGT'N CLO
CHARDWELL CLO
King George V Park
Newham City Farm
Sports Amenity Centre
ROBSON CLO
ANDREWES CLO
DUND. CLO
OAKLEY CLO
ASHWELL CLO
CHELMSF'D CLO
EXETER CLO
GOOSE SQ
ARMSTRONG CLO
NEWLING CLO
GAUTREY SQ
BRANDRETH RD
DIXON CLO
OAKES CLO
KING GEORGE
ROAD
Will Thorne Pavillion
BAXTER
Albert Dock Hospital
CASPIAN WK
AVENUE
OPAL CLO
EMERALD CLO
GUILDFORD RD
HARPER RD
TRUSEDALE RD
BATTEN CLO
PORTER RD
SAVAGE
GARV
FELSTED RD
TASMAN WK
S'GASSO CLO
BERING WLK
JADE CLO
JASPER CLO
AGATE CLO
Sch
CHICHESTER CLO
BOULTWOOD RD
YORK CLO
WINCHESTER CLO
BAYNE CLO
New Be Par
ROYAL ROAD
Park Quays
South Beckton District Park
PARRY AVE
LEYES ROAD
Allotments
Allotments
CAMPION CLO
CONNAUGHT
STRAIT ROAD
Docklands Light Railway Proposed Extension
Royal Albert
Beckton Park
ROAD
Connaught
A112
Royal Docks Area Office
11
Royal Albert Dock
A B C D
1 2 3 4 5 6

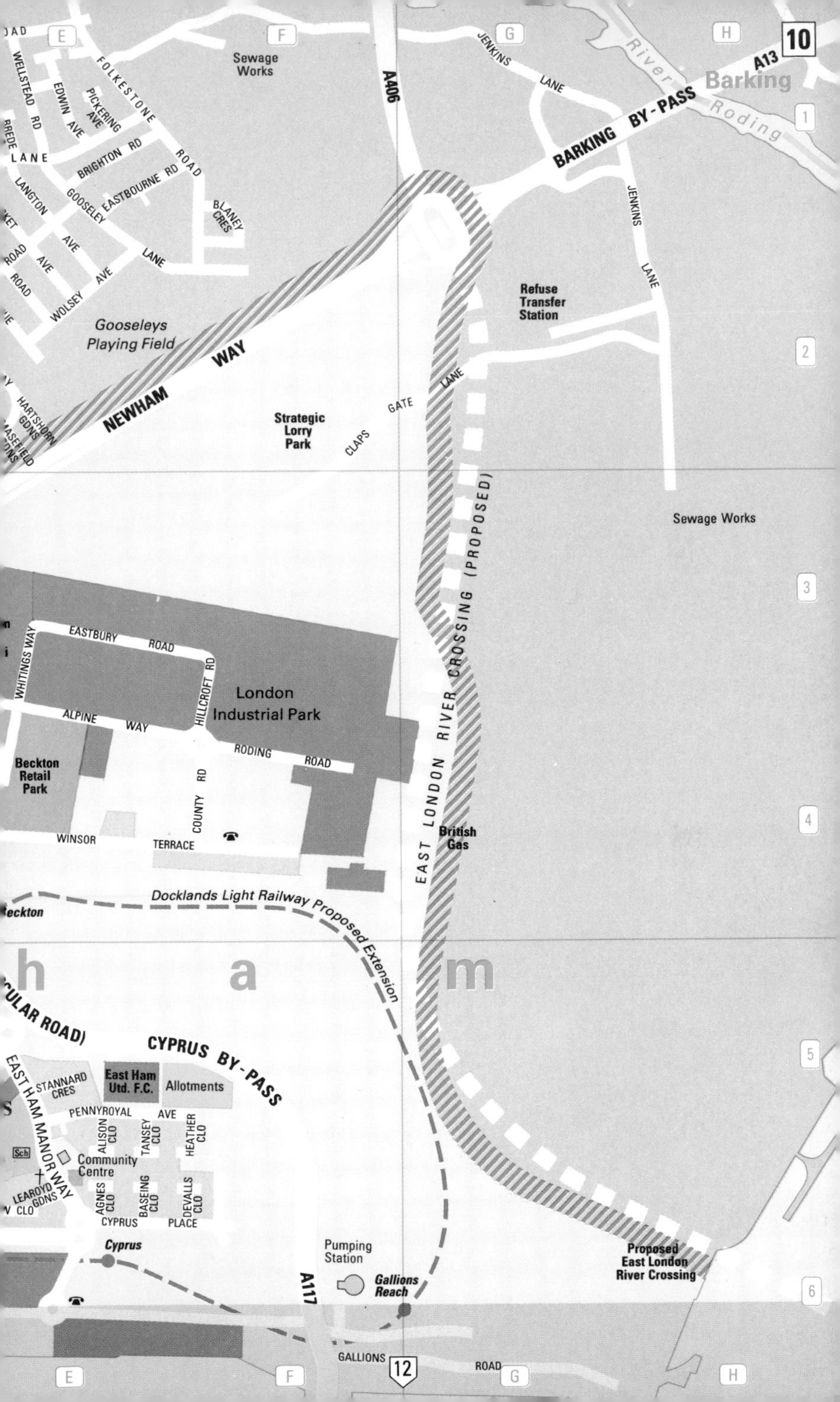

10
Sewage Works
Barking
BARKING BY-PASS
A13
River Roding
A406
JENKINS LANE
FOLKESTONE ROAD
WELLSTEAD RD
EDWIN AVE
PICKERING AVE
BRIGHTON RD
EASTBOURNE RD
GOOSELEY LANE
LANGTON AVE
WOLSEY AVE
BLANEY CRES
Gooseleys Playing Field
NEWHAM WAY
Strategic Lorry Park
CLAPS GATE LANE
Refuse Transfer Station
HARTSHORN GDNS
MASEFIELD GDNS
Sewage Works
EAST LONDON RIVER CROSSING (PROPOSED)
EASTBURY ROAD
WHITINGS WAY
HILLCROFT RD
London Industrial Park
ALPINE WAY
RODING ROAD
Beckton Retail Park
COUNTY RD
WINSOR TERRACE
British Gas
Docklands Light Railway Proposed Extension
Beckton
CYPRUS BY-PASS
EAST HAM MANOR WAY
STANNARD CRES
East Ham Utd. F.C.
Allotments
PENNYROYAL AVE
ALISON CLO
TANSEY CLO
HEATHER CLO
Sch
Community Centre
LEAROYD GDNS
AGNES CLO
BASEING CLO
DEVALLS CLO
CYPRUS PLACE
Cyprus
Pumping Station
Gallions Reach
A117
Proposed East London River Crossing
GALLIONS ROAD
12

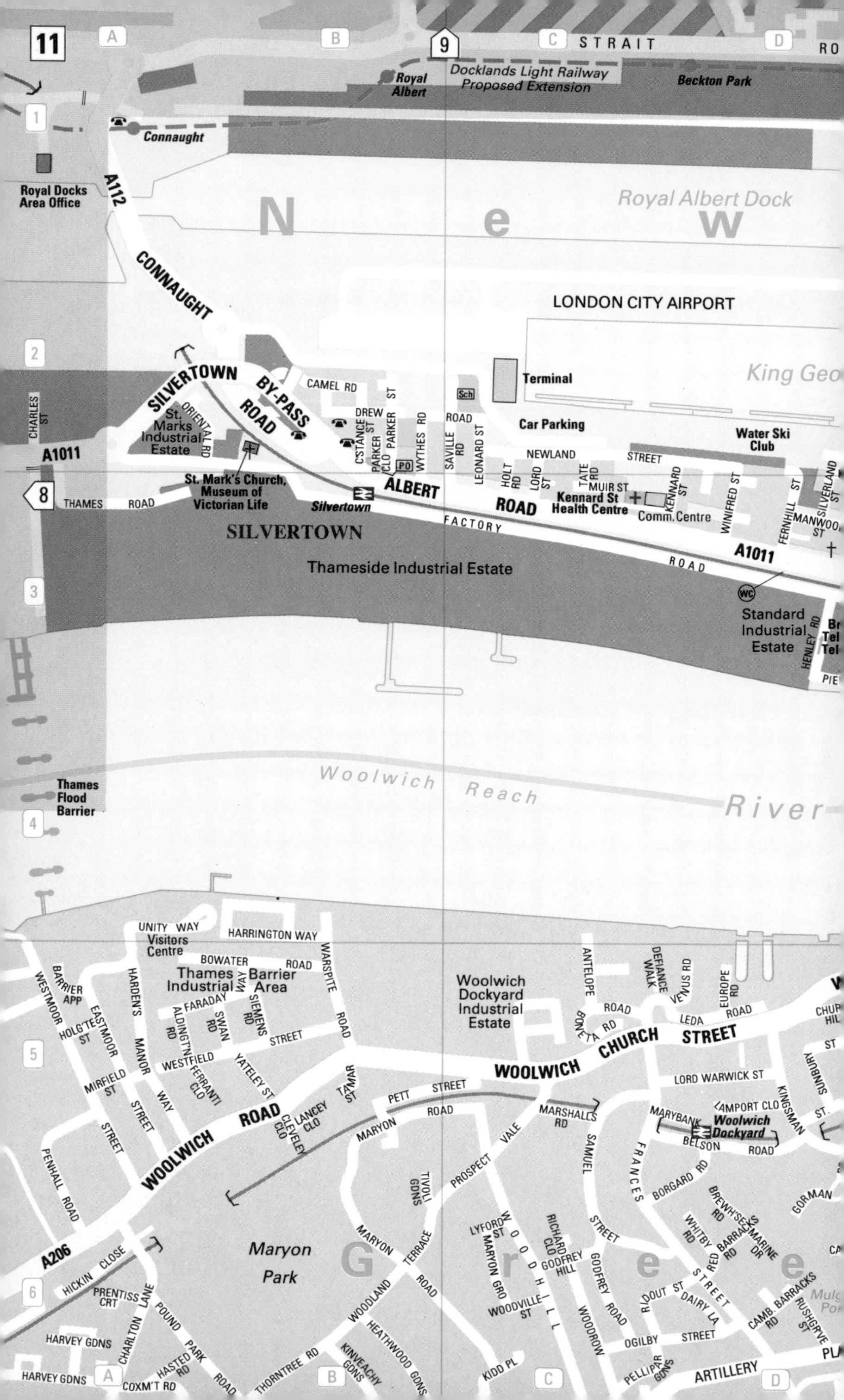

11
A
B
9
C
STRAIT
D
RO
Royal Albert
Docklands Light Railway Proposed Extension
Beckton Park
1
Connaught
Royal Docks Area Office
A112
Royal Albert Dock
N
e
w
CONNAUGHT
LONDON CITY AIRPORT
2
King Geo
Terminal
SILVERTOWN
BY-PASS
ROAD
CAMEL RD
CHARLES ST
St. Marks Industrial Estate
ORIENTAL RD
DREW ST
C'STANCE ST
PARKER CLO
PARKER ST
WYTHES RD
ROAD
Sch
SAVILLE RD
LEONARD ST
Car Parking
Water Ski Club
A1011
NEWLAND
STREET
HOLT RD
LORD ST
TATE RD
MUIR ST
KENNARD ST
WINIFRED ST
FERNHILL ST
SILVERLAND ST
PO
ALBERT
ROAD
Kennard St Health Centre
Comm. Centre
MANWOO ST
St. Mark's Church, Museum of Victorian Life
8
THAMES ROAD
Silvertown
FACTORY
SILVERTOWN
Thameside Industrial Estate
ROAD
A1011
3
Standard Industrial Estate
HENLEY RD
Br
Tel
Tel
PIE
Woolwich Reach
River
Thames Flood Barrier
4
UNITY WAY
Visitors Centre
HARRINGTON WAY
BOWATER ROAD
Thames Barrier Industrial Area
WAY
BARRIER APP
WESTMOOR
HARDEN'S
FARADAY
SWAN RD
SIEMENS RD
WARSPITE
ROAD
Woolwich Dockyard Industrial Estate
ANTELOPE
DEFIANCE WALK
VENUS RD
EUROPE RD
ROAD
BONETA RD
LEDA ROAD
CHURCH HILL
HOLG'TE ST
EASTMOOR
ALDINGTN RD
STREET
5
MANOR
WESTFIELD
FERRANTI CLO
YATELEY ST
WOOLWICH CHURCH STREET
ST
MIRFIELD ST
WAY
STREET
TAMAR ST
PETT STREET
LORD WARWICK ST
KINGSMAN
SUNBURY ST.
LAMPORT CLO
ROAD
LANCEY CLO
CLEVELEY CLO
MARYON ROAD
MARSHALLS RD
MARYBANK
Woolwich Dockyard
BELSON ROAD
STREET
WOOLWICH
PENHALL ROAD
PROSPECT VALE
SAMUEL
FRANCES
BORGARD RD
GORMAN
TIVOLI GDNS
BREWH'SE RD
WHITBY RD
A206
LYFORD ST
MARYON GRO
WOODHILL
RICHARD CLO
GODFREY HILL
STREET
RED BARRACKS RD
MARINE DR
Maryon Park
MARYON
TERRACE
G
r
e
e
CA
HICKIN CLOSE
ROAD
GODFREY ROAD
STREET
6
PRENTISS CRT
WOODLAND
WOODVILLE ST
RIDOUT ST
DAIRY LA
CAMB. BARRACKS RD
RUSHGROVE ST
Mulg Po
CHARLTON LANE
POUND PARK ROAD
HEATHWOOD GDNS
WOODROW
HARVEY GDNS
OGILBY STREET
PL
KINVEACHY GDNS
HARVEY GDNS
A
HASTED RD
THORNTREE RD
B
KIDD PL
C
PELLIPAR GDNS
ARTILLERY
D
COXM'T RD

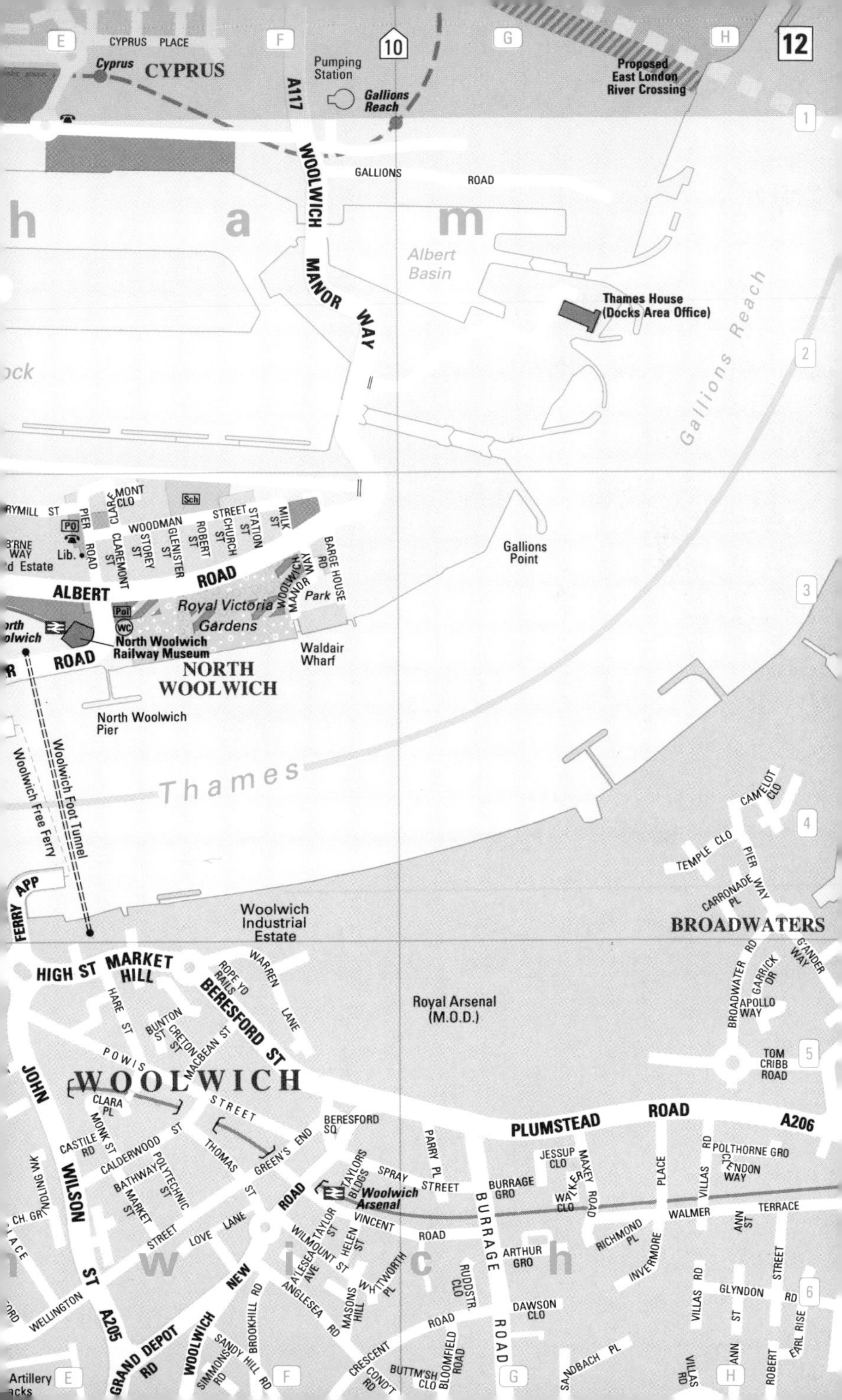

E
F
G
H
10
CYPRUS PLACE
Cyprus
CYPRUS
Pumping Station
Gallions Reach
A117
Proposed East London River Crossing
WOOLWICH MANOR WAY
GALLIONS ROAD
Albert Basin
Thames House (Docks Area Office)
Gallions Reach
Gallions Point
CLAREMONT CLO
Sch
PIER ROAD
WOODMAN STREET
MILK ST
STATION ST
CHURCH ST
ROBERT ST
GLENISTER ST
STOREY ST
CLAREMONT ST
BARGE HOUSE RD
Lib.
ALBERT ROAD
WOOLWICH MANOR WAY
Park
Royal Victoria Gardens
North Woolwich Railway Museum
Waldair Wharf
NORTH WOOLWICH
North Woolwich Pier
Woolwich Foot Tunnel
Woolwich Free Ferry
Thames
FERRY APP
Woolwich Industrial Estate
CAMELOT CLO
TEMPLE CLO
PIER WAY
CARRONADE PL
BROADWATERS
BROADWATER RD
GARRICK DR
APOLLO WAY
TOM CRIBB ROAD
HIGH ST
MARKET HILL
ROPE YD RAILS
WARREN LANE
BERESFORD ST
HARE ST
BUNTON ST
CRETON ST
MACBEAN ST
POWIS STREET
Royal Arsenal (M.O.D.)
WOOLWICH
JOHN WILSON ST
CLARA PL
MONK ST
CASTILE RD
CALDERWOOD ST
BATHWAY
POLYTECHNIC ST
MARKET ST
THOMAS ST
GREEN'S END
BERESFORD SQ
TAYLORS BLDGS
SPRAY STREET
Woolwich Arsenal
PARRY PL
PLUMSTEAD ROAD
A206
BURRAGE GRO
JESSUP CLO
MAXEY ROAD
WALKER CLO
PLACE
VILLAS RD
POLTHORNE GRO
WALMER TERRACE
ANN ST
CH. GR
LOVE LANE
STREET
ROAD
WILMOUNT ST
TAYLOR ST
HELEN ST
VINCENT ROAD
BURRAGE ROAD
ARTHUR GRO
RICHMOND PL
INVERMORE
ANGLESEA AVE
WHITWORTH PL
RUDDSTR. CLO
GLYNDON RD
STREET
WELLINGTON
A205
NEW ROAD
BROOKHILL RD
ANGLESEA RD
MASONS HILL
DAWSON CLO
ROBERT
EARL RISE
GRAND DEPOT RD
WOOLWICH
SANDY HILL RD
SIMMONS RD
CRESCENT
CONDT RD
BUTTM'SH CLO
BLOOMFIELD ROAD
SANDBACH PL
1
2
3
4
5
6

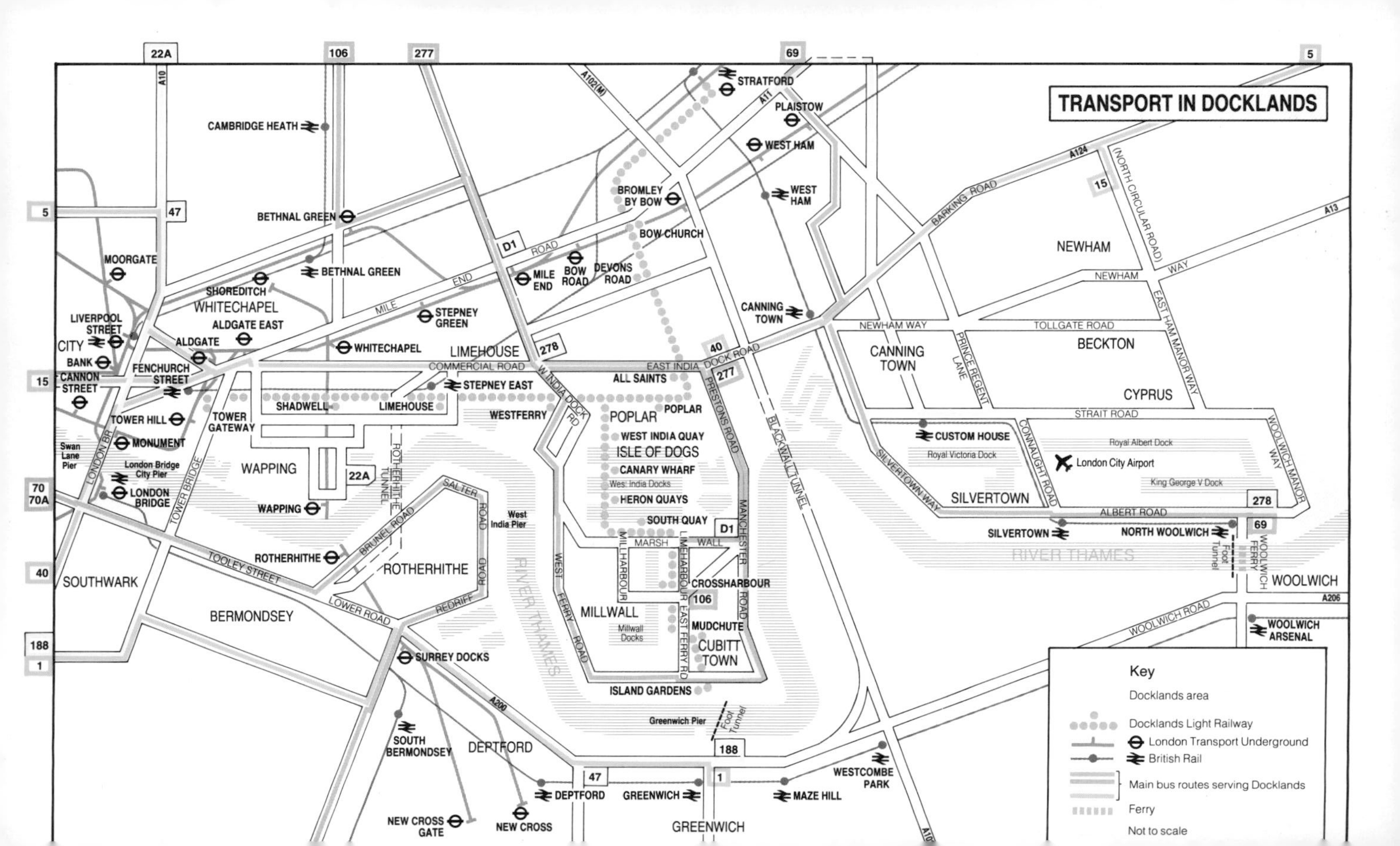
TRANSPORT IN DOCKLANDS
Key
Docklands area
Docklands Light Railway
London Transport Underground
British Rail
Main bus routes serving Docklands
Ferry
Not to scale
22A
106
277
69
5
47
15
40
70
70A
188
1
278
D1
CAMBRIDGE HEATH
BETHNAL GREEN
MOORGATE
SHOREDITCH
WHITECHAPEL
LIVERPOOL STREET
CITY
BANK
CANNON STREET
FENCHURCH STREET
ALDGATE
ALDGATE EAST
STEPNEY GREEN
MILE END
BOW ROAD
DEVONS ROAD
BROMLEY BY BOW
BOW CHURCH
STRATFORD
PLAISTOW
WEST HAM
CANNING TOWN
LIMEHOUSE
COMMERCIAL ROAD
STEPNEY EAST
SHADWELL
TOWER GATEWAY
TOWER HILL
MONUMENT
Swan Lane Pier
London Bridge City Pier
LONDON BRIDGE
WAPPING
ROTHERHITHE TUNNEL
WESTFERRY
ALL SAINTS
POPLAR
WEST INDIA QUAY
ISLE OF DOGS
CANARY WHARF
West India Docks
HERON QUAYS
SOUTH QUAY
CROSSHARBOUR
MUDCHUTE
CUBITT TOWN
MILLWALL
Millwall Docks
ISLAND GARDENS
Greenwich Pier
Foot Tunnel
West India Pier
ROTHERHITHE
SOUTHWARK
BERMONDSEY
SURREY DOCKS
SOUTH BERMONDSEY
DEPTFORD
NEW CROSS
NEW CROSS GATE
GREENWICH
MAZE HILL
WESTCOMBE PARK
RIVER THAMES
CANNING TOWN
BECKTON
CYPRUS
NEWHAM
CUSTOM HOUSE
Royal Victoria Dock
Royal Albert Dock
London City Airport
King George V Dock
SILVERTOWN
NORTH WOOLWICH
WOOLWICH FERRY
WOOLWICH
WOOLWICH ARSENAL
A10
A102(M)
A11
A124
A13
A200
A206
A102
MILE END ROAD
EAST INDIA DOCK ROAD
W INDIA DOCK RD
PRESTONS ROAD
MANCHESTER ROAD
BLACKWALL TUNNEL
MARSH WALL
LIMEHARBOUR
MILLHARBOUR
EAST FERRY RD
WEST FERRY ROAD
SALTER ROAD
REDRIFF ROAD
BRUNEL ROAD
LOWER ROAD
TOOLEY STREET
TOWER BRIDGE
LONDON BR
BARKING ROAD
(NORTH CIRCULAR ROAD)
NEWHAM WAY
EAST HAM MANOR WAY
TOLLGATE ROAD
PRINCE REGENT LANE
STRAIT ROAD
CONNAUGHT ROAD
SILVERTOWN WAY
ALBERT ROAD
WOOLWICH MANOR WAY
WOOLWICH ROAD

STREET INDEX

The letter and figures before a street name in the index and at the top of each entry in the text, eg **1** C3, indicate the page, followed by the grid reference, where the name or entry will be found. A street name in the index followed by the name of another street in italics is too small to be named on the map. It will be found leading off the street shown in italics.

I

J

K

11	C6	Lyford Street SE18
		M
12	F5	Macbean Street SE18
7	D2	McDowell Close E16
8	G1	Macgregor Road E16
1	D6	Macks Road SE16
5	D5	McMillan Street SE8
6	F3	Macquarie Way E14
4	E1	Maddams Street E3
10	E2	Magdalene Gardens E6
1	B3	Magdalen Street SE1
1	C4	Maguire Street SE1
3	B5	Mahogany Close SE16
2	E5	Major Road SE16
5	D1	Malabar Street E14
4	E3	Malam Gardens E14
7	C1	Malmesbury Road E16
7	C1	Malmesbury Terrace E16
1	C4	Maltby Street SE1
4	G5	Managers Street E14
9	D2	Manbrough Avenue E6
6	F4	Manchester Grove E14
6	G4	Manchester Road E14
1	A4	Manciple Street SE1
3	D3	Mandarin Street E14
1	B6	Mandela Way SE1
3	D6	Manilla Street E14
7	B1	Manor Road E16
1	C1	Mansell Street E1
11	D3	Manwood Street E16
9	B5	Maplecroft Close E16
8	E2	Maplin Road E16
2	E6	Maria Close SE1
2	E4	Marigold Street SE16
6	H2	Mariner's Mews E14
11	D6	Marine Drive SE18
1	D5	Marine Street SE16
12	E5	Market Hill SE18
4	E4	Market Road E14
4	F3	Market Square E14
12	E6	Market Street SE18
4	F2	Market Way E14
1	B2	Mark Lane EC3
9	C2	Marlow Road E6
2	H3	Marlow Way SE16
3	B2	Maroon Street E14
11	C5	Marshalls Road SE18
6	G2	Marshfield Street E14
6	E3	Marsh Street E14
		(Cahir Street)
4	F6	Marsh Wall E14
3	D4	Marsh Wall E14
2	F1	Martha Street E1
2	G1	Martineau Street E1
1	A1	Martin Lane EC4
		(Lukin Street)
5	D6	Mary Ann's Gardens SE8
11	D5	Marybank SE18
9	D4	Mary Rose Mall E6
7	C1	Mary Street E16
11	C6	Maryon Grove SE7
11	B5	Maryon Road SE18
11	B6	Maryon Road SE7
10	E2	Masefield Gardens E6
7	D3	Mason Close E16
12	F6	Masons Hill SE18
1	A6	Mason Street SE17
1	B6	Massinger Street SE17
9	B2	Masterman Road E6
3	A1	Master's Street E1
6	E3	Masthouse Terrace E14
4	E6	Mastmaker Road E14
10	E1	Mathews Avenue E6
		(Folkestone Road)
3	B2	Matlock Street E14
7	C2	Maud Street E16
12	G5	Maxey Road SE18
7	C2	Mayfield Road E13
5	A2	Mayflower Close SE16
		(Greenland Quay)
2	F4	Mayflower Street SE16
6	G6	May's Building Mews SE10
5	D6	Mechanics' Passage SE8
2	F3	Meeting House Alley E1
		(Watts Street)
9	D2	Melford Road E6
1	A3	Melior Street SE1
6	E1	Mellish Street E14
5	A5	Mercury Way SE14
1	D3	Mews Street E1
3	A6	Middleton Drive SE16
1	A3	Middle Yard SE1
6	G4	Midland Place E14
		(Ferry Street)
3	C1	Midlothian Road E3
12	F3	Milk Street E16
2	G2	Milk Yard E1
6	E1	Millharbour E14
3	C4	Milligan Street E14
3	C3	Mill Place E14
8	F5	Mill Road E16
1	C4	Millstream Road SE1
1	D4	Mill Street SE1
5	D1	Millwall Dock Road E14
		(Tiller Road)
5	B5	Milton Court Road SE14
1	B1	Mincing Lane EC3
3	D4	Ming Street E14
1	C1	Minories EC3
11	A5	Mirfield Street SE7
9	C1	Mitcham Road E6
1	B1	Mitre Street EC3
3	C3	Mitre, The E14
5	D1	Moiety Road E14
7	C1	Mona Street E16
9	B5	Moncrieff Close E6
		(Linton Gardens)
7	D3	Monk Drive E16
12	E5	Monk Street SE18
9	C2	Monmouth Road E6
1	D6	Monnow Road SE1
1	A2	Montague Close SE1
4	F3	Montague Place E14
9	B1	Montpelier Gardens E6
1	A2	Monument Street EC3
2	G2	Monza Street E1
2	G5	Moodkee Street SE16
4	E3	Morant Street E14
7	C2	More Close E16
7	D1	Morgan Street E16
1	B3	Morgan's Lane SE1
5	C6	Mornington Road SE8
1	B4	Morocco Street SE1
4	F1	Morris Road E14
2	F1	Morris Street E1

Page	Grid	Street
11	C6	Pellipar Gardens SE18
11	C6	Pellipar Road SE18
		(Artillery Place)
2	F2	Penang Street E1
11	A5	Penhall Road SE7
2	E2	Pennington Street E1
3	D3	Pennyfields E14
10	E5	Pennyroyal Avenue E6
1	B1	Pepys Street EC3
7	B1	Percy Road E16
9	C4	Peridot Street E6
2	E5	Perryn Road SE16
7	C3	Peto Street North E16
7	D4	Peto Street South E16
11	B5	Pett Street SE18
6	G6	Peyton Place SE10
2	E1	Philchurch Street E1
1	A1	Philpot Lane EC3
10	E1	Pickering Avenue E6
1	B3	Pickle Herring Street SE1
		(Vine Lane)
12	E3	Pier Road E16
6	G2	Pier Street E14
12	H4	Pier Way SE18
3	D3	Piggot Street E14
1	A4	Pilgrimage Street SE1
2	E1	Pinchin Street E1
3	D3	Pinefield Close E14
12	B4	Pintail Close E6
8	F5	Pirie Street E16
3	A3	Pitsea Place E1
		(Pitsea Street)
3	A3	Pitsea Street E1
3	C2	Pixley Street E14
6	F1	Plevena Street E14
4	E3	Plimsoll Close E14
5	A3	Plough Way SE16
12	G5	Plumstead Road SE18
8	E2	Plymouth Road E16
6	H3	Plymouth Wharf E14
7	D3	Pollard Close E16
12	H5	Polthorne Grove SE18
12	E5	Polytechnic Street SE18
2	E1	Ponler Street E1
2	H4	Poolmans Street SE16
2	G1	Poonah Street E1
1	C4	Pope Street SE1
4	F3	Poplar Baths Street E14
4	E4	Poplar High Street E14
1	A4	Porlock Street SE1
3	C1	Porta Way E3
9	D5	Porter Road E6
2	E3	Portland Square E1
7	A2	Portree Street E14
1	C1	Portsoken Street E1
1	A5	Potier Street SE1
1	B3	Potters Fields SE1
2	E4	Pottery Street SE16
11	A6	Pound Park Road SE7
12	E5	Powis Street SE18
11	A6	Prentiss Court SE7
1	C1	Prescot Street E1
2	E2	President's Drive E1
1	B6	Preston Close SE1
4	G6	Preston's Road E14
6	F6	Prince of Orange Lane SE10
		(Greenwich High Road)
8	G3	Prince of Wales Street E16
8	G1	Prince Regent Lane E13
8	G2	Prince Regent Lane E16
5	D5	Prince Street SE8
1	A5	Prioress Street SE1
2	E5	Priter Road SE16
2	F4	Prospect Street SE16
11	C5	Prospect Vale SE18
2	F3	Prusom Street E1
1	A2	Pudding Lane EC3
9	C1	Pulleyns Avenue E6
1	B5	Purbrook Street SE1

Q

Page	Grid	Street
3	D6	Quarterdeck, The E14
5	A1	Quebec Way SE16
1	C4	Queen Elizabeth Street SE1
4	H4	Quixley Street E14

R

Page	Grid	Street
3	B2	Raby Street E14
7	D3	Radland Road E16
2	H4	Radley Court SE16
1	A3	Railway Approach SE1
2	G4	Railway Avenue SE16
1	B1	Railway Place EC3
		(London Street)
2	F2	Raine Street E1
5	B3	Rainsborough Avenue SE8
4	G5	Raleana Road E14
9	C1	Rancliffe Road E6
6	F6	Randall Place SE10
8	H2	Randolph Approach E16
3	A3	Ratcliffe Cross Street E1
		(Commercial Road)
3	A3	Ratcliffe Lane E14
7	C2	Rathbone Street E16
7	D1	Ravenscroft Close E16
		(Hayday Road)
8	E1	Ravenscroft Road E16
2	F6	Raymouth Road SE16
2	F3	Reardon Path E1
2	F2	Reardon Street E1
2	G5	Rebecca Terrace SE16
12	E5	Rectory Place SE18
3	A1	Rectory Square E1
11	D6	Red Barracks Road SE18
2	G1	Redcastle Close E1
1	D3	Redmead Lane E1
5	A2	Redriff Road SE16
9	C4	Redstart Close E6
3	B5	Redwood Close SE16
7	D2	Reed Close E16
6	H2	Rembrandt Close E14
9	B4	Remington Road E6
2	G4	Reneforth Street SE16
10	E6	Renfrew Close E6
1	A5	Rephidim Street SE1
3	B2	Repton Street E14
3	B6	Reveley Close SE16
1	D6	Reverdy Road SE1
3	B1	Rhodeswell Road E14
4	E3	Ricardo Street E14
11	C6	Richard Close SE18
2	E1	Richard Street E1
12	G6	Richmond Place SE18
3	D3	Rich Street E14
4	E3	Ridgen Street E14
8	G1	Ridgwell Road E16

Page	Grid	Street
7	D2	Scoulding Road E16
3	C1	Seager Place E3
1	A6	Searles Road SE1
1	B2	Seething Lane EC3
9	B4	Selby Close E6
8	F1	Selby Road E13
3	D1	Selsey Street E14
1	C6	Setchell Road SE1
2	G4	Seth Street SE16
6	H3	Sextant Avenue E14
6	G3	Seyssel Street E14
1	C3	Shad Thames SE1
2	G2	Shadwell Pier Head E1
2	F1	Shadwell Place E1
1	B3	Shand Street SE1
3	A1	Shandy Street E1
9	A4	Sheerwater Road E16
3	D1	Shelmerdine Close E3
1	A1	Sherborne Lane EC4
2	F1	Sheridan Street E1
1	A4	Ship and Mermaid Row SE1 *(Snowsfields)*
8	F3	Shipman Road E16
5	B1	Shipwright Road SE16
1	B3	Shipwright Yard SE1 *(Tooley Street)*
4	E3	Shirbutt Street E14
7	C2	Shirley Street E16
1	C2	Shorter Street E1
3	B3	Shoulder of Mutton Alley E14
10	E1	Sidney Elson Way E6 *(Edwin Avenue)*
11	B5	Siemens Road SE18
11	D3	Silverland Street E16
11	A2	Silvertown By-Pass E16
7	C2	Silvertown Way E16
3	G5	Silver Walk SE16
5	B5	Simla Close SE14
12	F6	Simmons Road SE18
4	F4	Simpson's Road E14
9	D2	Skipsey Avenue E6
2	F5	Slippers Place SE16
2	E3	Smeaton Street E1
2	H3	Smith Close SE16
4	F3	Smythe Street E14
1	A4	Snowsfields SE1
3	B6	Somerford Way SE16
8	F2	Sophia Road E16
9	B3	Sorrel Gardens E6
9	D1	Southchurch Road E6
8	E2	South Moulton Road E16
5	C2	South Sea Street SE16
1	D1	South Tenter Street E1
1	D6	Southwark Park Road SE16
3	C2	Southwater Close E14
1	C5	Spa Road SE16
3	A3	Spert Street E14
4	F2	Spey Street E14
6	E3	Spindrift Avenue E14
2	E3	Spirit Quay E1
12	F5	Spray Street SE18
1	A3	Stainer Street SE1
3	D2	Stainsby Place E14
3	D2	Stainsby Road E14
2	F5	Stalham Street SE16
10	E5	Stannard Crescent E6
9	A4	Stansfield Road E16
1	C4	Stanworth Street SE1 *(Millstream Road)*
3	B5	Staples Close SE16
1	A4	Staple Street SE1
6	E1	Starboard Way E14
7	C1	Star Lane E16
7	D1	Star Street E16
12	F3	Station Street E16
5	C5	Staunton Street SE8
3	A5	Stave Yard Road SE16
6	G3	Stebondale Street E14
2	G1	Steel's Lane E1
3	B6	Steers Way SE16
7	B1	Stephenson Street E16
2	H1	Stepney Causeway E1
3	A1	Stepney Green E1
3	A2	Stepney High Street E1
3	A2	Stepney Way E1
1	B5	Stevens Street SE1
6	G1	Stewart Street E14
3	D3	Stocks Place E14
6	G6	Stockwell Street SE10
9	B3	Stokes Road E6
9	C4	Stonechat Square E6
4	E4	Stoneyard Lane E14
12	E3	Store Road E16
6	H3	Storers Quay E14
12	E3	Storey Street E16
2	E5	Stork's Road SE16
6	E5	Stowage SE8
3	D6	Strafford Street E14
9	C6	Strait Road E6
6	F6	Straitsmouth SE10
1	D6	Strathnairn Street SE1
6	F2	Strattondale Street E14
4	F3	Sturry Street E14
2	E1	Stutfield Street E1
8	H1	Sullivan Avenue E16
11	D5	Sunbury Street SE18
2	G5	Surrey Quays Road SE16
2	H3	Surrey Water Road SE16
4	F3	Susannah Street E14
2	G1	Sutton Street E1
9	C4	Swallow Street E6
9	B4	Swan Approach E6
1	A2	Swan Lane EC4
1	B5	Swan Mead SE1
2	G4	Swan Road SE16
11	B5	Swan Road SE18
2	E1	Swedenborg Gardens E1
5	B2	Sweden Gate SE16
1	C4	Sweeney Crescent SE1
7	B1	Sycamore Close E16

T

Page	Grid	Street
1	A5	Tabard Street SE1
6	E3	Taeping Way E14
11	B5	Tamar Street SE7
1	B4	Tanner Street SE1
10	E5	Tansey Close E6
7	C2	Tant Avenue E16
7	D3	Tarling Road E16
2	F1	Tarling Street E1
5	B3	Tarry Lane SE8
6	F6	Tarves Way SE10
8	H3	Tasman Walk E16
11	C3	Tate Road E16

Y

Z

LONDON DOCKLANDS GUIDE

Acknowledgements

We would like to thank the following people for their invaluable assistance during the compilation of this guide: Bob Aspinall of the Museum of London (Docklands Project); Deborah Archer, Russell Grossman, Neil Hilkene, Chris Pullen, Kate Stott, Stuart Tanner, Barbara Tyrer and Rhonda Wootten of the LDDC; David Chapman of the Docklands Settlement; Eve Clark; Brian Gill; Ron Howes of the London Borough of Tower Hamlets; Mike Green of Southwark Leisure and Entertainment; Ted Johns; Anna Moffat of Marketing Support Partnership; Dr David Parker of the Dickens House; Graham Woodall of London Regional Transport and the many others who spared the time to talk to us, answer our questions and show us round the churches and other places of interest in Docklands.

J.A. & J.C.

DOCKLANDS: PAST, PRESENT AND FUTURE

London's Docklands, covering a total of 8½ square miles, is really several areas, each with its own character, strung out along both sides of the Thames. On the north bank it stretches seven miles from Tower Bridge eastwards to Bow Creek and on the south, about a third of this length, from London Bridge as far as Deptford.

The system of enclosed docks which grew up from about 1800 made the Port of London a thriving commercial and industrial centre. Modernisation of cargo handling methods, larger ships and changes in world trading patterns led to the docks' decline, and they closed one by one between 1967 and 1981. Docklands became a depressing wasteland of derelict buildings, high unemployment and a disintegrating community.

Now, in an ambitious and controversial programme of regeneration under the London Docklands Development Corporation (LDDC), Docklands has become

Dockside Cranes

'Europe's largest building site'. Nevertheless, much of the old is being preserved, refurbished and put to new use, so that a rich variety of images is emerging: massive Victorian warehouses on the riverfront; jazzy modern office buildings; redundant dockside cranes perched by the water's edge; dark narrow streets and worn stairs leading down to the river; white towers of splendid 18thC churches rising above treetops; bascule bridges and lock gates; hundreds of modern redbrick houses; glimpses of the Thames sliding past deserted wharves; and the immense stretches of water of the docks themselves – 400 acres (182 ha) in all – where windsurfers have replaced the cargo ships.

The Port of London's history goes back to the Romans, who built the first bridge across the Thames and some quays on the north bank, but it was under the Normans that trade became important, with exports of wool, hides and cereals, and imports of wine, cloth, flax and hemp. Later, silks, spices and ivory arrived from the East via Constantinople.

Throughout the Middle Ages and up to the reign of Elizabeth I, the City merchants grew in wealth and power. They gradually wrested control of the port from the monarchy, in return for political and financial support, and built quays along the north bank west of the Tower of London.

The 16thC was the age of exploration and commercial expansion. Merchant companies were formed to finance the voyages which opened up new routes and new areas for trade in both the East and the New World, and were rewarded by the Crown with trading monopolies. One of the most powerful was the East India Company, founded in 1600, whose charter gave it the monopoly of trade with India and beyond.

London's port became the busiest in the world and, with thousands of large and small vessels jostling for room on the river, smuggling was rife and revenue was being lost. In 1558, just before Elizabeth's accession, an Act of Parliament established the system of legal quays, in an attempt to regulate shipping and cargo handling. All goods had to be landed at one of the designated quays on the north bank between London Bridge and the Tower, under the supervision of customs officers. Eventually there were 20 of these quays, including Billingsgate, which handled fish.

During the next two centuries, however, the chaos on the river worsened as trade continued to expand. London's convenient location between the New World and Europe made it an important commercial centre for cargoes of sugar, rum and tobacco, as well as furs from Nova Scotia. To relieve the congestion, some goods were allowed to be handled at 'sufferance wharves', mostly on the south bank. At any one time there would be at least 1,400 ships and 3,500 small craft in the Pool of London, the stretch of river from Wapping to London Bridge. Some 500 people a year drowned as boats collided; a very large proportion of cargoes disappeared through thieving – from small-scale pilfering to organised rackets; and ships sometimes had to wait a week to enter the Pool. The shortage of berths meant that goods had to be transferred to lighters or barges which then carried them to the quays.

In the mid-17thC the East India Company built an enclosed dock at Blackwall where it had established its own moorings, wharf and shipyard, but the dock was for fitting out, not cargo handling. At the end of the century the Howland Great Wet Dock, covering 10 acres (4 ha), was built among the marshy wastes of Rotherhithe. This, too, was for fitting out and repairs, although during the next century it was adapted for the whaling fleet and its name was changed to Greenland Dock. Eventually, the merchant companies realised that enclosed docks for unloading and loading cargo would solve many of the problems encountered on the river. Several schemes were put before Parliament and fiercely opposed by wharfingers, who owned the riverside quays, and by the watermen and lightermen. In 1799 the West India Dock Company was granted the right to build its own enclosed docks. It selected the marshy and virtually uninhabited Isle of Dogs as the site for two parallel docks. Five-storey warehouses were built round their edges and the whole area was surrounded by 20ft (6m) high walls, which were to become a characteristic, oppressive feature of Docklands and sections of which survive to this day. The company was also given the right to form an armed guard as additional security. The docks opened in 1802 and immediately their worth was proved by the dramatic fall in losses from thieving and in the much faster turnround time. The system of bonded warehouses also began at this time: duties were paid on goods such as wine and tobacco only when they were withdrawn from the warehouse, not when landed. This removed the pressure to sell goods as soon as possible in order to defray the duties liable.

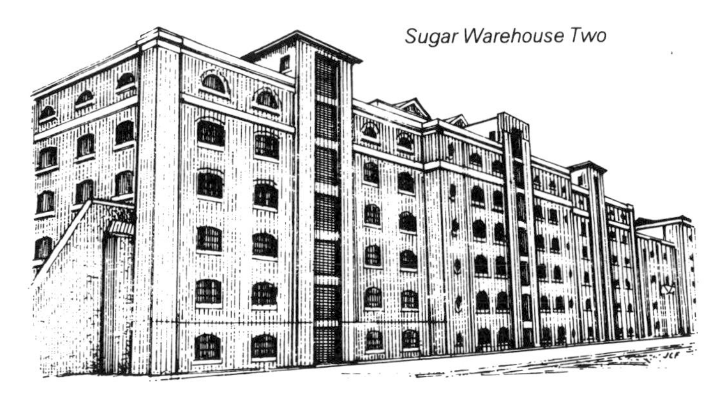

Sugar Warehouse Two

In 1805 the London Docks complex opened at Wapping, specialising in high-value goods such as tobacco, wine, brandy and furs as well as wool, tea and, later, rubber. The following year the East India Company completed two basins on the site at Blackwall, one for import and the other for export, for its trade with China and the East Indies. Its warehouses, however, were in the City and not at the docks.

South of the river, development started when Greenland Dock was purchased by the Commercial Dock Company in 1807, and began to handle timber and grain. Four companies built docks in haphazard fashion all over the Rotherhithe peninsula and eventually there were nine docks, six timber ponds and 3½ miles of canal (all that was ever built of a grandiose plan to link the Thames with Portsmouth). The separate companies, which specialised in trade with the Baltic and North America, merged first into two and then into one company, the Surrey Commercial Dock Company, formed in 1864.

St Katharine Docks were opened in 1828, with specialist warehouses for luxury goods such as coffee, sugar, spices, gums, spirits and wine. As with the London Docks, the scheme involved the removal of thousands of slum-dwellers, and in this case it also meant the demolition, amid public protests, of the medieval hospital of St Katharine.

On the Isle of Dogs, in 1805, the Corporation of London had opened the City Canal just south of the West India Docks, as a short cut across the peninsula for shipping. It was not a success, however, and in 1829 was bought by the West India Dock Company which widened it and made it into a third dock.

The number of ships using the port grew from 14,000 in 1794 to 23,600 in 1824, encouraging the continuing spate of piecemeal dock-building. However, this was the age of *laissez-faire*: the merchant companies lost their monopoly rights and the fierce competition between them, far from being healthy, was to lead to bankruptcies and mergers. Another major cause of their financial difficulties was the 'Free Water Clause' included in the Acts which authorised building of the docks. This allowed barges and lighters to enter the docks without paying dues. The end result was that up to 80 per cent of imports were being unloaded inside the docks on to small craft which then carried them off to riverside wharves, the dock owners receiving no revenue.

Nevertheless, more docks were built. The Victoria (later Royal Victoria) Dock opened in 1855 and was the first to be linked to the new rail network, the first to

Thames Sailing Barge

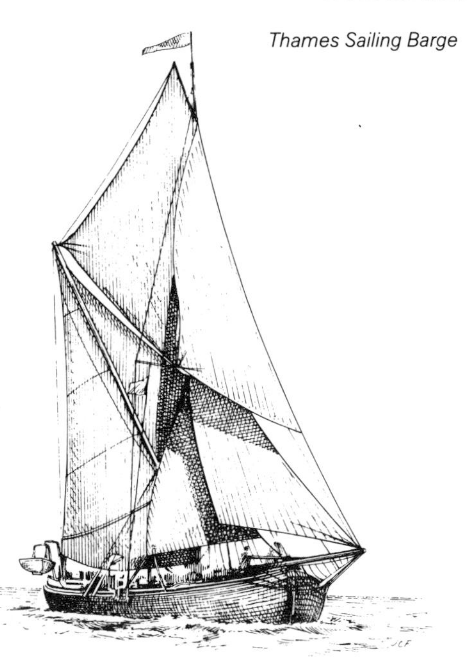

The Bosses, the Workers and the Villains

During the years when the docks were active numerous people were associated with them in various ways and some are still remembered in street names.

The bosses at first were individual ship owners-cum-merchants; later, Dock Companies came into being and employed Dock Managers to live on site and run things. The merchants who provided and maintained the Thamesside wharves and warehouses were known as wharfingers.

The majority of *the workers* were the dockers, who unloaded incoming cargo, and the more skilled stevedores who packed cargo for export. There were also shipwrights, engineers, ballast men, coopers, rope-makers, sack-makers, tally-clerks – and lightermen and watermen. In the days when incoming ships moored in mid-river and passengers and goods were taken ashore in smaller craft, the passenger craft were in the care of watermen, while the goods-carrying barges, or lighters (so-called because they 'lightened' cargo vessels as goods were discharged overside) were operated by lightermen.

The villains fell into distinct groups. The river pirates were armed and favoured the full frontal assault; the night plunderers were usually crooked watermen who bribed night watchmen; the scuffle-hunters took on casual work as porters and disappeared as soon as they'd concealed enough produce under their long aprons; the light and heavy horsemen conducted organised raids but favoured bribery over violence; the mudlarks pretended to search the silt for legitimate finds but often collected bags of stolen cargo dropped discreetly overboard by accomplice dockers.

be equipped with hydraulic machinery, the first with a telegraph service and the first to be purpose-built for the new iron steamships. These had first appeared on the Thames in 1815, but it was not for another 60 years or so that sail was to be supplanted by steam, and some cargoes still came up the river in square-rigged sailing ships even into the 1920s.

The Millwall Dock Company was formed with an eye to the growth in cheap grain imports following the repeal of the Corn Laws, and opened its docks on the Isle of Dogs in 1868. The Royal Albert, completed in 1880, was 1¾ miles long and the largest dock in the world. The merged East and West India Dock companies went 20 miles downstream to build new docks at Tilbury but the scheme was not a success and caused the company to go into liquidation – Tilbury's day was yet to come. By 1901 all the dock companies on the north bank, with the exception of the Millwall Dock Company, had merged into one.

Throughout the second half of the 19thC there had been great industrial activity around the docks: flour milling, rope making, lead refining and works producing bridges and girders, ships' propellors, boilers and machinery. Ship-building, which predated the docks, flourished only until the 1860s, when yards in the north of England, with their access to cheap iron and coal, became pre-eminent. Until then, the yards of Blackwall and Rotherhithe were busy producing sailing ships and Millwall became famous for the new iron steamships, including Brunel's unlucky *Great Eastern*. The introduction of hydraulic power in the docks was to have far-reaching consequences: by replacing manual labour needed for turning capstans, operating cranes and lockgates and other machinery it reduced the human drudgery but also the number of men required.

Thousands of workers, particularly from Ireland, Scotland and rural areas of England, had moved into Docklands during the 19thC. Work was scarce and uncertain, however, wages were very low and families lived in appalling poverty and squalor, not only in the docks but all over London's East End. Their plight inspired the work of social reformers such as Dr Barnardo, Arnold Toynbee and Passmore Edwards and numerous welfare halls and educational institutes were built. The Docklands Settlement, which eventually set up branches in several parts of London's Docklands and also in other British ports, grew out of the Mayflower Club, founded in Canning Town in 1905 by West End playwright Reginald Kennedy Cox and supported by Malvern College. The Oxford and Cambridge university missions worked with the churches here and still have links with Docklands. Numerous sailors' hostels were opened to provide clean and safe accommodation for both British and foreign seamen who came ashore at the port. One is still functioning on the Isle of Dogs.

The spread of education was to lead, in the latter years of the 19thC, to the organisation of labour under the leadership of men whose names are still honoured in Docklands: John Burns, Will Thorne and Ben Tillett among them. The dock companies forced down wages in an effort to undercut one another in the frantic competition for business. There were numerous strikes but the most famous was in 1889, demanding 'the dockers' tanner' – a wage of sixpence an hour – and a minimum engagement of four hours. Dock labour was employed on a casual basis and this system was to remain a cause of bitter discontent until it was phased out after World War II. Labour was hired on a daily or twice-daily basis through a degrading system of 'calling on' in which men had to present themselves for selection, like cattle at a market. The six-week strike in 1889 won public sympathy, the employers gave way, and the first-ever union of unskilled labourers was formed.

Management of the Port of London was in the hands of the Thames Conservancy Board, created in 1857. As the volume of shipping continued to increase, the port became more disorganised and inefficient and in 1900 a Royal Commission was set up to investigate the problems of the enclosed dock companies. The Port of London Authority (PLA) was set up in 1909 as a result of the Commission's findings. It took over all the docks, including Tilbury, and was made responsible for regulating navigation on the river, licensing private wharves, jetties, barges, lighters and other small craft, dredging channels, and providing mooring points – duties which it still carries out. Its income was to be raised from dues on vessels and goods entering and leaving the port. The PLA opened the King George V dock, the last dock to be built, in 1921 and made

'Calling On'

'It's 7.35 now. Hundreds of men stream in through the gates, making their way to the various places for the general call-on, facing the firm's foremen and labour superintendents who will exactly at 7.45 am walk over to the waiting labour force and make their selection . . . at times, particularly if there is a fall-off in shipping, the crowd on the "stones" can be four or five men deep and about 500 yards long . . . All of a sudden there is a complete hush . . . Over walk the ship and quay foremen, like a sheriff's posse in a Western . . . There is a rush and a flurry, arms are outstretched with registration books in the hands (without the registration book you can't go to work) . . . When there's been a heavy spell of unemployment, the call-on reminds you of a flock of seagulls converging on a morsel.' Jack Dash, *Good morning, brothers*, Lawrence and Wishart Ltd, 1969.

many improvements at the other docks. Despite disruption caused by numerous dock strikes, the General Strike of 1926 (when goods were handled by volunteers protected by armed soldiers) and the Depression in the 1930s, trade through the port remained at a high level for most of the inter-war period, and passenger liners of P&O, Royal Mail, Ellerman, Union Castle, Shaw Savill and many other lines plied between London (especially the Royal and Tilbury Docks) and every continent of the world.

Then came World War II. From 7 September 1940 London's docks were set ablaze by 57 consecutive nights of bombing. Despite losing many warehouses and storage facilities the docks continued to function and nearly all of them were reinstated after the war; for some years there was intense activity on the river and industries were working at full capacity. However, there were radical changes on the horizon which foreshadowed the docks' demise. The appearance in the 1950s of the first forklift truck heralded mechanisation of cargo handling.

Yet closure of the docks still seemed unimaginable. Despite innumerable strikes by dockers, and the decline in passenger traffic, business was still booming in the early 1960s. In 1964 a peak of over 61 million tons of cargo was handled. The PLA was still making improvements and even had plans to expand the docks on the Isle of Dogs, at the same time that trade started to shift downriver to Tilbury. The East India Docks, not fully reinstated after the war, closed down in 1967 and were quickly followed in the next two years by St Katharine and London Docks. Next to go were the Surrey Commercial Docks, in 1970. On the river, strikes had finally killed off Hay's Wharf in 1969. West India and Millwall Docks were to survive until 1980 and a large private timber firm on Millwall Dock ceased operating only in 1984. At the Royals – which were still very busy in the 1970s, having taken some of the trade from the closed upstream docks – the last ship to discharge cargo, the Chinese vessel *Xingfeng*, left in October 1981. (During the next few years several ships were laid up in the Royals and the very last ship movement was in October 1985 when a vessel being transformed into a floating restaurant sailed out into Gallion's Reach.)

Containerisation had been the fatal blow. The first container ship on the Thames to use purpose-built facilities arrived at Tilbury in 1968. It took 2 shifts, of 15 men each, 12 hours to unload 82 containers and load another 120; in the conventional way it would have taken over 100 men 4 or 5 days. As more and more cargo was moved in containers and by roll-on, roll-off ('ro-ro') vessels, trade shifted downstream to Tilbury and to other ports which were being developed for container handling and were accessible by large modern ships.

The closure of the docks was accompanied by the departure of most of the riverside industries, although a few working wharves remained. Many families had moved away: 150,000 jobs had disappeared since the mid-1960s. What was left was 5,000 acres (2,025 ha) of dereliction, decaying housing, no employment and apparently no hope. The silent warehouses and deserted docks seemed to have no possible purpose.

When the docks' end was clearly in sight, however, various proposals for the area's redevelopment were put forward by local borough councils and community groups. Already a few of the docks had been filled in and the Tower Hotel opened at St Katharine Docks in 1973 to the accompaniment of demonstrators' placards calling for 'Homes before Hotels'. In the mid-1970s the GLC and five boroughs produced the Strategic Plan for Docklands which was based on the needs and skills of existing communities in the area and was to have started in 1979. That same year, however, the Conservative government was returned to power and its view was that Docklands should be regenerated by private enterprise. It saw the proximity to the City of London as Docklands' major advantage.

In 1981 the government established the LDDC with a mandate to carry out a ten-year programme of regeneration, but as an enabling body rather than a planning authority. It was given a budget to use as 'leverage': to attract private investment, public money would be used to provide infrastructure – drainage, communications and transport networks. The LDDC was also empowered to acquire land from the PLA and other bodies, to which it would then attract private developers of commercial and residential schemes.

Heron Quays

At the heart of the programme is the Enterprise Zone on the Isle of Dogs which covers 500 acres (203 ha), including 130 acres (53 ha) of water. A package of incentives is on offer until 1992: exemption from local rates, relaxation of planning controls (virtually no planning permission is needed except for buildings over 120ft – 37m – high), simplified customs procedures, and up to 100 per cent allowance against corporation tax for capital expenditure on construction.

The boom in the financial sector and the expansion of financial services resulting from the deregulation of the City, or 'Big Bang', provided the momentum for the rush of investment into Docklands in the first few years. The stock market collapse in the latter part of 1987 placed a question mark over the future pace of development, however. The most controversial scheme in the whole of Docklands is Canary Wharf in the Enterprise Zone. The £3,000-million project, dubbed 'Wall Street on the Water', will be the largest single commercial development in Europe. If its 10 million square feet (930,000 square metres) of office space is eventually all let, it promises 46,000 new jobs. Its proposed design has provoked anger and dismay in some circles: one of its three towers, at 850ft (260m), would be half as tall again as the NatWest building in the City, and the tallest in Europe. Critics complain that it will be quite out of scale with surrounding buildings and that its new 'brutal' style of architecture will contrast painfully with the sublime elegance of Greenwich across the water.

The story since 1981 has been one of achievement but also of bitter conflicts between the LDDC and private developers on the one hand and, on the other, local community groups, conservationists and the three borough councils concerned – Tower Hamlets, Newham and Southwark. There are many bones of contention: the alleged lack of jobs for local people; the absence of an overall physical plan and resulting hotchpotch of architectural design; the 'relocation' of small businesses such as car breakers, which were firmly rooted in local tradition but which do not fit the LDDC image; the activities of speculators taking advantage of soaring land prices which increased, for example, from about £60,000 an acre in Wapping in 1982 to well over £4 million by 1987; the demolition of several historic buildings and structures; the lack of rented housing; and the invasion of the area by the newly rich from the City, who live in luxury apartment blocks or converted warehouses with privileged river views, such as Cascades on the Isle of Dogs, nicknamed 'Yuppie Towers'.

However, some local residents have recognised the new opportunities and have been able to benefit from them. The LDDC's 'affordable housing policy' in theory requires that a certain proportion of homes built on its land by private developers be offered at a low price to local tenants. To prevent quick profiteering, the LDDC has now tightened the rules to ensure that capital gains tax is paid on profits made on these homes if resold within five years. Many young Docklanders have been helped by Skillnet, set up jointly by the LDDC, Newham Council and the ILEA to promote vocational education courses in the area, and others have attended courses at the Docklands New Technology Centre (ITEC). Contrasting local views are evident in the graffiti to be seen all over Docklands: 'The LDDC can seriously damage your health', 'Another victim of the LDDC', 'Canary Wharf is for the birds'; but also, 'STOL is our lifeline', and 'STOL means jobs'.

London City Airport, the short take-off and landing (STOL) airport with its runway spectacularly placed between the Royal Albert and King George V docks, is primarily for business travellers and has aroused strong local protest. However, the Docklands Light Railway, which will eventually link north Docklands directly with the City, serves not only commuters and tourists but also local residents. The latter were previously poorly served by public transport and were used to long delays with road traffic regularly held up while bridges were raised to let ships enter and leave the docks. New roads and road improvements are already ending the isolation. Local people will also benefit from the many new amenities such as sport and leisure facilities and shopping centres; as well as from the LDDC's funding of community centres and restoration of churches and other historic buildings.

More telling than the LDDC's liberal use of words such as 'staggering', 'unparalleled' and 'exceptional' to describe its achievements are the statistics showing what has been attained between 1981 and 1987: 12,000 new homes built or under way on LDDC or privately owned land (and, the LDDC claims, 40 per cent of homes on the land it owns have been bought by local residents); an inflow of £2,200 million in private investment; 660 new firms in Docklands by 1985 – and probably about 800 by the end of 1987; an estimated 10,000 new jobs created by 1987. However, local people occupy only a very small proportion of the new jobs and unemployment in Docklands is believed to be as high as 25 per cent. The total number of jobs in the area in 1987 – 30,000 – was only 2,000 more than in 1985, because the 'old' jobs are still disappearing. The LDDC claims that the employment opportunities are still to come: the total number of jobs is expected to reach 80,000 by 1991 and the potential for the year 2000 is 200,000.

Ivory House

Docklands today is a rapidly changing world, full of powerful images of both past and future. The historic buildings and structures are reminders of the Port of London's former bustle and wealth. The poverty, violence, dirt and sweated labour of the old days are, perhaps fortunately, difficult to conjure up but evocative names such as Hope Sufferance Wharf, Penang Street, Ivory House, and East India Dock impart still a faint romantic aura of exotic cargoes, faraway places and Imperial glory. Slowly taking shape around the surviving images of the past is the new Docklands, which is being heralded as 'the Water City of the 21st Century'.

SURREY DOCKS

The area once covered by the Surrey Commercial Docks is a broad peninsula in a loop of the river. It has always been rather remote, bypassed by the main traffic routes and not linked with the north bank until the turn of the century. On its western edge is Rotherhithe Village, a small corner with a much older history. Stretching westwards to London Bridge is the long tail of land which is Bermondsey's river front, with a history dating back to the early Middle Ages.

Until the closure of the docks in 1969, the peninsula had nearly 460 acres (186 ha) of water: nine docks and six timber ponds. Now, most of the docks have been filled in, and the dereliction which set in during the late 1960s is gradually being replaced by new, predominantly residential, developments and by refurbished old council estates. The mix of private and local authority development is the outcome of years of wrangling between the LDDC and Southwark Council. The local residents, with their strong sense of community, have also been active in opposing some of the private developers' plans. One area, around Surrey Docks tube station in the south west, seems to be stubbornly hanging on to its individual and scruffy character.

War damage and extensive demolition in recent years means that there are only isolated examples of great warehouses or historic buildings and structures on the peninsula. Of the old docks, only Greenland and South Docks (part of Canada Dock and the Surrey Basin) have been retained, as attractive features and for use as watersports centres. Overall, however, there is a great sense of spaciousness, created in particular by the Russia Dock Woodland, Stave Hill and the Ecological Park in the centre. There is also the planned riverside walk for almost the whole length of shoreline which will ensure public access to the superb river views.

This part of London was mostly deserted marshland until the Howland Great Wet Dock was built in 1697, the first of its kind on the Thames. It was designed only for mooring and refitting but during the 18thC it became a whaling base and was renamed Greenland Dock. Later, grain and timber became the main imports and during the 19thC many more docks were built, haphazardly, by four separate companies which amalgamated in 1864 as the Surrey Commercial Dock Company. Quebec Dock was the last to be built in London, in 1926. Many of the dock names echoed the cargoes' origins: Greenland, Norway, Baltic, Russia, Canada and Quebec. There is still a strong Scandinavian connection, with Danish firms prominent among the developers, and a few Scandinavian churches and seamen's missions remain.

Rotherhithe Village, a conservation area, is a quiet and unspoiled little corner, rich in historic buildings and maritime tradition. The *Mayflower*, commemorated in the name of the attractive riverside pub, moored here in 1620 before starting her voyage to Plymouth from where she sailed to the New World. There are some impressive warehouses, now converted into flats, studios and workshops, an award-winning new housing development, and pre-war blocks of council flats. Among all these are Rotherhithe's little-known treasures: the beautiful St Mary's church, built in 1715, an 18thC charity school, and the small, brick pumping engine house for the Thames Tunnel, standing as a modest reminder of the mighty engineering feats of Marc and Isambard Brunel.

Bermondsey presents yet another picture. There has been commercial activity here since medieval times when the nearby Benedictine Abbey was one of the richest in England and flour-mills lined the river banks. By Victorian times it had become a Dickensian place of busy wharves and towering warehouses, overcrowded tenements and appalling poverty and violence. When the docks downstream began to close in the 1960s, so did the riverside wharves. Now, Bermondsey's proximity to the City of London and its fine riverside location make it a prime area for redevelopment, and the big money has moved in. London Bridge City is cited as the largest single commercial development in Europe. Here, most of the old warehouses have been sacrificed to make way for spectacular new office buildings, marking yet another phase in Bermondsey's long commercial history. East of Tower Bridge, other large-scale projects are under way but they incorporate the great Victorian warehouses and maze of narrow streets around Shad Thames and St Saviour's Dock, which have been designated a conservation area, so the unique character of the place will not be entirely erased.

Shad Thames

At the western end of Bermondsey lies an area of low-density housing and the new Cherry Garden residential scheme. The recently discovered remains of a 14thC manor house, believed to be Edward III's palace, together with the historic Angel pub, are the main attractions.

Charles Dickens
Several writers have been inspired by the starkly evocative scenery of the docks in their heyday, but it was Charles Dickens who seemed to make them his own, so much so that 'Dickensian' is one of the most frequently used descriptive terms for the 19thC alleys, wharves and warehouses.

Dickens knew London well and walked its streets – especially the poorer back streets – regularly, and it is possible to trace his wanderings, to an extent, by references in the novels. The area around Marshalsea, in Southwark, was important to him, but is outside the area covered by this guide; however there are plenty of references within the chosen boundaries.

London Bridge (the previous not the present structure) is mentioned in several of the books including *David Copperfield, Oliver Twist, Great Expectations, Our Mutual Friend* and *Martin Chuzzlewit*; Quilp's grisly wharf was somewhere east of Tower Bridge in the Surrey Docks area; Jacob's Island where Bill Sikes met his awful end, was in Rotherhithe 'beyond Dockhead'; Limehouse Church (St Anne's) has a scene in *Our Mutual Friend* and the Grapes in Narrow Street appears in the same book as the 'Six Jolly Fellowship Porters'; an opium den in Shadwell High Street plays a role in *Edwin Drood*; and *The Uncommercial Traveller* has a lengthy description of the area around London Docks, which Dickens says is 'known to the initiated as "Down by the Docks"'.

These Docklands areas south of the river retain their own atmosphere and their separate identities, and are harder to understand perhaps than Docklands across the water, which is recognisably part of the East End community. In Bermondsey it will be difficult for the old identity to survive beside the overwhelming presence of new luxury housing and office developments. Rotherhithe Village now has the feel of an artists' colony, which preserves much of the past spirit of the place. It is less easy to predict what kind of place the old Surrey Commercial Docks will become: dreary, Milton Keynes-type suburbia, cut off from the mainstream of London life, or perhaps an area highly desirable for its wealth of open spaces and superb river frontage, together with the advantage of being nearer than even the Isle of Dogs, as the crow flies, to the City of London.

Bermondsey

The Anchor Brewhouse **1** C3
Shad Thames SE1. John Courage built his brewery here in 1789, replacing an earlier one. After a fire in 1892 it was largely rebuilt and extended, and continued operating until 1982. Its distinguishing feature is the tower on top, an imitation of those on the Tower of London across the river. The brewhouse and the old Boilerhouse with its large central chimney are Grade II listed and have been converted into very desirable flats. The best view of them is from the north end of Tower Bridge. No public access.

Bermondsey Square **1** B5
SE1. Bermondsey Abbey which once stood on this site was founded in the 11thC by Cluniac monks and became one of the richest in England. The square, which contains some early 19thC houses, is now the venue for the New Caledonian Antiques Market. *Market open 07.00-12.00 Fri.*

Butler's Wharf **1** C3
Shad Thames SE1. Separated from the old Courage Boilerhouse by a narrow alley leading to the river, Maggie Blake's Cause, this is a series of Grade II listed warehouses dating from the 1870s. They

occupy what was once the largest wharf on the Thames. It closed in 1972 and is now being developed as a major complex of offices, flats, studios, workshops, leisure units, a sports centre and a Covent Garden-type shopping area. The Conran Foundation is opening a major Design Museum and Resource Centre here in May 1989 and a children's museum and exhibition centre is also planned. A Business Centre of starter industrial and commercial units is run by a private concern, Skillions. There will be a riverside walk and possibly a new pier.

Cherry Garden **2 E4**
Bermondsey Wall East SE1. The area is named after the cherry gardens which existed in Elizabethan times, and the 18thC pleasure gardens, remembered also in the name of nearby Paradise Street. Pepys visited the gardens, and Turner sat on Cherry Garden Pier to paint *The Fighting Temeraire* as she returned from the Battle of Trafalgar to be broken up at Rotherhithe. The new development here represents a compromise mix of private and council housing, following four years of local opposition to the original plans for an all-private scheme. At Platform Wharf, archaeologists have found some exciting remains of a 14thC manor house, possibly Edward III's Rotherhithe palace. A Delftware factory stood on the same spot in the early 18thC.

Cottons Centre **1 A3**
Tooley St SE1. The enormous cream building is occupied mainly by the Canadian Imperial Banking Corporation and Citibank, with a leisure centre, Cottons Club, in the basement. The building's two great arms enclose a spectacular glassed-in atrium filled with palm trees and other tropical vegetation. During construction, remains of a Roman stone building, rubble from the 13thC London Bridge and a medieval anchor were found at the site.

Grange Walk **1 B5**
SE1. A row of attractive houses, of which Nos 5, 6 and 7 are 15th-16thC and were originally part of Bermondsey Abbey's south gatehouse. Some boast bits of Norman wall in their cellars and No 7 has two of the gate hinges still protruding from its wall. Nos 8-11 date from c1700. There is also a charity school of 1830, now in disrepair. Opposite, the Museum of London has been carrying out an investigative dig on another part of the Abbey site, to see if they can uncover anything before the developers move in. No public access.

Hay's Galleria **1 B3**
Tooley St SE1. Billed as 'London's new shopping and eating experience', this elegant and lofty arcade with barrel-vaulted glass roof is reminiscent of Victorian railway architecture or perhaps the Crystal Palace. The façades of the Victorian warehouses which surrounded the small Hay's Dock have been retained and the filled-in dock forms the floor of the Galleria, which has a range of upmarket high street shops, a wine bar, brasserie and brasserie/pub. There are hanging baskets and bay trees in tubs, real red telephone kiosks and some bijou handcarts with striped canopies.

But the real star of the show is its fountain, a 60ft (18m) high kinetic sculpture in bronze called *The Navigators*, by Cornish artist David Kemp (engineering by Norman Waldren OBE). It is a wonderfully imaginative and witty creation, a sea monster-cum-ship made of diverse marine and navigational objects, with parts which move and then stop, and water spouting from unexpected places. Worth a special visit. *Galleria open 06.00-23.30 Mon-Sun. Shops open normal hours.*

Hay's Galleria

HMS Belfast **1 B2**
Morgans Lane, Tooley St SE1. 01-407 6434. The largest cruiser ever built for the Royal Navy is most suitably reached by gangway from the south bank, or else by a regular ferry from Tower Pier. She is now a permanent museum, and her bridge, engine rooms, gun turrets, decks, galley and sick-bays may all be explored. Much of the original equipment is still in place and realistic dummies make it easier to imagine life on board. The keepers, all retired Navy men, will answer questions and there is a museum shop. *Open 11.00-17.00 Mon-Sun. Closed 16.30 winter. Charge.*

King's Stairs Gardens **2 F4**
Jamaica Rd SE1. A small, pleasant park with a riverside terrace and children's playground. On its east side is the Angel pub and on the west, the award-winning Elephant Lane housing scheme. Across the main road is the large Southwark Park

which has an open-air swimming pool and an art gallery.

London Bridge 1 A2

SE1. There has been some kind of bridge here since the 1stC. The present concrete structure by Harold Knox King, built 1967-73, has two particularly illustrious predecessors: the early 13thC stone one with its wooden houses and shops and, sometimes, traitors' heads on poles, familiar from old woodcuts; and John Rennie's construction of 1825-31 which was sold to America and now spans an artificial lake in Arizona.

London Bridge City 1 B3

Tooley St SE1. A major new development along the river from London Bridge to Tower Bridge, on the site of the old Hay's Wharf. The latter was founded in 1651 and was once known as 'the larder of London' because of the vast quantities of foodstuffs from all over the world unloaded and stored here. The Great Fire of Tooley Street in 1861 lasted two weeks and destroyed most of the original warehouses. Nearly all the Victorian warehouses which replaced them have, in turn, been demolished to make way for the largest single commercial development in Europe. The developers are the Kuwaiti-owned St Martin's Property Corporation.

Phase 1, from London Bridge to HMS *Belfast*, was completed in mid-1987 and includes No 1 London Bridge, London Bridge Hospital, Cottons Centre and Hay's Galleria. Dividing it from Phase 2 is the uninteresting new Crown Courts building, not part of London Bridge City but occupying a prime riverside site, to the chagrin of the developers. Phase 2, due for completion in 1989, will be a mix of offices, retail and residential units. A park has already been created beside Tower Bridge.

London Bridge Hospital 1 A3

Tooley St SE1. A non-matching pair of buildings, the Victorian Chamberlain's Warehouse and the 1930s Emblem House, have been combined in this conversion into a private hospital run by the St Martin's Group. No public access.

London Dungeon 1 B3

34 Tooley St SE1. 01-403 0606. Gruesomely realistic exhibition of the dark side of British history in a dank, vaulted cellar; sacrifices, tortures, plagues, murders, executions – everything you need for a really vivid nightmare, or several. Unsuitable for adults or those of a sensitive disposition. *Open 10.00-17.30 Mon-Sat, 14.00-17.30 Sun. Charge.*

Most Holy Trinity Church 1 D4

Dockhead, Jamaica Rd SE1. 01-237 1641. A Roman Catholic church by H.S. Goodhart-Rendel, built in 1960 to replace one destroyed in World War II. A chapel commemorates two local 16thC martyrs, John Felton and his son Thomas, tortured and executed for their faith. *Closed* except for services. Services: Mass *07.30, 10.00 & 18.00 Sun, 9.30 Mon-Wed & Fri, 20.00 Thur & 18.30 Sat.*

No 1 London Bridge 1 A3

Tooley St SE1. An uncompromisingly austere office building of pink granite, powerful but not lovable. It covers nearly one acre (0.4 ha) and comprises two towers, one of twelve storeys, in the form of an arch, and the other of nine storeys. They are linked by an asymmetrical atrium. No public access.

St James's Church 1 D5

Old Jamaica Rd SE1. 01-232 2329. One of the grandest of the 'Waterloo' churches (built as a thanks-offering for victory), designed by James Savage and built 1827-9. It has an impressive portico on the west front and a baroque-style spire with a golden dragon on top. The chancel contains a large Ascension of Christ painted in 1844 by John Wood. The church was built to seat 2,000; today's congregation is a fraction of that, but growing, due largely to the new housing developments in the area. There is a long-standing connection with the Cambridge University Mission. *Closed* except for services. Services: *11.00 & 18.30 Sun* (alternate between ordinary services and communion). Communion *07.30 Tue.*

St Martin's Walk 1 B3

London Bridge City, Tooley St SE1. A broad riverside path with benches and greenery, running in front of London Bridge City. It is reached by steps down from London Bridge or from Tooley Street. Eventually it will go as far as Tower Bridge. Superb views of the Tower of London, Tower Bridge, HMS *Belfast* and many other landmarks. The London Bridge City pier has been built as a stop for the new riverbus service.

St Mary Magdalen 1 B5

Bermondsey St SE1. 01-232 2329. The parish church of Bermondsey, standing on part of the site of Bermondsey Abbey, was founded in the 13thC. The present building is partly 15thC but was mostly rebuilt in the 17thC, and much restored in the 19thC. The beautifully kept churchyard makes this a pleasant corner. The church has some 12thC carved capitals, probably from the

Abbey, two large late-17thC candelabra and a 17thC wooden reredos, possibly carved by a pupil of Grinling Gibbons, as are the panels in the churchwardens' pew. There is an excellent 19thC organ by Joseph Walker in an 18thC case. The church's greatest treasure, the 14thC silver Bermondsey Dish, reputed to be from the Abbey, is now in the Victoria & Albert Museum. *Closed* except for services. Services: Communion *10.30, 18.00 & 19.30 Sun (plus 08.00 second Sun in the month), 13.00 Tue.*

St Olaf House **1 B3**
Tooley St SE1. A striking art deco building of 1931, designed by H.S. Goodhart-Rendel as offices for Hay's Wharf. It was built on the site of a church dedicated to St Olave (or Olaf), king and patron saint of Norway, who helped to defend London against the invading Danes in the 11thC. On one corner there is a mosaic picture of the saint and on another, an inscription telling the story. Tooley Street is probably a corruption of St Olaf Street (Olaf would have been pronounced 'Oolaf' at one time). No public access.

St Saviour's Dock **1 D4**
Jamaica Rd SE1. A tidal inlet, originally the mouth of the River Neckinger which has now disappeared. Grain, spices and peas used to be unloaded from lighters. The 19thC warehouses backing on to Shad Thames on the west side, Mill Street on the east, are being converted into luxury flats and studios. New Concordia Wharf, Mill Street, with its massive brick chimney at one corner, won a Europa Nostra medal in 1986. There is something romantically gloomy about the dank and sunless dock, which can be viewed from the end of an alleyway between Unity and Lloyds Wharves on Mill Street. The surrounding streets were once notorious for their violence and poverty and the area fascinated Dickens. Jacob's Island, now a new development site, was the rookery where Bill Sikes met his grisly end in *Oliver Twist*.

Milling had been the main commercial activity since the early Middle Ages, but that tradition ended in 1987 with the closure of Vogan's rice and lentil mill.

Dr Alfred Salter Conservation Area **2 E4**
Wilson Grove SE1. A small estate of attractive cottage-style houses built in 1928 by Bermondsey Council. It was a showpiece, part of the Council's attempts to turn Bermondsey slums into a garden suburb. Alfred Salter was a local doctor, an MP and a Quaker, who was deeply involved in this and other community work.

Shad Thames **1 C3**
SE1. A unique and dramatic bit of streetscape. The towering warehouses of St Saviour's Dock and Butler's Wharf on either side of this dark, narrow street are linked by overhead footbridges, which were used to transfer tea, spices and foodstuffs from riverside to landward warehouses. The powerful sense of the past which this eerie street evokes will probably fade as the area is redeveloped and the footbridges, pulleys and winches are transformed into pretty 'features'. The only working survivor is one of the spice mills, and the aroma still hangs in the air. Several of the warehouses have already been converted into flats. The land here was owned in medieval times by the Knights of St John and the street's name is thought to be a corruption of St John at Thames.

Shad Thames

South London College **1 C3**
Tooley St SE1. A very handsome Grade II listed building in red brick and white stone, built in 1893 to house St Olave's Grammar School. It was designed by E.W. Mountford and shows the influence of the 19thC Arts and Crafts Movement. No public access.

Southwark Cathedral **1 A3**
Borough High St SE1. 01-407 3708. Officially the cathedral and collegiate church of St Saviour and St Mary Overie (the last word meaning 'over the water'). It has had cathedral status only since 1905. Founded in the 12thC and restored and partially rebuilt over the years, its 13thC choir and retrochoir are superb examples of the Early English style, while the nave dates only from the late 19thC. Among the many treasures is a 13thC wooden effigy of a knight. One of the earliest English poets, John Gower who died in 1408, has an

elaborate and colourful tomb and there is a 20thC memorial to Shakespeare. A chapel commemorates the founder of Harvard University, John Harvard, who was christened here. Frequent concerts, organ recitals and other events. *Open 09.00-18.00 Mon-Sun.* Services: Holy Communion *09.00 Sun, 08.00 Tue & Thur, 12.45 Mon-Fri, 12.00 Sat.* Choral evensong *15.00 Sun, 17.30 Tue & Fri.* Evensong *17.30 Mon, Wed & Thur, 16.00 Sat.*

Tower Bridge **1 C3**
EC3. Splendid Victorian Gothic structure, with hydraulically operated drawbridge, by Jones and Wolfe-Barry, 1894. The lattice work footbridges with their wonderful river views are open to the public and there is a small exhibition inside on the history and operational abilities of the bridge, which still opens up to allow tall ships to pass through. *Open Apr-Oct 10.00-18.30 Mon-Sun; Nov-Mar 10.00-16.45 Mon-Sun. Charge.*

Eating and Drinking
Hay's Galleria for a choice of Balls Bros wine bar or two brasseries, Café Pelican or the Horniman; light meals at Byron's; pub food at the Anchor Tap, the Angel (which also has a restaurant) or the Old Justice. See Pubs and Restaurants.

Rotherhithe

Associated Newspapers **5 A1**
Redriff Rd SE16. Another of the big names of Fleet Street moves to Docklands – the printing works and editorial offices of the Daily Mail were being built here as this book went to press.

Brunel Pumping Engine House **2 G4**
Tunnel St SE16. Built in 1842 to house the machinery which pumped water out of the Thames Tunnel engineered by Marc Brunel. It was restored in 1976 and now contains a small exposition on the construction of the tunnel – the first underwater tunnel for traffic ever to be completed and now a part of the London Underground system's Metropolitan Line. At the moment opening of the engine house is a rare event – one Sunday afternoon a month – but there are plans to develop the immediate area for tourism and to establish more convenient opening times. Limited access. *Small charge.*

Canada Water **2 H5**
SE16. Once a working dock exporting machinery and general cargo and importing plywood, Canada Water is now temporarily stranded in the middle of a building site. Its interesting freshwater ecology – unusual because the rest of the docks are estuarine – was badly damaged when a section at one end was filled in for the Tesco building project. Potassium in the in-fill turned the water alkaline and though it has now been neutralised back to its original state the water plants and wildlife don't seem to be rushing to re-establish themselves. The London Wildlife Trust are monitoring progress.

Charity School **2 G4**
St Marychurch St SE16. Elegant 18thC timber-panelled house. Soon after it was built it was taken over by a Charity School, founded by Peter Hill a Rotherhithe sailor, and the traditional Charity School statues of a demure boy and girl are preserved above the door. It is now used as offices by another charity, the East End Community Trust, which funds community projects and will preserve the fabric of the house. No public access.

Durand's Wharf **3 C6**
Rotherhithe St SE16. An attractively landscaped public open space, with grass and trees sloping gently upwards to a brief riverside promenade which gives views across the Thames to the Isle of Dogs.

Ecological Park **3 B5**
SE16. The largest (7 acres – 3 ha –) man-made ecological park in Britain curves around Stave Hill and is backed by the thick strip of trees that is known as Russia Dock Woodland. It is being laid out and monitored by the Trust for Urban Ecology, partly as a showpiece, and partly as a research project where those in charge of other such areas can watch theory become practice. In the end, of course, it has to be left to the flora and fauna of Rotherhithe to decide on the degree of its success.

Finnish Seamen's Mission **2 G4**
33 Albion St SE16. 01-237 4668. One of the three Scandinavian churches in the area, built by Yorke, Rosenberg and Mardall, with white walls and an attractive campanile. There are Sunday services in Finnish, and

social events in the afternoons and evenings, principally for Finnish sailors, though all expatriate Finns (and, indeed, other nationalities) are welcome. *Centre open 14.00-22.00 Mon-Fri; 14.00-20.00 Sat & Sun.* Service: *11.00 first Sun in the month, 18.00 other Suns.*

Greenland Dock **5 B2**
SE16. The Howland Great Wet Dock, constructed at the end of the 17thC, was the first of the docks in this area. By 1763 it had become a base for the whaling trade and was renamed Greenland Dock. By 1900 it was receiving grain from Canada and in the

The London Docklands Development Corporation
The London Docklands Development Corporation (LDDC) was set up by the government in 1981 to manage and co-ordinate a programme of regeneration of London's Docklands, following the closure of all the docks and most of the associated industries.

It was established under the 1980 Local Government Planning and Land Act which empowered the Secretary of State for the Environment to create Urban Development Corporations. The then Secretary of State, Michael Heseltine, is credited with having had the original idea for these corporations when, some years earlier, he had flown in a helicopter over London's dying docks and was apparently inspired with a vision of how these and similar wastelands might be transformed through private enterprise.

The LDDC's specific task is 'to bring land and existing buildings into effective use and to encourage the development of new industry and commerce; to create an attractive environment; and to ensure the availability of housing and social facilities.' It acts as a catalyst: by investing a certain amount of public money into reclaiming land, upgrading it and releasing it for development sites, and into the improvement of infrastructure and communications, it attracts private investment into the area. In the first six years, the LDDC's net investment of £257 million brought in £2,242 million of private funds – a 'leverage' rate of 1:9, which is considered highly successful.

Although the Corporation is the planning authority for the area, there is no overall physical plan and developments are carried out on a market-led basis.

A certain amount of land has been vested in the LDDC. However, the Corporation also has the power to acquire the freehold or, in some cases, the leasehold of land from the Port of London Authority (PLA), formerly the main landowner in Docklands, from other public bodies such as British Rail or the Central Electricity Generating Board, or from private owners, and in due course sells or leases the land to developers. In 1987 it owned about 1,000 acres (405 ha) of the total 5,000 acres (2,025 ha) of land. A considerable area has remained in private hands or as the property of public bodies.

Of the 400 acres (182 ha) of water in Docklands, the LDDC owns the Royal Victoria, West India and Millwall Docks and what remains of Surrey Docks; it has a long lease on the Royal Albert and King George V Docks; a Taylor Woodrow subsidiary owns St Katharine Docks; the British Waterways Board owns Limehouse Basin.

The Board of the LDDC consists of up to 13 members, including the Chairman, all appointed by the Secretary of State for the Environment for a 3-year period, which can be extended. It meets monthly and is advised by officers of the Corporation. It also has several more specialised committees.

Members include business people (with property developers to the fore), industrialists and retired local government officials and civil servants. There is only one woman on the Board at present (early 1988).

Originally it was thought that the LDDC would have a life of 15-20 years; now it is believed that its task will be completed more quickly than expected and that it can be wound up at an earlier date. The creation of a new Docklands Borough has been mooted, but it is more likely that planning powers will revert to the three existing councils.

The Corporation has about 90 people on its permanent staff and another 200 or so on fixed-term contracts or on secondment from private or public organisations. The Chief Executive is appointed by the Board and, it is assumed, will also be made a Board member by the Secretary of State.

1960s, just before it closed down, it was docking general cargo vessels, paper from Scandinavia, marble from Italy and wines from France and Spain. Now its 22.5 acres (9 ha) of water surface are to be used for quiet watersports, its quays have been attractively landscaped with trees and lollipop street lights, and many of the new developments which are to surround it are already complete. On the north bank Brunswick Quay, Russia Court East and Norway Dock are principally residential, and Greenland Passage to the west and Greenland Quay and Swedish Quays to the south are entirely residential. The old hydraulically operated entrance lock remains as a reminder of the old working days.

Brunswick Quay

Greenland Dock Pier **5** C2
SE16. Docklands' newest pier, built by the LDDC to serve the new riverbus. It was opened in 1987 by Princess Margaret who was officially the first person ever to set foot on it.

Greenland Dock Swing Bridge **5** B1
Redriff Rd SE16. The old iron swing bridge which crossed the canal between Greenland and Russia Docks is to be preserved as an intriguing piece of industrial archaeology.

Holy Trinity Church **3** C6
Rotherhithe St SE16. 01-237 3963. Modern Anglican church built on the site of a predecessor obliterated by World War II bombs. An ancient stone slab, under a tree in the churchyard, has become a focal point for the recently bereaved whose relatives have been cremated, and is often decorated with posies of fresh flowers. Inside, on the east wall, is a striking Hans Feibusch mural.

Lavender Pond **3** B4
Lavender Rd, Rotherhithe St SE16. 01-232 0498. Lavender Dock was the largest, in terms of water area, of the Surrey Commercial Docks and was used principally as a timber pond. When the Docks closed it was filled in, though the lock, and the yellow stock-brick pumping station which served it, both remain.

There is now a 2-acre (0.8 ha) nature park on the site, with a pond, reed beds, meadowland and mixed woodland. It is run jointly by the Borough of Southwark and the Trust for Urban Ecology, and is primarily a community educational facility. There is a warden on site and a teacher is available to encourage school parties to identify water beetles, dragonflies and birds. Fishing here is not illegal, but neither is it encouraged (if you must, at least don't use lead weights, which have been responsible for more than one tragedy among the swans). *Open till dusk Mon-Sun.*

LDDC Surrey Docks Area Office **2** G5
Surrey Quays, Lower Rd SE16. 01-237 6666. This, the former Dock Manager's Office, built in 1892 of yellow stock brick with red detailing and a pleasing clock tower (also of brick), has been restored to good effect by the LDDC and at present provides appropriate premises for their area office. No public access.

The London Glass Blowing Workshop **2** G4
109 Rotherhithe St SE16. 01-237 0394. Here craftsmen create unique decorative 'pieces' in blown glass. Watch them at work, or cross to the Gallery in the restored granary building where the finished products are on sale. *Open 11.00-18.00 Mon-Fri.*

Nelson Dock and Nelson Dock House **3** C5
Rotherhithe St SE16. Nelson Dock was a shipbuilding yard which was turning out warships as early as the 17thC. It had various owners and by the middle of this century was used solely for ship repair. The Danish developers, Islef, plan to put up housing here. They are also considering filling the dock with water, which would be a shame because it is at present one of only two surviving riverside dry docks.

The elegant 18thC mansion, Nelson Dock House, was built for one of the owners of the shipyard. As a Grade II listed building it is currently being restored and will be used as offices.

Norwegian Seamen's Church **2** G4
1 Albion St SE16. 01-237 5587. The Norwegian Seamen's church has been active in London for over 100 years, and has been based here, at St Olave's, for the past 60. Services are conducted in Norwegian every Sunday and there are social gatherings in the afternoons and evenings for Norwegian sailors and for other

Norwegian visitors and residents. Built in 1927, by John Seaton Dahl, its spire with golden Viking-ship weathervane is a landmark in the area. *Open 15.00-22.00 Mon-Fri, 10.00-18.00 Sat, 10.00-22.00 Sun.* Service: *11.00 Sun.*

Rope Knots Garden **2 G4**
St Marychurch St SE16. This bleak concrete area with its riverside wall which is awkward to look over, its raised seat, and its three massive knots made from stout hempen rope, was the result of a nationwide 'Art into Landscape' competition. The local authority governing each of the designated sites was committed to creating the winning design. Possibly there weren't many other entries for this one. The LDDC plans to refurbish in the future.

Rotherhithe Pier **2 H2**
SE16. Gravel dredged from sea-channels and river-mouths is docked here and taken by road to customers all over the country. The LDDC plans to build a new bridge nearby to serve the riverbus.

Rotherhithe Pier (Ventilation Shaft) **2 H2**
SE16. The large and mysterious brick drum at the waterside is a ventilation shaft for the 4,860ft (1,482m) Rotherhithe Tunnel.

Rotherhithe Tunnel **2 H3**
SE16. Here the road plunges underground to offer cars and pedestrians a quick, if unappealing, route to Wapping. It was built by Maurice Fitzmaurice in 1904-8 using a technique known as the Greathead shield method, after J.H. Greathead who improved upon the shield method pioneered by Marc Brunel. The shield had separate working compartments, making it rather like a massive iron honeycomb. Each man dug out the clay and earth in front of him and the shield was jacked steadily forwards as they worked. The arch at the tunnel entrance is part of the shield itself.

Rotherhithe Workshops **2 G4**
61 St Marychurch St SE16. 01-237 5299. Community workshops offering classes in art and craft-related subjects; workshop space for professionals; and facilities – such as computer literacy training, photocopying and secretarial services – for local businesses. The Woodwork Shop makes toys and frames pictures, and the River Gallery provides a welcome exhibition space for local artists. *Open 09.00-17.30 Mon-Fri. Weekends by appointment only.*

Russia Dock Woodland **3 B6**
SE16. A long woodland park, richly planted with mixed deciduous trees by Southwark Borough Council, on the site of the old Russia Dock. It has a walkway, comfortingly provided with benches, and leads from Greenland Dock to Stave Hill and the Ecological Park, the three together forming an unexpected and wholly welcome green belt in the middle of the thoroughly urbanised peninsula.

St Mary's Church **2 G4**
St Marychurch St SE16. 01-231 2465. There has been a church in Rotherhithe Village for 1,000 years, but the present St Mary's was finished in 1715. Its impressive interior is beautifully maintained, the John Byfield organ is magnificent and Grinling Gibbons' handiwork can be seen in the reredos.

Maritime connections are strong. The crew of the *Mayflower* worshipped here and her Captain, Christopher Jones, was buried in the churchyard in 1622. Unfortunately most of the graves were lost during the rebuilding and part of the churchyard is now a playground. The communion table and two bishops' chairs are carved from oak taken from the warship *Fighting Temeraire*, whose voyage to the Rotherhithe breaker's yard is the subject of a famous Turner painting in the National Gallery. *Open 07.00-18.00 Mon-Sat.* Services: Eucharist *10.00 Sun, 07.30 Mon-Thur, 09.45 Sat.* Evensong *17.30 Sat.*

South Dock **5 B2**
SE16. A marina is planned where general cargo vessels once docked, and the old bollards and capstans will be kept *in situ* as interesting features. Most of the development in this area will be residential.

Southwark Park **2 G6**
Lower Rd, Rotherhithe SE16. Although it lies just outside the area covered by this guide, the 63 green acres (25 ha) of Southwark Park are too important and attractive to leave out. It is exceptionally well-equipped for sports, with 12 full-sized football pitches and 2 junior ones, a cricket pitch, tennis and netball courts, bowling and putting greens, a floodlit running track – and also an outdoor swimming pool (*open from Jun-Sep*). Those with a less energetic approach to life can simply stroll beneath the trees – mercifully largely undamaged by the hurricane force winds of 1987 – or enjoy the changing art exhibitions in the Café Gallery, 01-232 2170. *Park open 07.00-dusk or 20.00. Please ring for details of Café hours.*

While in the park, take a look at the fish farm, off Gomm Rd (01-232 1777, *before 10.00 or after 19.00*). Here Doug Potter breeds freshwater fish to restock the ponds of Southwark, and also barn owls which the

British Bird Council then releases into suitable habitats around Britain. There are rabbits, goats, peacocks, geese, ducks and a donkey to see, too. It's free, run by volunteers, and if it looks crowded when you arrive that may be because a party of children or OAPs is being shown around. *Open 10.00-16.00 Mon-Sat. Free.*

Stave Hill **3 B6**
SE16. Man-made, in the image of a small Silbury Hill, from earth dug out of the new Albion Channel (built 1985-6) which links Canada Water and Surrey Water. There are good views from the top – downwards to the Ecological Park and Russia Dock Woodland and outwards to Tower Bridge, St Paul's Cathedral, the NatWest Tower and the City. In the other direction are glimpses of the river with the Isle of Dogs beyond.

Surrey Docks Farm **3 C6**
Rotherhithe St SE16. 01-231 1010. Goats, pigs, donkeys, ducks, quail, geese and hens mill about together in entertaining disarray on this 2 acre (0.8 ha) site, which also has a small orchard, vegetable garden, wild area, duckpond and new riverside walk. The atmosphere is informal although the purpose is educational; the classroom with resident teacher is used by local schools and there are schemes to provide work experience and community service. The children observe the animals, calculate feed requirements and analyse the farm's budget. There is no room for sentimentality – a report on the pig-keeping year begins: 'We took June and Betty to the slaughterhouse in the Easter holidays.' Run by a Provident Society and funded by the LDDC, ILEA, Southwark Council and other bodies, the farm moved here in 1986 from its old site near Greenland Dock. The farm shop sells organic honey, goat's milk and yoghurt, soft cheese and eggs. *Open 10.00-13.00 & 14.00-17.00 Tue-Sun. Closed Mon & Fri in school holidays. Free.*

Surrey Docks Watersports Centre **5 B2**
Gate 6, Greenland Dock, Redriff Rd SE16. 01-237 4009. At the moment the centre is for schools and youth groups only, but there are plans to expand it considerably. *Open 09.00-dusk Mon-Sun. Please ring for details.*

Surrey Quays Shopping Centre **2 H5**
SE16. Tesco's huge retail development is due to open at the end of 1988. As well as an enormous Tesco hypermarket there will be a general department store and about 30 smaller shops, including branches of W.H. Smith, Boots and BHS.

Surrey Water **2 H3**
SE16. Once Surrey Dock Basin, this is now an attractive water feature at the edge of the Surrey Quays Residential Development. Its fountain was ceremonially switched on by Princess Margaret. Surrey Water is linked to Canada Water by the new Albion Channel. Not so much a canal, more a linear water feature, this follows the line of the old Albion Dock which is now filled in.

Surrey Water Bridge **2 H3**
SE16. The spectacular red contraption over the entrance canal to Surrey Water is a restored iron bascule bridge. In its working days it was hydraulically operated and swung right back on its counterpoise to allow boats and ships to pass.

Surrey Water Bridge

Swedish Seamen's Church **2 H5**
120 Lower Rd SE16. 01-237 1644. The church may look closed but the entry-phone system admits genuine callers at any time of day. There is one service in Swedish a week, bed and breakfast accommodation, a cafeteria and Swedish books and magazines. Though primarily for seamen – the church visits all Swedish ships here and in the Medway – all are welcome. The cross outside, formed of an anchor and a fish, is particularly attractive. *Open 14.00-22.00 Mon-Sun* Service: *18.00 Sun.*

The Watch House **2 G4**
St Marychurch St SE16. The local watchman or constable operated from here and could take wrongdoers into custody in the watch house pending their appearance before the magistrate. This one was well placed for watching over new graves in the churchyard – a temptation to early-19thC body snatchers who sold fresh cadavers to hospitals for dissection by students. No public access.

Eating and Drinking
Pub food at the Blacksmith's Arms (which also has a restaurant), the Gun, the Mayflower (restaurant, too), the Ship or the Ship Yorke; an unusual dinner at the Rogue's Kitchen.
See Pubs and Restaurants.

Services

All services closed Sat & Sun unless otherwise stated.

ADULT EDUCATION

Southwark Institute of Adult Education
Headquarters Branch, Queens Road Centre, St Mary's Rd SE15. 01-639 1178.
Aylwin Branch **1** D6
55 Southwark Park Rd SE16. 01-237 1491. Offers a variety of classes including cookery, dressmaking and keep fit. *Open 10.00-16.00 & 18.30-22.00 Mon-Fri.*
Grange Branch **1** B5
12 Grange Rd SE1. 01-237 3716. Offers usual mainstream classes but also has wide programme of courses for people with special learning difficulties. *Open 10.00-16.00 & 18.00-21.30 Mon-Fri.*
Scott Lidgett Branch **2** E5
Drummond Rd SE16. 01-237 4029. Courses include car maintenance, dog training, keep fit and swimming. *Open 18.30-22.00 Mon-Fri.*

BANKS

Barclays Bank **1** B5
104 Tower Bridge Rd SE1. 01-231 3636. *Open 09.30-15.30 Mon-Fri.*
Barclays Bank
29 Borough High St SE1. 01-403 0666. *Open 09.30-15.30 Mon-Fri.*
Barclays Bank **2** E5
180 Jamaica Rd SE16. 01-237 5115. *Open 09.30-15.30 Mon-Fri.*
Barclays Bank **5** A3
1 Plough Way SE16. 01-231 7222. *Open 09.30-15.30 Mon-Fri.*
Lloyds Bank **5** B5
67 Tower Bridge Rd SE1. 01-407 3251. *Open 09.30-15.30 Mon-Fri.*
Lloyds Bank
69-73 Borough High St SE1. 01-407 7731. *Open 09.30-15.30 Mon-Fri.*
Midland Bank
28 Borough High St SE1. 01-407 0575. *Open 09.30-15.30 Mon-Fri.*
Midland Bank **2** E5
98 Jamaica Rd SE16. 01-237 5972. *Open 09.30-15.30 Mon-Fri.*
Midland Bank **5** A3
196 Lower Rd SE16. 01-237 1705. *Open 09.30-15.30 Mon-Fri.*
National Westminster Bank **1** C4
201 Tooley St SE1. 01-403 4722. *Open 09.30-15.30 Mon-Fri.*

BUILDING SOCIETIES

Abbey National
51 Borough High St SE1. 01-403 6822. *Open 08.30 (09.00 Wed)-16.30 Mon-Fri.*
Abbey National **2** E6
210 Southwark Park Rd SE16. 01-237 4974. *Open 09.00 (09.30 Wed)-17.00 Mon-Fri, 09.00-12.00 Sat.*
Woolwich Equitable **2** F5
264 Southwark Park Rd SE1. 01-231 1126. *Open 09.00 (09.30 Thur)-17.00 Mon-Fri, 09.00-12.00 Sat.*

CHEMISTS

Campion & Co **2** G4
38 Albion St SE16. 01-237 1193. *Open 09.00-18.30 Mon-Fri, 09.00-17.30 Sat.*
Carefield Ltd **1** D4
Wade House, Dickens Estate, Parkers Row SE1. 01-231 1100. *Open 09.00-18.30 Mon-Thur (to 18.00 Fri).*
James of Rotherhithe **5** A3
182-184 Lower Rd SE16. 01-237 1896. *Open 09.00-18.30 Mon-Sat.*
T. P. Patel **2** E5
182 Jamaica Rd SE16. 01-237 3483. *Open 09.00-18.30 Mon-Fri, 09.00-16.00 Sat.*
Sur-dock Chemists **5** A3
162 Lower Rd SE16. 01-237 2512. *Open 09.00-19.00 Mon-Fri, 09.00-18.30 Sat.*

CHIROPODISTS

James of Rotherhithe **5** A3
182-184 Lower Rd SE16. 01-237 1896. Appointment necessary. *Open 09.00-18.30 Mon-Sat.*

COMMUNITY AND YOUTH CENTRES

Docklands Settlement **5** B1
Rotherhithe St SE16. 01-237 3621. Community and youth centre. Sporting facilities on the site. *Open 09.00-15.00, 18.00-22.00 Mon-Fri.*
Rotherhithe Civic Centre **2** G4
Albion St SE16. 01-231 1025. Can be booked by all members of the community for weddings, parties, local interest group meetings etc. *Open 07.00-21.30 Mon, Thur & Sat, 07.00-21.00 Tue, 07.00-17.00 Wed &*

Fri. Times may vary depending on function, phone for details.

Rotherhithe Community Workshop 2 G4
61 St Marychurch St SE16. 01-237 5299. Offers picture framing facilities and office facilities. *Open 09.00-17.30 Mon-Fri.*

Time and Talents Association 2 G4
The Old Mortuary, St Marychurch St SE16. 01-231 7845. A neighbourhood centre offering many different facilities and *open 10.00-18.00 Mon-Fri. Also open weekends and later in evenings* depending on functions. Phone for details.

COUNCILLORS

Members of London Borough of Southwark. Council offices at the Town Hall, Peckham Rd SE5. 01-703 6311. The local councillors for the Riverside Neighbourhood are Michael Hannon (Liberal), Michael Heaney (Liberal) and Joan Price (Liberal). The local councillors for the Dockyard Neighbourhood are Ronald Kendrick (Liberal), Patricia Mattheson (Liberal) and Pat Sullivan (Labour). If you have any complaints, suggestions or queries write to your councillor at the Town Hall.

DENTISTS

. N. Hampleman & Associates 2 G5
04 Lower Rd SE16. 01-237 7902. *Open 09.00-18.30 Mon, Tue & Thur, 09.00-13.00 Wed, 09.00-17.00 Fri, 10.00-13.00 Sat.*

. V. & J. L. Jenkins 2 E5
86 Jamaica Rd SE16. 01-231 2883. *Open 09.00-17.30 (closed 13.00-14.00) Mon, Tue, Thur & Fri, 09.00-13.00 Wed.*

. J. Southcott & Associates 2 E5
64 Jamaica Rd SE16. 01-237 3413. *Open 09.00-19.30 Mon-Wed, 09.00-17.00 Thur & Fri (closed 13.00-14.00 Mon-Fri), 09.00-12.00 Sat.*

DHSS OFFICES

Southwark DHSS Office
Wedge House, Blackfriars Rd SE1. 01-928 949. Covers Surrey Docks area. *Open 09.30-15.30 Mon-Fri.*

DOCTORS

Drs J. & E. Hickey 2 G4
Albion Health Centre, Albion St SE16. 01-237 2092. *Open 09.30-11.00 & 16.30-18.00 Mon-Fri (to 11.00 Thur).*

Dr A. Ross 1 D4
2 Wade House, Parkers Row SE1. 01-237 0898. *Open 09.30-10.30 Mon-Fri, 17.00-18.15 Mon-Wed.* Emergency no: 01-689 6811.

Dr Rosser & Dr Cook 1 E5
6-8 Drummond Rd SE16. 01-237 1857. *Open 09.00-12.00 & 15.00-18.00 Mon-Fri.*

Dr T. Stack & Dr Das 2 H6
34 Rotherhithe New Rd SE16. 01-237 4091. *Open 09.00-11.00 & 16.00-18.00 Mon-Fri.*

DRY CLEANERS

Four Hour Clean-In 5 A3
194 Lower Rd SE16. 01-237 3725. *Open 07.00-17.30 Mon-Wed & Fri, 09.00-13.00 Thur, 08.00-17.30 Sat.*

Sarah Drycleaning 2 F4
198 Jamaica Rd SE16. 01-237 6866. *Open 08.00-18.00 Mon-Fri, 08.00-14.45 Sat, 08.00-12.45 Sun.*

State Express 2 E4
176 Jamaica Rd SE16. 01-237 7134. *Open 08.00-18.00 Mon-Sat (to 13.00 Thur).*

Toptower Dry Cleaners 1 B5
110 Tower Bridge Rd SE1. 01-237 7135. *Open 08.00-18.00 Mon-Sat.*

EMPLOYMENT AGENCIES

Atlas
18 Borough High St SE1. 01-407 8311. Agent for temporary and permanent office staff. *Open 09.00-17.00 Mon-Thur, 09.00-18.00 Fri.*

ESTATE AGENTS

Docklands Property Centre 2 H6
Southside House, 128 Lower Rd SE16. 01-237 5454. Residential property only. *Open 09.00-18.00 Mon-Fri, 10.00-17.00 Sat & Sun.*

Field & Sons
54 Borough High St SE1. 01-407 1375. Residential and commercial property. *Open 09.30-17.30 Mon-Fri.*

Michael Kalmar & Co 1 C4
1 Jamaica Rd SE1. 01-403 0600. Residential and commercial property. *Open 09.00-18.00 Mon-Fri, 10.00-14.30 Sat.*

Keith Cardale Groves (Docklands) 1 C3
212 Tower Bridge Rd SE1. 01-407 2790. Mainly residential but handle commercial property in association with their Mayfair office. *Open 09.00-17.30 Mon-Fri.*

Lennard, Headley & Chandler 2 G5
1 The Dock Offices, Surrey Docks SE16. 01-232 0233. Residential and commercial

property. *Open 09.00-18.00 Mon-Fri, 10.00-17.00 Sat & Sun.*

Parris & Quirk 2 G4
City Business Centre, Albion St SE16. 01-232 0752. Commercial property only. Residential office on Isle of Dogs. *Open 09.30-17.30 Mon-Fri.*

E. A. Shaw & Partners 1 C3
216 Tower Bridge Rd SE1. 01-403 7250. Residential and commercial property. *Open 09.00-17.30 Mon-Fri, 11.00-16.00 Sat & Sun.*

HAIRDRESSERS

Diamond Cut 5 A3
243 Lower Rd SE16. 01-237 1031. Unisex. *Open 09.00-18.00 Mon, Wed & Thur, 09.00-19.30 Fri, 08.30-18.00 Sat. Closed Tue.*

C. George 2 H6
195 Lower Rd SE16. 01-237 1051. Unisex. *Open 09.00-18.00 Mon-Thur & Sat, 09.00-18.30 Fri.*

Lords & Ladies 2 F5
361 Southwark Park Rd SE16. 01-231 8665. Unisex. *Open 09.00-17.00 Mon-Thur & Sat, 09.00-19.00 Fri.*

Shobiz 2 F5
230 Southwark Park Rd SE16. 01-231 8077. Unisex. *Open 09.30-17.30 Mon-Thur, 09.30-20.30 Fri, 08.30-16.30 Sat.*

Spenlows 2 E5
129 Jamaica Rd SE16. 01-237 3302. Unisex. *Open 10.00-16.00 Mon, 09.30-17.30 Tue-Fri, 08.00-18.00 Sat.*

HEALTH CENTRES

Albion Street Health Centre 2 G4
87 Albion St SE16. 01-231 2296/7. Facilities include child healthcare, district nurse, family planning, physiotherapist and well woman clinic. *Open 09.00-17.00 Mon-Fri* but some clinics run later. Phone for details.

John Dixon Clinic 2 F5
Drummond Rd SE16. 01-237 5006. Services include chiropody and dental treatment (for children and older people), infant welfare (including the sale of infant foods), family planning, speech therapy and antenatal care. *Open 09.00-17.00 Mon-Fri.* Phone for details of individual clinic times.

Surrey Docks Health Centre 3 B6
Downtown Rd, off Salter Rd SE16. 01-231 3085. Services include GP surgery, chiropody, child and toddler sessions, child healthcare, dental care, expectant and nursing mothers clinic, family planning, health visitor & speech therapy. *Open 09.00-17.00 Mon-Fri.* Phone for details of individual clinic times.

HOSPITALS

Guy's Hospital 1 A3
St Thomas St SE1. 01-407 7600. 24hr general hospital with casualty department.

London Bridge Hospital 1 A3
London Bridge City, 27 Tooley St SE1. 01-407 3100. Private general hospital but specialises in renal problems. No casualty department.

JOB CENTRES

Bermondsey Employment Office 2 G4
Brunel Rd SE1. 01-237 2864. *Open 09.00-13.00 & 14.00-16.00 Mon-Fri.*

Borough Job Centre
92 Borough High St SE1. 01-403 2055. *Open 09.00-17.00 Mon-Thur, 10.00-17.00 Fri.*

LAUNDERETTES

J. Toone 1 B5
44 Tower Bridge Rd SE1. 01-231 7583. *Open 08.30-18.30 Mon-Fri, 08.30-18.00 Sat, 08.30-11.30 Sun.*

LIBRARIES

Bermondsey Library 1 C5
Spa Rd SE16. 01-237 6677 (01-237 690 *after 17.00 Mon-Fri & all day Sat*). Senior library and music library *open 10.00-20.00 Mon, Tue & Thur, 10.00-17.00 Fri & Sat. Closed Wed.* Junior library *open 15.30-19.00 Mon, Tue & Thur, 15.30-17.00 Fri.* Bermondsey library also has a housebound library service which delivers books at home to those who cannot get to the library. Phone 01-237 6677 for details.

Mobile Library
01-237 6677. Stops in Surrey Docks area: *10.45-11.45 Mon* Scott Lidgett School Drummond Rd, *13.30-14.45 Mon* Surrey Docks District Centre, *15.00-16.30 Mon* St Helena Rd, *10.45-11.45 Tue* Redriff School (pupils only), *13.30-14.45 Thur* Globe Pond Rd, *15.00-16.30 Thur* Russia Dock Rd, *12.15-13.15 Fri* Tooley St, *14.45-16.00 Fri* Plough Way.

Rotherhithe Library 2 G
Albion St SE16. Books and cassettes. 01-237 2010. *Open 09.30-12.30 & 13.30-20.00 Mon & Thur, 09.30-12.30 & 13.30-17.00 Tue, 09.30-12.30 Sat. Closed Wed & Fri.*

Toy Library **5** C1
Docklands Settlement, Rotherhithe St SE16. £2 membership per term. Includes a playgroup session and a toy exchange for parents with children under five. *Open 13.00-15.00 Thur.*

MINI-CABS

Blue Anchor Cars **2** F6
270 Southwark Park Rd SE16. 01-237 3687/0202. *Open 24hrs Mon-Sun.*
M.J.'s Car & Van Service **2** H6
124 Lower Rd SE16. 01-237 9955/231 1234. *Open 24hrs Mon-Sun.*
Red Lion Car Hire **2** G5
192 Lower Rd SE16. 01-237 4402. *Open 24hrs Mon-Sun.*
Star Cars **2** F6
393 Southwark Park Rd SE16. 01-237 0543/1763 & 01-231 1007. *Open 24hrs Mon-Sun.*
Toby Car Service **1** B5
18 Tower Bridge Rd SE1. 01-237 4221/8211/8383. *Open 24hrs Mon-Sun.*

PETROL STATIONS

Hopfields Self-Service **2** F6
3 Raymouth Rd SE16. 01-237 2140. *Open 08.30-17.30 Mon-Fri, 08.30-12.30 Sat.*
Star Service Station **1** B5
Grange Rd SE1. 01-237 4171. *Open 24hrs Mon-Sun.*
Tooley Street Service Station **1** C4
271 Tooley St SE1. 01-407 1315. *Open 06.45-19.30 Mon-Fri, 08.00-15.00 Sat.*

PLACES OF WORSHIP

Many churches have to remain closed except for services. Where this is the case anyone can get in by arrangement if they phone the number given.

Bermondsey Churches (C of E) Office **1** C5
107 Grange Rd SE1. 01-232 2329. This office covers St Anne's, St James's and St Mary Magdalen.
Finnish Seamen's Mission **2** G4
33 Albion St SE16. 01-237 4668. This is a Finnish centre as well as a church selling Finnish items and newspapers. Also has a canteen. *Centre open 14.00-22.00 Mon-Fri, 14.00-20.00 Sat & Sun.* Services: *11.00 first Sun in the month* conducted in Finnish and English. *Other Suns 18.00* Finnish only service.
Most Holy Trinity **1** D4
Dockhead SE1. 01-237 1641. *Closed* except for services. Services: Mass *07.30, 10.00 & 18.00 Sun, 09.30 Mon-Wed & Fri, 20.00 Thur & 18.30 Sat. The Mercy convent next door holds mass at 07.00 Mon-Fri.*
Norwegian Seamen's Church **2** G4
1 Albion St SE16. 01-237 5587. *Open 15.00-22.00 Mon-Fri, 10.00-18.00 Sat, 10.00-22.00 Sun.* Service: *11.00 Sun.*
Rotherhithe Evangelical Free Church **2** H9
Lower Rd SE16. 01-692 5949. *Closed* except for services. Services: *11.00 & 18.30 Sun.* House meetings are held in the area on *Wed.*
St Anne's **1** D6
Thorburn Sq SE1. 01-232 2329. *Closed* except for services. Services: *10.00 every Sun & 16.00 first Sun in the month.*
St James's **1** D5
Thurland Rd SE16. 01-232 2329. *Closed* except for services. Services: *11.00 & 18.30 Sun* (alternate between ordinary services and communion). Communion *07.30 Tue.*
St Mary Magdalen **1** B4
Bermondsey St SE1. 01-232 2329. *Closed* except for services. Services: Communion *10.30, 18.00 & 19.30 Sun (plus 08.00 second Sun in the month), 13.00 Tue.*
St Mary's **2** G4
St Marychurch St SE16. 01-231 2465. *Open 07.00-18.00 Mon-Sat. Open at service times on Sun.* Services: Eucharist *10.00 Sun, 07.30 Mon-Thur, 09.45 Sat.* Evensong *17.30 Sat.*
Southwark Cathedral **1** A3
Tower Bridge Rd SE1. 01-407 3708. *Open 09.00-18.00 Mon-Sun.* Services: Holy Communion *09.00 Sun, 08.00 Tue & Thur, 12.45 Mon-Fri, 12.00 Sat.* Choral Evensong *15.00 Sun, 17.30 Tue & Fri.* Evensong *17.30 Mon, Wed & Thur, 16.00 Sat.* Regular events in the cathedral: organ recitals *13.10 Mon,* live music recitals *13.10 Tue,* dialogue discussion *13.10 Wed,* recorded music *13.10 Thur,* readings & meditation *13.10 Fri.*
Swedish Seamen's Church **2** G5
120 Lower Rd SE16. 01-237 1644. *Open 14.00-22.00 Mon-Sun.* Services: *18.00 Sun.* Morning prayers *09.15 Mon-Sun.* Evening prayers *20.00 Mon-Sun.*

POLICE STATIONS

Rotherhithe Police Station **2** G5
99 Lower Rd SE16. 01-237 0582.

POST OFFICES

Dockhead **1** D4
35 Dockhead SE1. 01-237 3308. *Open*

09.00-13.00 & 14.00-17.30 Mon, Tue, Thur & Fri, 09.00-13.00 Wed & Sat.

Jamaica Road **2 E4**
181 Jamaica Rd SE16. 01-237 4387. *Open 09.00 (09.30 Wed)-17.30 Mon-Fri, 09.00-13.00 Sat.*

Lower Road **2 H6**
193 Lower Rd SE16. 01-237 2945. *Open 09.00-13.00 & 14.15-17.30 Mon, Tue, Thur & Fri, 09.00-13.00 Wed & Sat.*

PUBLIC CONVENIENCES

Cherry Garden Pier **2 E4**
Off Cherry Garden St SE16. *Open 24hrs Mon-Sun.* Men only.

Redriff Road **2 H5**
By the Old Fire Station SE16. *Open 24hrs Mon-Sun.* Men only.

Rotherhithe Tunnel **2 G4**
Entrance to Rotherhithe Tunnel, Rotherhithe Approach Rd SE16. *Open 08.00-18.00 Mon-Sun.*

Southwark Park **2 G6**
Hawkstone Rd side (by Astroturf pitch) SE16. *Open 08.00-18.00 Mon-Sun.*

Southwark Park Gates **2 G5**
Lower Rd side (by police station) SE16. *Open 08.00-18.00 Mon-Sun.*

Trident Street **5 A2**
SE16. *Open 08.00-18.00 Mon-Sun.*

SCHOOLS AND COLLEGES

Albion School **2 G4**
Albion St SE16. 01-237 3738. State primary school for ages 3-11.

Peter Hills with St Mary's & St Paul's School **3 A4**
2 Beatson Walk SE16. 01-237 2654. Church of England primary school for ages 5-11.

Redriff School **3 C5**
Rotherhithe St SE16. 01-237 4272. State primary school for ages 3-11.

Riverside School **2 E4**
Janeway St SE16. 01-237 3227. State primary school for ages 4-11.

St Joseph's School **1 D4**
George Row SE16. 01-237 4267. Roman Catholic school for ages 5-11.

St Michael's School **1 D4**
John Felton Rd SE16. 01-237 6432. Catholic secondary school for ages 11-16.

Southwark College **1 C4**
Bermondsey Branch, Tanner St SE1. 01-928 9561. Further and higher education college offering some evening classes.

SHOE REPAIRS

J. & W. Croft **1 D5**
23 Old Jamaica Rd SE16. 01-237 1939. *Open 09.00-14.00 & 15.00-17.30 Mon-Fri, 09.00-12.00 Sat.*

R. N. Goulding **2 E6**
289 Southwark Park Rd SE16. 01-237 5821. *Open 09.00-17.30 Mon-Sat.*

Quickie Heel Bar **2 E6**
236 Southwark Park Rd SE16. 01-232 1672. *Open 08.00-17.15 Mon-Sat.*

SHOPPING CENTRES

Local Shopping Areas
The main shopping areas are Lower Road, Albion Road and Jamaica Road which provide a range of local shops and services such as banks, chemists, bakers and newsagents.

London Bridge City **1 B3**
Tooley St SE1. Includes Hay's Galleria which has a selection of upmarket shops plus wine bars and restaurants. See London Bridge City entry p. 46.

Surrey Quays Shopping Centre **2 H5**
Canada Water SE16. A 280,000 sq ft (26,000 sq m) covered shopping centre which is to include an enormous Tesco and a variety of other household name stores including Boots and BHS. The centre is scheduled to open in late 1988.

SOLICITORS

Baldwin & Co **2 F4**
236-238 Jamaica Rd SE16. 01-237 3035. General practice. *Open 09.30-17.30 Mon-Fri.*

Baldwin & Co **1 C4**
National Westminster Bank Chambers, 185 Tower Bridge Rd SE16. 01-403 4366. Mainly criminal practice. *Open 09.30-17.30 Mon-Fri.*

Elmore & Co **2 G4**
19 Smith Close SE16. 01-232 0272. Mainly commercial/conveyancing practice. *Open 09.30-17.30 Mon-Fri.*

WAPPING AND LIMEHOUSE

This long, narrow strip of Docklands, between Tower Bridge and the beginning of the Isle of Dogs peninsula, can be seen as three main sections, all of which come under the local authority of Tower Hamlets. The first section includes St Katharine Docks – which has been on the tourist circuit for some time – and also the area immediately to the west, which is outside Docklands but has been included for the sake of Britain's best-known fortress, the Tower of London. The second section is Wapping, site of the old London Docks, incorporating Radcliff and Shadwell; the third is Limehouse in the old London Borough of Stepney.

There are two principal roads: the Highway and Commercial Road. The former links at Limehouse with the aptly named Narrow Street, and offers a quick under-river route to Surrey Docks by way of the Rotherhithe Tunnel. The latter runs parallel to the Highway, to the north of the strip. Both roads are extremely busy, pervaded by the roar of diesel engines and the gasp of air brakes. The Docklands Light Railway operates here, between the Minories (Tower Gateway Station) to the west and the Isle of Dogs and Stratford to the east, and London Underground's Metropolitan Line has stations at Shadwell and at Wapping by the riverside. The launch of the new riverbus service in 1988 will reinstate the Thames itself as the important thoroughfare it once was.

Monumental architecture is the most obvious characteristic of the St Katharine Docks area. The oldest and most impressive structure is the Tower itself, still a royal palace though not a royal residence, heavy with history, a museum of dramatic objects – the Crown Jewels, the executioner's block and axe – and of tradition – the Yeomen Warders engaged in the Ceremony of the Keys. Here, too, are the Gothic splendours of Tower Bridge; the macabre associations of Trinity Square Gardens; the grey bulk of the grim-faced Tower Hotel and, around the Docks themselves, the extensive modern buildings of the World Trade Centre and Futures Exchange, the 19thC warehouse still called the Ivory House, and the ever-popular Dickens Inn.

The origin of names is often a vexed question, but St Katharine Docks took the name of the 12thC religious foundation of St Katharine which was forcibly removed (first to Regent's Park, later to Limehouse) to make way for it. The dock system was designed by Thomas Telford and Philip Hardwick and soon after opening in 1828 began trading in luxury goods such as ivory and spices, ostrich feathers, carpets and cigars. These docks were not hugely successful – it was said that the entrance locks were too narrow from the start – and the St Katharine Dock Company merged with the London Dock Company in 1864. In 1968 the docks ceased trading and were the first to be developed with an eye to tourism. The Historic Ships Collection which was moored here in the 70s has been dispersed to other sites, leaving only the Nore lightship and the steam tug, *Challenge*, but the Thames barges, the dockside walkways, the restaurants and bars, and the shops on the ground floor of the Ivory House, which was built in 1858, thirty years after the opening of the Dock, are a strong attraction. All the original warehouses have been demolished, some due to enemy action in World War II, others due to redevelopment of the site.

Wapping is unique in having a High Street without shops (though current proposals will change this), just a wall of 19thC warehouses between road and river, many of them now converted into luxury flats, studios and offices. Wapping Lane, the heart of Wapping Village, has far more of a High Street feel about it.

Early trading here was from wharves and jetties with cargo ships moored in the river, at the mercy of thieves. In 1798 the West India Company of Merchants set up the Marine Police (still functioning here as the Thames Division of the Metropolitan Police) to resolve the problem. They were only partially successful and the enclosed London Dock at Wapping was built at the beginning of the 19thC, to Daniel Alexander's and John Rennie's designs, as a means of protecting the goods more effectively. Wine was one of the principal imports, but wool had been arriving here for generations and there was also trade in fruit, wax, gums, tea and coffee. London Dock was closed down in 1969 and since then has been almost entirely filled in, with Shadwell and Hermitage Basins and the magnificent Skin Floor warehouse at Tobacco Dock remaining as the chief memorials.

Narrow stairways leading to the river can be glimpsed beside a few warehouses; Wapping Old Stairs beside the Town of Ramsgate pub is one of the best examples. They were used by passengers who wanted to be ferried across the river by watermen and are still public rights of way, though so dangerously slippery that in most cases they are barred by locked gates.

The Town of Ramsgate and, further east, the Prospect of Whitby, are two famous survivors of the inordinate number of pubs Wapping once boasted. Their associations with numerous pirates, and with Colonel Blood and Judge Jeffreys, have been drawing visitors for many years. In contrast, the streets around the Highway were more or less a no-go area throughout the 18th and 19th centuries and into the beginning of the 20th: sad and dangerous slums, the haunts of prostitutes and drunks, where robbery and even murder were relatively commonplace.

Limehouse's sinister reputation as an exotic world of its own, all smoky opium dens and thin knives in the back, was at least partially created by fiction writers,

Thames Sailing Barges
The history of craft on the Thames is long and fascinating, but the Thames sailing barge – unique to this river – is probably the most romantic of those still functioning; more elegant than the flat-bottomed 'dumb barges' or lighters, still to be seen moored at buoys in the river or on the move in groups; more glamorous than the chunky tugs, which still manoeuvre the lighters.

The sails get their distinctive dark reddish-brown colouring from the mixture of red ochre, linseed oil, fish oil and horse fat with which they are traditionally treated to keep them supple.

Some of the sailing barges are still at work, while others have become floating function rooms.

See Pubs and Restaurants.

Town of Ramsgate

especially Sax Rohmer and Conan Doyle. The existence of the large Chinese community, mostly seamen and their families, sparked off these stories – a few of which were justified. The Chinese influence is still here, most noticeably in the form of excellent and authentic restaurants, but Limehouse may now be more widely known for its moment of modern history when Dr David Owen announced 'The Limehouse Declaration', on the formation of the SDP, from his converted warehouse home in Narrow Street.

The medieval lime houses, or lime kilns, which gave the area its name, are long gone and its history since Tudor times has been tied up with shipbuilding and related crafts. The hugely impressive but strangely ominous tower of St Anne's church has been a landmark for shipping on the river since it was built in the early years of the 18thC. The coming of the docks brought new roads and greater prosperity. Since their closure the mixed community has been in a state of flux as the development programme takes hold.

Although there has already been a great deal of development in all three sections, and well-heeled newcomers are settled in many a riverside home, much is still promised. The parks and open spaces are to be perked up; the old hydraulic pumping station at Shadwell Basin is to be refurbished as a rehearsal room and recording studio for the Academy of St Martin-in-the-Fields; the slithery stairs are to be made safe and opened to the public; watersports are promised on the three dock basins; and a riverside walkway is to be established where possible. In common with those in the other three Docklands areas, people here wait to see the effect of the immense input of money and the emphasis on luxury and leisure, and whether the newcomers and the established residents will ever merge into one community.

St Katharine Docks and Wapping

All Hallows by the Tower **1 B2**
Byward St EC3. 01-481 2928. A church was founded on this site in AD675 and over the centuries different buildings were added, demolished and rebuilt. World War II bombs made further restoration necessary, but the tower is still the one from which Pepys watched the Great Fire of London in 1666. Its memorial brasses, dating from the 14th-17th centuries, are particularly fine and its heraldic stained glass is exceptional.

The 14thC undercroft has a museum with a collection of Saxon crosses and Roman artefacts, and the only Roman mosaic floor in London which has not been resited – in fact it has lain here undisturbed since AD122. The refectory upstairs serves light lunches between *12.00-14.00 on weekdays. Church open for services and 10.00-17.00 Mon-Sat, 12.30-17.00 Sun; museum open by prior arrangement. Charge for museum.*

Coronarium **1 D2**
St Katharine Docks E1. The glass rotunda, with the crystal crown set above its door, was unveiled by the Queen in 1977, the year of her Silver Jubilee. It was planned as a multi-faith chapel though, at the moment, the only regular service is the Thursday lunchtime communion organised by All Hallows by the Tower. Locked when not in use, but there is no need to go inside to see all there is to see.

East London Marine Venture, Shadwell Basin Project **2 G2**
Shadwell Pier Head E1. 01-481 4210. A registered charity, launched in 1976 to provide adventure activities for young people not simply in the immediate locality but throughout Tower Hamlets. Fishing, canoeing, sailing and windsurfing have been going since the start and recently they have acquired traditional Peacock Boats from Bangladesh and Hong Kong Dragon Boats which they plan to race. Adults may use the facilities at specially allocated times (*18.00-21.00 Tue, 10.30-17.00 Sat*), but in return are required to weigh in with some voluntary help. *Open 17.00-21.00 Mon, Wed & Thur, 10.30-17.00 Sun.* (In school holidays *open 10.30-17.00 Mon-Sun.*) *Closed Christmas and some Bank hols*–phone for details.

Futures and Options Exchange **1 D2**
Commodity Quay, St Katharine's Way E1. 01-365 0561. The London Commodity Exchange was founded in 1954, though trading in commodities has been part of the London business scene since the 10thC. Originally in the City, it moved here in the mid-1980s and began trading at Easter 1986. It is now called the London Futures and Options Exchange – or FOX. No public access except on business.

Hermitage Basin **1 D3**
Redmead Lane E1. Only two stretches of enclosed water remain of what was once the extensive London Dock system – Shadwell Basin to the east, and Hermitage Basin. Hermitage Basin, its entrance lock still in place, is now surrounded by local authority housing. A perky garden centre, displaying bedding plants, moulded planters and desperately cheerful gnomes, stands at its southern edge.

The Highway **2 E2**
E1-E14. The Highway is a continuation of East Smithfield, which ends beside Limehouse Basin, and was notorious in the 19thC under its earlier name of Ratcliffe Highway. In *London's River* (Hamish Hamilton, 1975), Philip Howard quotes Montagu Williams, an East End Magistrate, who: 'described it in the 1860s as "a scene of riots, debaucheries, robberies and all conceivable deeds of darkness. From the public houses there constantly issued the sounds of loud laughter, mingled with shouting and fearful imprecations . . . If the sailors were not entirely fleeced inside the saloons, the process was completed by bullies and fighting men when they staggered out into the street."'

Severely bomb damaged in the war, its main claim to notoriety now is its heavy, noisy traffic – though there are those who still get a grisly satisfaction from telling the tale of the Ratcliffe Highway murders of 1811, in which two families were butchered for no clear reason. John Williams, a lodger from the local Pear Tree public house, was suspected and arrested but committed suicide before the trial.

Ivory House **1 D2**
East Smithfield E1. This is one of the earliest dock buildings and is listed Grade II. The entrance gateposts are also original, but the elephants on top are effective fibreglass reproductions. The ground floor is now equipped with shops where you can buy jerseys, souvenirs, nautical equipment

Ivory House

and ships' furniture; the mezzanine floor is given over to offices; and the four storey's above are smart residential properties.

London Dock House **1 D2**
East Smithfield E1. Corner of Thomas More Street. Grade II listed building standing at what was once the entrance to the old London Docks. It will be preserved and used as office accommodation. No public access.

The Minories **1 C1**
EC3. The street took its name from the religious foundation of nuns of the order of St Clare whose abbey stood in the area until the Minoresses relinquished it to Henry VIII in 1539. At the southern end of the street is the most westerly station of the Docklands Light Railway, Tower Gateway.

News International **2 E2**
1 Pennington St E1. 01-481 4100. This is the vast and plain-faced printing and publishing works whose presses roll seven days a week and long into the night to produce *The Times, The Sunday Times, The Sun, The News of the World* and *Today*. Disputes with print workers over the use of new technology at the plant resulted in heavy picketing between January 1986 and February 1987. The defensive measures taken to try to ensure that the pickets kept their distance inspired the nickname 'Fortress Wapping.' No public access except on business.

The Old Royal Mint **1 D2**
East Smithfield E1. The Royal Mint has been functioning since about AD895 and from 1300 until the beginning of the 19thC was sited between the inner and outer walls of the Tower. This particular building by James Johnson and Robert Smirke, on the remains of a medieval Cistercian monastery, was its home from 1810 until 1968 when it moved to Llantrisant in Wales because of lack of space.

The current joint development, between the Crown Estate Commissioners and British Telecom, is resulting in the refurbishment of the Smirke building as a conference centre. The scheme includes a restaurant and wine bar; an exhibition on the Cistercian Abbey; and a pedestrian underpass to give direct access from St Katharine Docks. When the dock development excavations began in 1971 an underground passage was discovered leading from St Katharine Docks to the Mint (probably part of a planned robbery) and this showed that an underpass was possible. The first phase of the scheme should be completed by late 1988. No public access.

Riverside Self-Build Housing Association **2 F2**
Garnet St E1. There are 18 houses here, on just under an acre (0.4 ha) of land, built by local people for themselves – those with relevant skills guiding and teaching those who could offer only energy and enthusiasm. The scheme was funded by loans from the Housing Corporation which will be repaid by means of mortgages.

St George in the East **2 F1**
Cannon St Rd E1. Extraordinarily impressive and imaginatively designed church-within-a-church.

Between 1714 and 1726 an imposing church rose on this site, at the same time massive and elegant, with a turreted tower rising 160ft (48m). It was designed by Nicholas Hawksmoor with east windows by Sir Joshua Renolds.

The interior was gutted by a World War II incendiary bomb, but the exterior remained untouched and, especially since its recent face-lift, must look exactly as it did when first consecrated. After the bomb, services continued in a shed and then, in the early 1960s, Arthur Bailey designed a modern church which was built within the outer walls, leaving space for an inner courtyard between the original west front and the new, which is entirely glass. As you cross the courtyard the imposing tower behind you is reflected in the glass in front of you.

The old galleries were blocked off from the new building and converted into four flats, one of them the rectory, and there are plans to develop the extensive crypt with its stage, kitchen and lavatories – an arts or exhibition centre is the most likely outcome. *Open 08.00-17.00 Mon-Sun.* Services: Morning Prayer *08.00 Mon-Sun.* Evening Prayer *17.00 Mon-Sun.* Eucharist *10.15 Sun.* Holy Communion *20.00 Thur.*

St John's Church **2 F3**
Scandrett St E1. Scandrett Street was named for the Reverend John Scandrett who was rector of St John's from 1900 to 1908. The street remains but the World War II bombs left little of the church except its north wall and its substantial tower. Built in 1756, to a design by Joel Johnson, it stands within the Wapping Pier Head Conservation Area and will be preserved and given some suitable new role.

The melancholy little graveyard across the street, protected by mature trees and lushly overgrown, has been used as a location by the makers of horror films, who equipped it for the duration of filming with man-made mists and plywood headstones. It will eventually be landscaped.

St Katharine Docks **1 D2**
St Katharine-by-the-Tower Ltd, St Katharine Docks E1. 01-488 2400. In the 1820s the Royal Foundation of St Katharine, with its church and hospital, was removed to Regent's Park and then to Limehouse, and St Katharine Docks were built on the cleared site. There were protests at the time – the foundation had been granted this land at its inception in 1148 – and numerous small houses were also demolished, with little thought for the futures of the occupants and no compensation for those without freehold or leasehold. One of the only survivors was part of a small brewery.

The docks, by Thomas Telford and his architect Philip Hardwick, were designed with warehouses right at the water's edge so goods could be transferred directly to or from ships. Ivory, ostrich feathers, carpets and cigars arrived here, but the docks were never economic to run because large ships could not get through the lock into the dock area. The St Katharine Dock Company merged with the London Dock Company in 1864, and they ceased to trade in 1968.

In the early 1970s the firm of Taylor Woodrow won an architectural competition organised by the then GLC, and were awarded a 199-year lease on the 30 valuable acres (12 ha). The dock, run by their subsidiary St Katharine-by-the-Tower Ltd, is now a yacht haven with long-term and transient berthing. Here too are several large, distinctive Thames barges, with their red ochre sails, mainly used by companies for promotional purposes but still able to compete in traditional summertime barge races in the Thames Estuary. The Nore lightship and the *Challenge* steam tug – no access to either – are reminders of the late 70s when historic ships were moored here.

The two earliest buildings are the Ivory House and the Dockmaster's House by the pierhead which is now private residential property – though the old King's Brewery was only moved 100 yards or so before being refurbished as the Dickens Inn. Major buildings around the site are the Tower Hotel, opened in 1973; the World Trade Centre; the London Futures and Options Exchange (FOX); and the 93,000 square feet (8,370 square metres) of riverside office development, half-way to completion, which is the only UK site on the shortlist of

Thames Sailing Barge

Cosmopolitan Cargoes
'Working in the docks was to me like geography come to life. At St Katharine Docks we handled ivory from Africa and perfume from France. At Cutler Street, Persian carpets. When I crossed over to the Surrey Docks (by walking through Rotherhithe Tunnel) there were hoops to tighten on German barrels of apple pulp. At the Victoria and Albert Docks we handled melons from Spain, peaches from Italy, tobacco in hogshead and case . . .'

Bob Gilding in *The Journeymen Coopers of East London*, History Pamphlets No 4, History Workshop, Ruskin College, Oxford, quoted in *London Docks* by John Pudney, Thames and Hudson, 1975.

four hoping to house the EEC Trade Marks Office.

St Paul's Church **2 G2**
The Highway E1. Many of the historical associations are with the previous St Paul's, on the same site. The mother of Thomas Jefferson and the eldest son of Captain James Cook were baptised in it, in 1718 and 1763 respectively; John Wesley gave his last known sermon in it; and more than 75 sea captains and their wives were buried in the churchyard.

The present symmetrical brick building with the delicate stone-faced tower went up between 1818-21, one of the Waterloo churches, designed by John Walter and built as a thanksgiving for the defeat of Napoleon. Originally back to front, with the altar to the west, it was put right in the 1950s and given attractive, modern, stained-glass east windows by John Hayward.

Most of the organ is the original made in 1712 by Abraham Jordan, few examples of whose work still exist.

The church plays an active role in the community. There are plans to develop the crypt into a community centre; the Tower Hamlets *Talking Newspaper for the Blind* is recorded in a room at the top; and the churchyard is to be linked with the public walkway around Shadwell Basin. *Closed* except for services. Services: Eucharist *10.00 Sun & 10.30 on fourth Sun in month.*

St Peter's Church **2 F3**
Wapping Lane E1. Anglo-Catholic church designed by F.H. Pownall in 1866, its polychromatic brickwork, vivid stained-glass windows, brightly coloured altar rails and statues, glimmering candles and haze of incense a deliberate contrast to the plain grey drabness of the docks. Though only the eastern end was completed, and there is no churchyard, the interior is exceedingly striking and the entrance, through part of a convent building facing on to Wapping Lane, unusual. Note the rose windows, each depicting one of the first four vicars. Charles Lowder, shown carrying a child, was one of the most important figures in the Anglo-Catholic movement, regarded as controversial by Protestants and Roman Catholics alike. The Madonna at the new altar is known as Our Lady of Wapping. *Open* for services and *08.30-18.00 Mon-Sun*. Services: Mass *07.30 Mon, Wed & Fri, 18.00 Tue, 09.30 & 11.00 Thur, 08.30 & 10.00 Sun.*

Shadwell Basin **2 G2**
E1. One of the two remaining basins which served the London Dock, before it was closed down and filled in, with most traces hidden by new developments. It is proposed to extend the canal, which has been constructed as part of the housing development of Western Dock to act as a rainwater reservoir, through to Shadwell Basin. This will recreate the linked waterways between Hermitage and Shadwell Basins which existed when the London Dock was in operation and which made old Wapping an island surrounded by water.

Tobacco Dock and the Skin Floor **2 F2**
Pennington St E1. The huge early 19thC warehouse at Tobacco Dock is known as the Skin Floor because, although designed by D.A. Alexander to hold tobacco, it was used to store imported sheep skins with the wool still on them. It is one of the few survivors of old London Dock – though not a complete survivor since parts were demolished at the closure of the Dock in 1969 – and is listed Grade I. The extensive wine vaults below, and the vast above-ground structure with its forest of cast-iron supports, is to be developed into a 'shopping village' with bars and restaurants, High Street-style shops, and craft and gift shops. There has been mention, inevitably, of a new Covent Garden and by the end of 1988 the public should be able to make up its own mind.

Tower Bridge **1 C3**
EC3. 01-403 3761. Splendid Victorian Gothic structure, with an hydraulically operated drawbridge, by Jones and Wolfe-Barry, 1894. The lattice work footbridges with their wonderful river views are open to the public and there is a small exhibition inside on the history and operational abilities of the bridge, which still opens up to allow tall ships to pass through. *Open Apr-Oct 10.00-18.30 Mon-Sun; Nov-Mar 10.00-16.45 Mon-Sun. Charge.*

Tower of London **1 C2**
Tower Hill EC3. 01-709 0765. This is London's oldest museum and the most popular. Visitors can see the Bloody Tower, the Traitor's Gate, the armouries, the instruments of torture, the tragic graffiti, the executioner's block and axe and, of course, the Crown Jewels. The impressively plain Norman chapel of St John is the oldest church in London.

Begun by William the Conqueror – the White Tower, or Keep, is his (although it only became known as the White Tower after it had been whitewashed in 1240) – it has been added to by many of the

Tower of London

sovereigns who followed. It has been one of the most impregnable fortresses in England, an arsenal and a prison. It is still designated a royal palace and was a royal residence until the time of James I. Those forcibly detained within it include the young Princess Elizabeth, Sir Walter Raleigh, Roger Casement and Rudolf Hess, and those beheaded on Tower Green include Anne Boleyn, Catherine Howard and the 17-year-old Lady Jane Grey. Others were taken from it to public execution on Tower Hill. Today it is guarded by Yeomen Warders and by six ravens (with clipped wings), who are also on the nation's payroll on account of a legend that their departure will cause the whole edifice to topple. *Open Mar-Oct 09.30-17.00 Mon-Sat, 14.00-17.00 Sun; Nov-Feb 09.30-16.00 Mon-Sat. Closed Sun. Charge.*

Tower Pier **1 B2**

EC3. 01-488 0344. Regular daily passenger launch service travels to and from Westminster and Greenwich, and there is a frequent ferry service to HMS *Belfast* (which can also be reached by gangway from the south side of the river). This will be one of the ports of call of the riverbus service, due to begin operation in 1988.

Trinity Square Gardens **1 C2**

EC3. The small park on Tower Hill was named after Trinity House, on its south side, which was designed by Samuel Wyatt in 1793-5 and which is the headquarters of the authority responsible for the lighthouses, lightships and pilotage in British waters.

Despite the mature trees and grassy lawns the gardens have an oddly malevolent air – which may or may not be explained by the fact that this was the site of the Tower Hill scaffold, which was in use from 1388-1747, dispatching those convicted of treason. The atmosphere is not relieved by the presence of the old headquarters of the Port of London Authority, an example of early 20thC oppressive architecture, from the top of which a buoyant Father Thames waves his trident at his river. The building has been likened to a wedding cake, a thought which induces instant indigestion.

Wapping Hydraulic Pumping Station **2 G2**

Wapping Wall E1. The red brick building resembles a large church, with its square accumulator tower romantically clad in ivy. The London Hydraulic Company's station, designed by Green and Homan, was the world's last public supply hydraulic pumping station and closed only in 1977. Opened in 1892, it operated the bascules of Tower Bridge, lifts all over London and the London Palladium safety curtain as well as lock-gates, cranes and other dock machinery. Now listed Grade II and undergoing an exciting transformation into a home for the orchestra of the Academy of St Martin-in-the-Fields. There will be a rehearsal room and a glass-walled public viewing gallery; a recording studio; a shop selling records and London concert tickets; a museum of hydraulic power; a classroom for educational projects; restaurant; conservatory and a terrace overlooking Shadwell Basin.

At the entrance gates is the Engineer's House. The company's last station engineer, who started working here in

Hydraulic Pumping Station

1946, has continued to live on site among the ghosts of the past, and is now enjoying playing an active role in the pumping station's reincarnation. No public access.

Wapping Pier Head **2 E3**
Wapping High St E1. This was the original ship entrance to the London Dock, and even though the old lock has long since been filled in it is easy to see where it was. The elegant Georgian houses built in 1811, to house senior dock officials, flank the line of the lock at a discreet distance, and careful landscaping has preserved the rows of bollards once used for mooring ships.

The original houses are listed Grade II, and the new local authority-owned flats have been sensitively designed to match them.

A few hundred yards to the east is the historic Town of Ramsgate pub and, beside it, Wapping Old Stairs. This is where watermen used to land passengers and Ramsgate fishermen used to land their catches and the steps are noticeably green and slimy at the bottom. The nearby Execution Dock marks the spot where condemned pirates were hung in chains on the foreshore for three tides – an early example of overkill.

Wapping Police Station **2 F3**
98 Wapping High St E1. 01-488 5212. This is the headquarters of the world's oldest uniformed police force. In the 1790s the West India Company of Merchants formed the Marine Police to control the large-scale theft of cargoes. The Metropolitan Police, who were not formed until 1829, incorporated the Marine Police in 1839, as the Thames Division. They are now the 'motorway' police of the river, with a 54-mile beat from Staines to Dartford Creek and with their official boundary extending to Thames high water. From Wapping, and the stations at Waterloo Pier, Barnes, Hampton and Shepperton, they enforce the rules and regulations of the river, keep an eye on regattas and races, attend accidents, perform rescues and, by way of their Underwater Search Unit, recover bodies, stolen cars and even guns. As ever, they watch out for thieves, whose targets these days are private boats and wealthy riverside houses.

The police launches are serviced in the Wapping boatyard behind the ultra-modern fibreglass-faced building. The present station itself, built 1907-10, is listed Grade II and has the added distinction that Buster Keaton's cousin served here as an Inspector. There is a small museum upstairs with pictures, models, documents and leg-irons. Apply in writing for permission to visit, ideally one month in advance. No one under the age of 12 is allowed in.

Wapping Underground Station **2 F3**
Wapping High St E1. The under-river tunnel that now carries the Metropolitan Line from Wapping to Rotherhithe was constructed by the Brunels between 1824 and 1843. It was begun by Marc Brunel and finished by his son, Isambard Kingdom Brunel, who took over the project when he was 20 and had his 21st birthday party inside it. It was the world's first underwater tunnel intended to carry traffic, but though it was an impressive bit of civil engineering it was not a success in its day. Money ran out when it was half-way across from Rotherhithe, and seven years passed before it was finished. It opened in 1843 but only for pedestrian use because there was not enough money to build carriage ramps. A small exhibition of pictures was mounted down there, but once the novelty wore off it degenerated into a hunting ground for prostitutes. In 1865 it was sold to the then East London Railway Company who converted it into a railway tunnel and it was not used for its proper purpose until after the death of both its engineers.

Wapping Wine Warehouse **2 E3**
The Old Pumping Station, 60 Wapping High St E1. 01-265 0448. The Great Wapping Wine Company was the first of the cash and carry warehouses which cut wine prices by selling direct to the consumer and cutting out the off-licence. When it finally closed down this new company moved into its premises and continued the tradition. Redevelopment pushed them out of the warehouse and they have settled in the old pumping station, which used to supply all the hydraulic power for Wapping High Street. Friendly and knowledgeable, they stock a wide range of wines, provide glasses and ice, run a delivery service for companies and local people, and put on occasional wine tastings. *Open 09.00-19.00 Mon-Fri, 09.00-18.00 Sat, 10.00-16.00 Sun.*

Wharves and Warehouses **2 E3**
Wapping High St and Wapping Wall E1. Many of the late 19thC riverside warehouses have been, or are currently being, refurbished and adapted to other uses. St John's and King Henry's Wharves, beside Wapping Police Station, will be a mixture of residential accommodation and storage for Samuel Smith's Brewery; Gun Wharves near Wapping Underground

Station are already luxury flats; and Metropolitan Wharf on Wapping Wall, its lifting gear still in good order, has been transformed inside into a series of studios and workshops. In many cases it has been possible to provide car parking space, under ground or at ground floor level – a necessity, considering how extremely narrow both roads are.

World Trade Centre **1 C2**
East Smithfield E1. 01-488 2400. International House and Europe House together form the World Trade Centre which was set up in 1971 as part of an international movement under the overall title of the World Trade Centers Association. This apolitical movement began in 1968 with the aim of promoting peace, trade and interdependence of trading countries. Members tend to be primarily involved with shipping, insurance and commodities (see Futures and Options Exchange above) and the facilities they can use include office space, all kinds of business and secretarial services, a health club, and a restaurant which is open to the general public in the evenings. No public access except on business.

Eating and Drinking
Simple sandwiches at Ma Averil's Riverside Café or the SS *Yarmouth*; pub grub at the Caxton, the Prospect of Whitby (which also has a restaurant), the Town of Ramsgate or the White Swan and Cuckoo; cold collations and wine at the Vineyard or the Ivories; a full meal at Harry's Java Brasserie, the Dickens Inn, one of the three restaurants in the Tower Thistle Hotel, or, in the evening at the Quayside Restaurant; a medieval banquet at Beefeater by the Tower.
See Pubs and Restaurants.

Limehouse

British Sailors' Society Building **3 C3**
Newell St E14. Now a private residence, this 18thC building used to house the Prince of Wales nautical training school (which has moved to Dover). No public access.

Former Limehouse Town Hall **3 C3**
Commercial Rd E14. This listed neo-classical building of 1881 was the home of the National Museum of Labour History from 1975-87. Now returning to its town hall function as the Wapping Neighbourhood Centre, part of Tower Hamlets Council's scheme to decentralise local authority power.

Free Trade Wharf **2 H2**
The Highway E1. The site, bordered by the river on one side and the Highway on the other, is being developed to provide new offices and housing with leisure and retail facilities. Some of the principal historic buildings are being preserved. These include the pair of East India Company saltpetre warehouses and the wharf entrance dating from 1795 flanked by warehouses of c1870, designed by Richard Jupp. Wooden jetties, stone stairs to the river and a barge dock have also survived. No public access before completion in late 1988.

Hydraulic Accumulator Tower **3 B3**
Limehouse Basin E14. The top of this octagonal brick tower resembles a castle keep, if glimpsed from Mill Street. It is all that remains of what is believed to have been London's first ever hydraulic power station, installed in 1852 by Sir William Armstrong. The Ragged School Museum hopes to convert it into an interpretation centre and possibly a museum of Limehouse history. No public access.

King Edward VII Memorial Park **2 H2**
The Highway E14. Better known locally as Shadwell Park and created in 1922 on the site of the old Shadwell Fish Market. This 9 acre (3 ha) riverside area has tennis and netball courts, a red gravel football pitch, bowling green, paddling pool and children's playgrounds as well as lawns and flowerbeds. There is a tablet commemorating Martin Frobisher and other explorers who set sail from this part of the river to discover new trade routes. Just to the south west of the park are the ventilation shaft and spiral staircase entrance to the Rotherhithe Tunnel. *Open 07.30 to 30 mins before sunset Mon-Sun.*

Limehouse Basin **3 B3**
E14. Also called the Regent's Canal Dock, it forms the entrance to Regent's Canal which was built to link the Port of London with England's canal network. It was completed in 1820, with several subsequent enlargements. Limehouse Cut leads out of

the basin's east side but predates it, having been built in 1770 to link the River Lea with the Thames at this point. The basin's northern edge is bounded by the viaduct which used to carry the London & Blackwall Railway and now the Docklands Light Railway runs along it. It spans the Limehouse Cut with three arches. The entrance lock on the south is crossed by Narrow Street via a swing bridge. At present the basin is a grim 10 acre (4 ha) area of water with debris bobbing about on the surface. Round its edges are decaying buildings and general junk.

Development plans drawn up by the basin's owners, the British Waterways Board, have been slightly modified and are now going ahead, after several years of fierce opposition from local groups who wanted a community-based scheme with some rented housing. Phase I is for private housing on the east and south sides of the basin and will include a pub and yacht marina. Further phases will be held up while part of the basin is temporarily infilled to enable a tunnel to be built under it, carrying a section of the new Docklands A13 relief road.

Limehouse Church Institute **3 C3**
Three Colt St E14. A Grade II listed building with terracotta decoration on the front elevation. It was opened in 1904 as a community centre aiming at moral improvement and was very active in pursuing this aim. Now it is being converted into flats. No public access.

Limehouse District Library **3 C3**
Commercial Rd E14. A Grade II listed building of 1900 in white stone and yellow brick. Two open books in stone appear on the Flemish-style gables. Formerly the Passmore Edwards Library.

Limekiln Wharf **3 C3**
Three Colt St E14. Several listed buildings front on to Limekiln Dock, itself listed. There is also a listed doorway: a white wooden door under a round arch with a triangular tympanum above. At present it stands alone in a brick wall, leading nowhere, like part of a stage set. It was in fact the front door of a vanished 18thC building occupied by lime and cement merchants and builders until demolished in 1935. The door will be transferred to the Ragged School Museum and replaced by a replica, which will be the entrance to a waterside walkway, planned as part of the development on the draw dock's south east side. Opposite is Dunbar's Wharf, founded in the 19thC by shipowner Duncan Dunbar. The first passenger liners for Australia left from here. The wharf is privately owned and still doggedly working. The firm has put forward its own proposals for redevelopment of the site. No public access at present.

Narrow Street **3 B3**
E14. One of the best-known roads in Limehouse, already colonised by actors, politicians and film producers. Between Dunbar's Wharf at the east end and converted warehouses and the recently closed Hough's Paperboard Mills at the west, is a row of fine early-18thC merchants' houses and the popular pub, the Grapes. Opposite is the open space of Ropemakers' Fields. At one time the road, simply called Limehouse, bustled with activity from the wharves, shipyards and factories which lined the river. There are good views from Limehouse Basin entrance, where the Pier Head Building and row of empty lockside cottages will be preserved.

Newell Street **3 C3**
E14. A quiet street with a row of pretty, listed houses which are mostly 18thC. It lies within the St Anne's Church Conservation Area and used to be called Church Row but was renamed in 1938 after a local councillor. St Anne's Passage is a cobbled way leading up to the church's west front. On its corner is a 17thC house with a curved front and first-floor balcony. Charles Dickens used to visit his godfather, Christopher Huffam, who lived in the house. Three underground passages are reputed to lead here: one from a house near the Grapes on the river, a second from the church and a third from the former lunatic asylum. This stood across the road on a site which is now King's Wharf, a small public garden with access to Limehouse Cut.

Prince's Lodge **3 C3**
Commercial Rd E14. This gigantic, prison-like building, formerly the Empire Memorial Hostel for Sailors, which glowers from its corner on the busy main road looks anything but welcoming but was opened in 1924 as a hostel for seamen. At present used as a DHSS hostel for the homeless, it is scheduled for eventual redevelopment as – hard to imagine – luxury flats. No public access.

Ragged School Museum **3 B1**
46-50 Copperfield Rd E3. 01-232 2941. The museum, still being set up at the time of going to press, is housed in a building once occupied by Dr Barnardo's Ragged School. It plans to tell the story of the East End, Lord Shaftesbury's Ragged School

movement, and the work of Dr Barnardo whose efforts for destitute children began in this area. It will have reconstructions of home, school and workshop interiors, written and recorded archives, a shop and a café. Visitors will be able to reach the museum by towpath walk or waterbus, calling in at the Hydraulic Accumulator Tower on the way from Limehouse. No 48 Copperfield Road is due to open to the public in June 1988 but before then public access only on *Open Days* or by appointment.

Rotherhithe Tunnel **2** H2
Tunnel Approach E14. The vehicular entrance to the tunnel, which was opened in 1908, is framed by segments of the Greathead shield used for cutting the northern half of the tunnel (see Rotherhithe Tunnel, Surrey Docks section p. 51).

Royal Foundation of St Katharine **3** A3
Butcher Row E14. 01-790 3540. Built in 1796 as a private residence for Matthew Whiting, a sugar merchant, the house later became St James's Vicarage but the church was destroyed by a bomb in World War II. It now houses the religious foundation which was created in 1148 beside the Tower of London, moved to Regent's Park in 1825 when St Katharine Docks were built, to Poplar in 1914 and to Butcher Row soon after World War II (see St Katharine Docks on p. 63).

The foundation continues its work in the community and organises conferences and retreats throughout the year. The house, standing in lovely, peaceful gardens, contains several landscape murals in the manner of Claude Lorraine. The 1950 chapel has some items preserved from the original medieval church, including 14thC carved choirstalls and a 17thC pulpit with carvings depicting four views of the ancient hospital. No public access.

The Sailors' Palace **3** D3
West India Dock Rd E14. The Cornish-born philanthropist Passmore Edwards financed this 1903 building designed by Niven and Wigglesworth. It is decorated in Arts and Crafts style with maritime motives above the entrance: the names of the Continents encircled by a rope, seagulls, anchors, dolphins and Britannia holding a ship in each arm. Formerly the headquarters of the British and Foreign Sailors' Society, now converted into flats and Grade II listed. No public access.

St Anne's Church **3** C3
Commercial Rd E14. 01-987 1502. One of Docklands' grandest churches, designed by

St Anne's Church

Nicholas Hawksmoor (although his first attempt was rejected) and built 1712-24. It was one of the 'coal churches' financed by a special tax on coal imposed in Queen Anne's reign. The enormous white tower dominates the whole area and in fact was once a landmark for ships sailing up the Thames.

Imposing from any angle, but particularly so from St Anne's Passage to the west. The multi-tiered, sharp-angled tower contrasts with the plain north and south elevations, but overall the church gives a sense of mass and grandeur. Its clock, added in 1839, is the highest public clock in Britain after Big Ben and is by the same makers. The vast space of the galleried interior is dramatic, but also dark and gloomy and in need of redecoration. Structural repairs are also urgently needed. The church was faithfully restored after fire caused extensive damage to the interior in 1850. The organ is one of the finest unaltered Victorian examples in the country, built for the Great Exhibition of 1851.

The churchyard is large and well kept, with mature trees. North west of the tower is a mysterious stone pyramid, about 9ft (3m) high. On its south side some all-but-effaced carving is believed to represent Masonic symbols, and one theory has it that Hawksmoor was a Freemason (as his master Wren was thought to be) and placed this strange object in the churchyard with a secret significance in mind. *Closed except for services. Services: 10.30 & 18.00 Sun, 07.30 Mon-Sat.*

Eating and Drinking
An appropriate Chinese meal at Good Friends, the Peking, Young Friends, Old Friends or New Friends; or pub food at the Five Bells and Bladebone, the Grapes, the House they Left Behind or Bootys.
See Pubs and Restaurants.

Services

All services closed Sat & Sun unless otherwise stated.

ADULT EDUCATION

Tower Hamlets Institute of Adult Education
Head Office, Smithy St E1. 01-790 3358.

Shadwell Centre **3** A3
The Highway E1. 01-790 5545/3358. Courses include boatbuilding, industrial machining, cookery and fitness training. Video facilities. Crèche *10.00-12.00 Mon-Fri. Open 10.00-17.00, 18.30-21.00 Mon-Fri.*

BANKS

Barclays Bank **3** D3
821 Commercial Rd E14. 01-515 2200. *Open 09.30-15.30 Mon-Fri.*

Midland Bank **3** C3
660 Commercial Rd E14. 01-538 5416. *Open 09.30-15.30 Mon-Fri.*

National Westminster Bank **1** C2
Europe House, World Trade Centre E1. 01-481 8713/709 9029. *Open 09.30-15.30 Mon-Fri.*

National Westminster Bank **3** D3
52 East India Dock Rd E14. 01-538 2363. *Open 09.30-15.30 Mon-Fri.*

CHEMISTS

Cormchoice **3** B2
132 Salmon Lane E14. 01-987 1791. *Open 09.00-18.30 Mon, Tue, Wed & Fri, 09.00-18.00 Thur & Sat.*

D.R. Ganatra **1** D2
Ivory House, World Trade Centre E1. 01-481 8375. *Open 10.00-18.00 Mon-Sun. No prescriptions Sat & Sun.*

Tower Pharmacy **2** F2
50 Wapping Lane E1. 01-488 9364. *Open 09.00-19.00 Mon-Fri, 09.00-17.30 Sat.*

CITIZENS ADVICE BUREAUX

Stepney Citizens Advice Bureau
Toynbee Hall, 28 Commercial St E1. 01-247 4172. *Open 10.00-12.30 Mon, Tue, Wed & Fri, 15.30-18.00 Thur.*

COMMUNITY AND YOUTH CENTRES

Wapping Youth Club **2** E3
Tench St E1. 01-488 4065. Facilities: playgroup, play centre, senior and intermediate clubs. *Open 09.30-22.00 Mon-Fri.*

COUNCILLORS

Members of the London Borough of Tower Hamlets. Council offices at the Town Hall, Patriot Sq E2. 01-980 4831. The councillors for the Wapping Neighbourhood are M. Ahmed (Labour), M. Ali (Labour), C. Mudd (Labour), J. Riley (Labour), J. Rowe (Labour) and A. Lilley (Liberal). If you have any complaints, suggestions or queries write to your councillor at the Town Hall.

DHSS OFFICES

Stepney DHSS Office
58 Nelson St E1. 01-790 3382. *Open 09.30-15.30 Mon-Fri.*

DOCTORS

Dr S.N. Basu **2 H1**
1 Barnado Gdns, Cable St E1. 01-791 1502. *Open 09.30-11.00 & 17.00-18.15 Mon-Fri (closed Thur evening).*

Drs Dumford, Killeen, Buszewicz & Mitchell **2 F3**
22 Wapping Lane E1. 01-481 9376. *Open 09.30-11.30 & 16.00-18.30 Mon-Fri, Sat morning emergencies only.*

Drs Kallaway, Livingstone and Widgery **3 C3**
11 Gill St E14. 01-515 2211. *Open 09.00-11.00 & 15.30-18.00 Mon-Fri, 16.30-18.30 Tue, Sat morning emergencies only.*

DRY CLEANERS

Salmon Dry Cleaners **3 B2**
135 Salmon Lane E14. 01-987 3520. *Open 08.00-18.00 Mon-Sat.*

EMPLOYMENT AGENCIES

Charterhouse Appointments **1 C2**
Europe House, World Trade Centre E1. 01-481 3188. Permanent professional appointments in banking, commodities and stockbroking. Also secretarial services. *Open 09.30-17.30 Mon-Fri.*

ESTATE AGENTS

Allied Cooklin Estates **3 B3**
Pier Head House, Narrow St E14. 01-790 7070. Mainly residential. *Open 09.00-18.00 Mon-Fri, 10.00-18.00 Sat & Sun.*

Carleton Smith & Co **1 D2**
London Dock House, 1 Thomas More St E1. 01-488 9017. Residential and commercial. *Open 09.00-18.30 Mon-Fri.*

Docklands Property Centre **3 A3**
487 The Highway E14. 01-790 9560. Residential only. (Commercial property dealt with by branch in Silvertown Way E16 01-474 1000.) *Open 09.00-18.00 Mon-Fri, 10.00-17.00 Sat & Sun.*

Egerton Docklands Centre **3 B4**
102-104 Narrow St E14. 01-538 3339/493 0676. Commercial and residential. *Open 09.00-18.00 Mon-Fri, 11.00-17.00 Sat & Sun.*

Anthony Gover **1 D2**
3-5 Dock St E1. 01-480 6815. Mainly residential. *Open 09.30-20.00 Mon-Sat.*

McDowalls **3 A3**
558 Commercial Rd E14. 01-790 9832. Residential only. *Open 09.30-17.30 Mon-Fri, 09.30-16.00 Sat, 10.00-13.00 Sun.*

McDowalls **3 A3**
530 Commercial Rd E14. 01-790 2777. Commercial only. *Open 09.30-17.30 Mon-Fri, 09.30-16.00 Sat, 10.00-13.00 Sun.*

Savills **1 E2**
34 The Highway E1. 01-488 9586. Residential only. *Open 09.00-18.00 Mon-Fri, 11.00-17.00 Sat.*

HAIRDRESSERS

Charm **3 B2**
112 Salmon Lane E14. 01-987 3581. Unisex. *Open 09.00-17.30 Mon-Thur, 09.00-18.30 Fri, 08.30-17.30 Sat.*

Chowrimootoo **3 B3**
633 Commercial Rd E14. 01-790 3972. Unisex. *Open 09.00-17.00 Mon, Tue, Thur & Fri, 09.00-16.30 Sat. Closed Wed.*

John Harding **1 D2**
1 Ivory House, World Trade Centre E1. 01-481 4730. Unisex. *Open 09.00-18.00 Mon-Thur & Sat, 09.00-20.00 Fri.*

Ricole **3 A3**
583b Commercial Rd E1. 01-790 1473. Unisex. *Open 09.00-21.30 Mon-Fri, 09.30-16.00 Sat..*

HEALTH CENTRES

Gill Street Health Centre **3 C3**
11 Gill St E14. 01-987 4433. Services include health promotion, health visitors, antenatal clinic, district nurse and baby clinic. *Open 09.00-18.00 Mon-Fri.*

St George's Clinic **2 F1**
Library Place, Cable St E1. 01-790 4711. Services include family planning and baby clinic. *Open 09.30-11.30 Tue, Wed & Thur.*

Wapping Health Centre **2 F3**
Wapping Lane E1. 01-488 0404. Services include maternity clinic, child development clinic and family planning. *Open 09.00-19.00 Mon-Fri.*

HOTELS

Tower Thistle **1 C2**
St Katharine's Way E1. 01-481 2575. 826 rooms each with private bathroom, central heating and television. The hotel accepts Access, American Express, Diners and Visa cards. Single room from £71-79; double room from £79-87.

LIBRARIES

Limehouse Library **3 C3**
638 Commercial Rd E14. 01-987 3183. Books plus records, cassettes and CDs.

Open 09.00-20.00 Mon, Tue & Thur, 09.00-17.00 Wed & Fri, 09.00-12.30 & 13.30-17.00 Sat.

Wapping Library **3** F3
103 Wapping Lane E1. 01-488 3535. Books only. *Open 14.30-18.30 Mon, Wed & Fri.*

MINI-CABS

City Car Service **1** D1
4 Cable St E1. 01-488 4223/3308. *Open 24hrs Mon-Sun.*

County Car Service **3** A2
80 White Horse Rd E1. 01-790 0559/8679. *Open 06.00-02.00 Mon-Thur & Sun, 24hrs Fri & Sat.*

Leeway **2** F1
143 Martha St E1. 01-790 6452/6453. *Open 24hrs Mon-Sun.*

St Katharine's Car Service **2** F3
99 Wapping Lane E1. 01-480 6239. *Open 08.30-20.00 Mon-Sat.*

Swift Cars **3** B2
106 Salmon Lane E14. 01-515 4886. *Open 08.00-24.00 Mon-Sun.*

Thames Cars Mini-cab Service **3** A2
80 White Horse Rd E1. 01-985 5999. *Open 24hrs Mon-Sun.*

PETROL STATIONS

Burdett Road Filling Station **1** C7
221 Burdett Rd E14. 01-515 1900. *Open 07.00-21.00 Mon-Sun.*

Thames Refueller **1** D3
Hermitage Wharf, Thomas More St E1. 01-481 1774. Boat fuel only. *Open 08.00-16.00 Mon-Fri.*

PLACES OF WORSHIP

Many churches have to remain closed except for services. Where this is the case anyone can get in by arrangement if they phone the number given.

All Hallows by the Tower **1** B2
Byward St EC3. 01-481 2928. *Open 10.00-17.00 Mon-Sat, 12.30-17.00 Sun.* Services: Sung Eucharist *11.00 Sun.* Evensong *16.00 last Sun in month.* Eucharist *12.15 Mon, 08.30 Tue, 12.35 Wed, 18.15 Thur, 13.10 Fri.* Spoken Evening Prayer *17.30 Mon-Fri.* Compline, Benediction and Healing *19.30 last Thur in month.* No services *Sat.*

St Anne's **3** C3
Commercial Rd E14. 01-987 1502. *Closed* except for services. Services: *10.30 & 18.00 Sun, 07.30 Mon-Sat.*

St George in the East **2** E1
Cannon Street Rd E1. *Open 08.00-17.00 Mon-Sun.* Services: Prayers *08.00 & 17.00 Mon-Sun.* Eucharist *10.15 Sun.* Holy Communion *20.00 Thur.*

St George's Methodist Church **2** G1
240 Cable St E1. 01-790 3927. *Open 12.30-16.00 Mon-Fri.* Services: *11.00 Sun.* Also a day centre for the homeless.

St Paul's **2** G2
The Highway, Shadwell E1. 01-488 4633. *Closed* except for services. Services: Eucharist *10.00 Sun, (10.30 on fourth Sun in month).*

St Peter's **2** F3
Wapping Lane E1. 01-481 2985. *Open 08.30-18.00 Mon-Sun.* Services: Mass *07.30 Mon, Wed & Fri, 18.00 Tue, 09.30 & 11.00 Thur, 08.30 & 10.00 Sun.*

POLICE STATIONS

Limehouse Police Station **3** D3
29 West India Dock Rd E14. 01-488 5212.

Wapping Police Station **1** D1
74 Leman St E1. 01-488 5441.

Wapping Police Station **2** F3
98 Wapping High St E1. 01-488 5212. This is the river police station. Only river matters dealt with here.

POST OFFICES

Wapping Lane **2** F3
52 Wapping Lane E1. 01-481 2192. *Open 09.00-13.30 & 14.30-17.30 Mon, Tue, Thur & Fri; 09.00-13.00 Wed; 09.00-12.00 Sat.*

PUBLIC CONVENIENCES

Tower Hill Underground Station **1** C2
E1. *Open 08.00-18.00 Mon-Sun.*

SCHOOLS AND COLLEGES

Blue Gate Fields School **2** G1
King David Lane E1. 01-790 3616. State primary school for ages 3-11.

City and East London College
Arbour Sq E1. 01-790 1066/1666. Higher and further education college.

Cyril Jackson School **3** C3
51 Three Colt St E14. 01-987 3737. Annexe at Gill St E14. 01-987 4426. State primary school for ages 3-11.

St Patrick's School **2** F3
3 Dundee St E1. 01-488 3910. Roman Catholic school for ages 5-11.

St Patrick's School **2** F3
Reardon St E1. 01-488 4010. This is the

nursery and reception branch of St Patrick's, Dundee St. Roman Catholic school for ages 3-5.

St Peter's School **2** F3

Garnet St E1. 01-488 3050. Church of England school for ages 3-11.

Our Lady School **3** C2

Copenhagen Place E14. 01-987 1798. Roman Catholic school for ages 5-11.

SHOE REPAIRS

S.A. Steptowe

80 Ben Jonson Rd E1. 01-790 1931. *Open 08.30-17.30 Mon-Fri, 08.30-17.00 Sat.*

SHOPPING CENTRES

Wapping Lane is currently the only area offering local shopping facilities. (Wapping High Street is unusual in that it is a High Street without shops but there are proposals to change this.) More specialist shops can be found on the ground floor of the Ivory House, St Katharine Docks. Tobacco Dock, Wapping Lane is being developed and there are plans for more speciality shops, restaurants and leisure facilities here – another 'Covent Garden' style development. The first phase will be open in mid-88.

ISLE OF DOGS AND POPLAR

The Isle of Dogs is not really an island but a peninsula pointing southwards into a loop in the Thames. Along its top stretches Poplar, as far as East India Docks and Leamouth in the east.

The core of the Island, which contains the West India and Millwall Docks, is now an Enterprise Zone, attracting spectacular developments, many from the City of London, with a package of incentives on offer until 1992. Here almost everything is new, or being built. A hotchpotch of office and warehouse buildings with a high-tech look, all gleaming glass and bright paintbox colours, is arrayed round the docksides. The blue and red Docklands Light Railway glides along its elevated track which threads across the length of the Island. The cheerful Toytown appearance belies the real nature of the area. Sites are quickly snapped up and over 200 firms had moved in by 1987. Crazily soaring land values mean that many of the first wave of speculative office developments are likely to be demolished and replaced with bigger and more costly buildings. The absence in the Enterprise Zone of an overall physical plan, and of nearly all planning controls (one of the incentives to attract businesses to the area), make it difficult to imagine the area's future appearance. Certainly it will be dominated by the gigantic Canary Wharf scheme for a new international financial centre, dubbed 'Wall Street on the Water'. This project, which will provide over 10 million square feet (930,000 square metres) of office space on 71 acres (29 ha) when completed in 1994, has been the subject of long and bitter debate as well as of financial negotiations. Its most controversial feature, three towers originally planned to be 850ft (259m) high, is now likely to be scaled down.

The older housing areas strung round the Island's perimeter are nearly all council-owned and alternate with expensive new residential developments. The south east corner is Cubitt Town and the south and south west is Millwall. In the middle is the extraordinary wild area of the Mudchute, fortunately preserved from the developers and run by the Islanders themselves. The numerous shipyards, ironworks, engineering works, sawmills and factories which once stood shoulder to shoulder all round the Island's riverfront have closed, following the demise of the docks in 1980 and most have been demolished to make way for luxury housing, although a few wharves still operate down the east side. One beneficial result of the industrial decline is that much of the riverside will be opened up as public walkways for the first time.

There is a strong sense of community among the Islanders, many of whom perceive the current transformation scene as a threat rather than an opportunity. They are accustomed to working together as well as living together, always rather cut off from the rest of the East End, with access to the Island restricted to two narrow roads.

However, the community's history dates back only to the early 19thC when the first docks were built. Before that, the Isle of Dogs was almost uninhabited, an area of marshy pastureland where cattle were kept by graziers renting land from absentee landlords. The Island, which lies 7ft (2m) below normal high-water mark, was repeatedly flooded until an extensive system of drainage ditches was built in the 17thC. At one time it was known as Stibenhithe or Stebunheath (later Stepney) Marsh. The origin of the later name is obscure. Of the various fanciful theories about royal hunting kennels at Greenwich, dead dogs on the shore, ducks etc, the most plausible is that 'dogs' is a corruption of the Flemish word for dyke, 'dijk' and that it came into use after Flemish experts were brought in to organise the drainage of the Island.

Since medieval times an embankment had been maintained round the shoreline and the name Millwall derives from the line of windmills which stood on the bank, pumping water from the drainage ditches as well as grinding corn. The only two buildings on the Island which have been recorded were a small stone chapel (built in the late 14thC) near what is now Millwall Outer Dock and the ferry house at the southern tip. The chapel, possibly built for pilgrims on their way to Canterbury, fell into disuse after severe floods drove away the few inhabitants of the Island in the mid-16thC, and later a farmhouse was built out of its ruins, together with a group of cottages. They survived until the construction of the Millwall Docks in the 1860s.

The Isle of Dogs was chosen as the site for London's first ever enclosed trading dock, the West India Dock, opened in 1802. Congestion in the Pool of London and rampant thieving were to be resolved by creating additional quayside space and by loading and unloading cargo into warehouses within an area surrounded by a high security wall. As the other docks were added during the 19thC, industries grew up round them and the population of the Island expanded, to reach 21,000 by 1900. By 1980 all the docks had closed and the area became one of appalling dereliction. The number of jobs fell from 8,000 in 1975 to only 600 in 1982.

Poplar, squashed between its 19thC High Street and the traffic-choked East India Dock Road, which is part of the A13, is a more integral part of the East End than is the Isle of Dogs. An impressive Victorian town hall and a few surviving rows of elegant Georgian houses, together with the splendid All Saints church, hint at former prosperity. Now, however, its small industries, many dependent on the docks, have gone into decline or disappeared, and the whole area has a down-at-heel appearance.

Further east, the area comprising Blackwall, Brunswick Wharf and what remains of the East India Docks, as far as the River Lea, is still at a very early stage of regeneration. There was a fitting-out dock at Blackwall from the early 17thC, built by the East India Company. An important shipbuilding industry grew up here and the East India Dock was opened in 1806. The large Financial Times printing works under construction is an early sign of future plans for the area. However, there are still dozens of small and distinctly 'informal' businesses to be relocated, as well as serious industrial contamination to be dealt with, and even the LDDC admits that redevelopment of the area presents quite a challenge.

Poplar and Isle of Dogs (North)

All Saints Church **4** F3
East India Dock Rd E14. Early 19thC church (built 1821-3) with an elegant spire and Portland stone facing, dramatically white as a result of the recent LDDC-funded cleaning operation. The interior is rather barn-like since the galleries which were extensively damaged by World War II bombs have been removed, but it is currently being redecorated to a high standard. The crypt, which served the local people as an air raid shelter in the war, will soon be smartened up and used as a community centre. *Closed* except for services: Mass *08.00 & 10.00 Sun; 07.00 Mon, Tue, Wed & Fri; 20.00 Wed; 09.30 Thur; 08.00 Sat.*

Billingsgate Fish Market **4** F4
West India Dock E14. 01-987 1118. This is Europe's principal inland wholesale fish market, which deals in over 35,000 tonnes of fish and shellfish a year, made up of more than 100 varieties, from anchovy to zander. A specialist fish market since 1699, it moved from the City to Docklands in 1982, but is still owned by the Corporation of London, in token of which the Lord Mayor of London makes a ceremonial gift of fish to the Mayor of Tower Hamlets each February. Samples are used for trading, while the bulk of any consignment remains in cold store, and all samples are inspected by the fishmeters (company officials) of the Fishmongers' Company, which is one of the 12 City Livery Companies and has 24 Royal Charters.

There is an annual open day of no fixed date, but it is possible, with permission, to visit on other occasions – and a smelly, slithery experience it is, too. *Trading 05.30-12.00 Tue-Sat, 05.30-10.00 Sun* (shellfish only). For permission to visit write to the Clerk and Superintendent, Room No 40, Billingsgate Market, West India Dock Road, Poplar, London E14.

Blackwall Basin **4** G5
Built in 1800-2 by W. Jessop as an entrance basin for the West India Docks. The modern housing development which overlooks it is called Jamestown Harbour to commemorate the fact that ships taking emigrants to Jamestown in the United States started from Brunswick Wharf, just to the north east of here.

The Blue Bridge **4** G6
Prestons Rd E14. The Port of London Authority installed this hefty drawbridge, over the eastern entrance to South Dock, as late as 1969.

Bridge House **4** G5
Prestons Rd E14. The superintendent of the West India Dock Company used to live in this impressive house, built in 1819 to a design by John Rennie senior (father of Sir John Rennie). It is being converted into six elegant flats, whose owners will have the added pleasure of admiring the listed cherry tree in the garden.

Canary Wharf **3** D5
E14. The quay which once docked ships from the Canary Islands is to be the site of the largest commercial development in Western Europe, under the auspices of a consortium led by the Canadian firm of Olympia and York. At the time of going to press, plans were still being finalised, but it will certainly be a mighty business and financial centre. Early models show a futuristic structure with buildings extending over the water on piers, a trio of towers which threaten to be the tallest in London and a complex of shops and restaurants with hidden parking. The whole development is extending as far as the river to the west.

The Docklands Light Railway station at Canary Wharf has already been dismantled to make way for building works, and will be reassembled as part of the new development.

Cannon Workshops **3** D4
Cannon Drive E14. Various small businesses rent accommodation in the low buildings behind Sir John Rennie's impressive entrance arch. Everything may have to be relocated, however, to make way for the outer edge of the vast Canary Wharf Development which, at this western end, will culminate in a two-tier roundabout the size of Trafalgar Square. Properly called the Quadrangle Building, its original sheds were put up in 1824-5 and used as workshops for coopers, engineers and farriers. The Trinity high water mark, indicating how low the surrounding land is, can be seen on the wall underneath the arch.

The roundhouse outside used to have a twin – one was a gunpowder magazine and the other a prison cell, but no one knows which one has survived.

The great curving brick wall opposite is the last remaining stretch of the boundary wall of the West India Dock Company, whose initials are still on the bollards by the blocked-off gateway.

Coldharbour **4** G5

E14. This lies within a conservation area, part of which is under some threat from the scheme to widen Prestons Road and to develop further the land around Blackwall Basin. Coldharbour itself, which will be preserved, is a narrow street with several listed 19thC houses and one supposedly haunted pub, the Gun. Apart from this the two most notable buildings are at the northern end. Isle House, large yet cosy-looking with its comfortably bowed frontage, was built in 1824 by Sir John Rennie for the Blackwall Dockmaster. Nelson House next door, plain but for its fanlight, is believed to have had the Admiral as a temporary visitor; certainly he and Lady Hamilton are said to have enjoyed assignations in a private room in the Gun.

Dockmaster's House **3** D3

West India Dock Rd E14. Built in 1807, to a design by the West India Dock Company's own engineer, Thomas Morris, this was never actually used as a dockmaster's house, though the name lingers on. First it was an excise office; then the Jamaica Inn; next a Port of London Authority office used by their Dock Manager; and until recently it was an LDDC office. Now there are plans to convert it into a high class restaurant to serve Canary Wharf and the other developments. No public access.

East India Dock **7** A3

E14. The LDDC regards this whole area as 'the last great challenge on the Isle of Dogs'. The dock has been under pressure since the last war when it was drained to supply additional dry docking and the walls, without the support of the water, collapsed. After that much of it was filled in, and the section that remained was the first of the working docks system to close down, in 1967.

Some of the surrounding land is heavily contaminated by mercury and other industrial waste from the nearby River Lea. It is now being cleaned, the remaining dock basin will be filled in, some of the impressive security walls retained, and the site taken up for commercial and light industrial development. The print works of the Financial Times newspaper are already at an advanced stage of construction.

Garford Street Cottages **3** D4

Garford St E14. The dock police used to live here with the sergeant in the middle and his constables on either side. Designed by John Rennie senior in 1819, they have survived well and are still nice places to live. No public access.

Heron Quays **4** E5

E14. Here stands the first of the new buildings to be extended out over the water on piles. The metal sculpture which stands on one leg in the water near the dock edge is called 'Spirit of Enterprise'; before building began herons stood one-legged on bollards watching for the fish which still live in the docks.

Heron Quays

Hydraulic Pumping Station **4** G4

Duthie St E14. The red brick structure with the cast-iron window frames was built in 1882 for the Midland Railways Dock, to provide power to operate the cranes and lock gates. The dock has since been filled in. No public access.

Ledger Building **3** D3

West India Dock Rd E14. Elegant early 19thC office block, built up against the West India Import Dock wall – although most of the latter has now been demolished. The LDDC, currently using it as one of its offices, is to preserve it as part of the proposed Port East Development, envisaged as the Isle of Dogs' answer to Covent Garden. George Gwilt, surveyor to the county of Surrey, designed it in 1803, but John Rennie senior added the portico in the 1820s.

Library of the Museum in Docklands Project **4** G3

Units C14-16 Poplar Business Park, 10 Prestons Rd E14. 01-515 1162. The Library has a large and unique collection of material on the London Docks and the Port of London together with some 10,000 photographs, historic prints and engravings. The staff are able to provide information on most aspects of Docklands past and present. The Library is *open to researchers 10.00-17.00 Mon-Fri by prior appointment with the Librarian.*

Limehouse Studios **4** E5

Canary Wharf, West India Docks E14. 01-987 2090. Britain's largest independent television studios operate from here. The output is diverse but probably the best-known production is that acidic adult puppet show, *Spitting Image*.

The *Sloop John D*, a well-known disco boat of the 60s, is moored alongside to do duty as a staff canteen, and another boat, renamed *Take Two*, is currently being refurbished to take the hungry overspill.

The studios may have to be relocated when the Canary Wharf project gets under way. No public access.

Mercury Communications **4** F5
West India Dock E14. High-tech businesses need high-tech communications, and the Mercury earth satellite station, linking its customers to European counterparts, has been so successful since it opened in 1984 that it is already adding a third dish. Since the privatisation of British Telecom, whose own teleport is in the Royal Docks, Mercury has been the principal competitor.

Poplar Dock **4** G4
E14. Established as a working dock in 1850 when it was leased to the North London Railway Company it had actually been dug out 20 years earlier as a reservoir to allow the mud from the incoming river water to settle before it was used to refill the docks. In 1850 it was enlarged and colliers delivered coal here to be transferred to the trains of the railway company. The two hydraulic accumulator towers, which powered the coal derricks, still remain intact. Proposed development here has not progressed beyond the discussion stage.

Poplar Town Hall **4** F4
Poplar High St E14. The former Poplar Town Hall, on the corner of Woodstock Terrace, is a Grade II listed building, a friendly Victorian-Gothic structure with a fairy-tale dome and pretty detailing. It is now used as offices by Tower Hamlets Council. No public access, except on business.

The Redbrick or Herringbone Road **3** D3
E14. Two landmarks denote the entrance to the Isle of Dogs; the gate piers of the original entrance to the West India Docks, and the beginning of the LDDC's three miles of road, made entirely of red bricks hand-laid in a distinctive herring-bone pattern. It is the first of its kind in Britain, designed so that sections can be easily lifted and relaid when service pipes underneath need repair or enlargement.

River Lea and Leamouth **7** C4
E14. The mouth of the Lea, which is navigable as far as Hertford, has suffered untold damage from the decision of succeeding councils to prevent chemical and heavy manufacturing companies moving any closer to the heart of London than this. The conglomeration of ugly, if necessary, structures have made the Lea Valley a sad and dirty place. Some of the smaller businesses are to be relocated, others will be cleaned up, but this will always be an industrial corner.

The Lea Flood Barrier, visible near Pura Foods, has to be activated at the same time as the Thames Barrier to prevent rising water using this as an escape route.

St Matthias Church **4** F3
Behind Poplar Town Hall, Poplar High St E14. Curious little church, rather like an ecclesiastical version of a gingerbread house, standing in a tangled country churchyard, hidden behind the old Poplar Town Hall. It can be glimpsed from Poplar High Street and Woodstock Terrace, or approached more closely through the gate between the churchyard and the recreation ground.

It was first built as a chapel in 1654, by the East India Company. It became a church in 1866 and soon afterwards was faced in Kentish ragstone and given a Victorian-medieval look by W.W. Teulon (brother of S.S., who designed St Mark's in Silvertown). It was abandoned to creeping dereliction in the late 1970s but, as the oldest complete building in Docklands, will be rescued as soon as plans can be finalised. The likelihood is that it will be refurbished as the permanent home of the Raglan Baroque Players. No public access.

Salvation Army Building **3** D3
West India Dock Rd E14. The attractive little building with the central green cupola went up in 1902, though the design, by Niven and Wigglesworth, suggests an earlier date. It began life as a mission for Scandinavian seamen, run on strict temperance lines by two elderly sisters, and was handed over to the Salvation Army in 1930.

South Dock **4** F5
E14. First conceived as a canal and built by William Jessop in 1805, the intention was to save shipping the time lost in sailing round the peninsula. It was very successful until tolls were introduced after three years and they and the double locks accounted for as much time as the voyage around the river loop. It was enlarged and modified as a dock in the 1870s.

South Dock Entrance Lock **3** D5
E14. This is the original lock (1803-5) leading to the City Canal, later to South Dock, not simply preserved but still in use to let in water from the Thames to the

impounding station between it and the dock. The impounding station (1914) releases the water as necessary, to replenish the docks.

South Quay Plaza **4 E6**
E14. South Quay Plaza is the site of major office developments, served by the South Quay station of the Docklands Light Railway. The first phase – the editorial building for The Daily Telegraph, the first national newspaper to move to the Isle of Dogs – is already complete. There will be two more building phases, the third of which will include some shops. The Telegraph's printing works are at the other end of Millharbour, beside Millwall Docks.

Visitor Centre **4 F5**
Canary Wharf, West India Dock Rd E14. 01-515 3000. The LDDC's temporary structure, shortly to move to a more permanent location, is a reception point for organised Docklands tours. Visitors can see architectural models of future schemes and also a regularly updated audio-visual show, which aims to explain the Corporation's own role; to impress with its exposition of the massive residential, retail and business development which has already taken place; and to generate enthusiasm about future opportunities still available for those prepared to take them. *Open 09.00-18.00 Mon-Fri & some weekends* (if special tours have been organised).

Warehouses 1 and 2 **4 E4**
E14. The old sugar warehouses c1802, with the viciously spiked window frames on their lower floors, are still an oppressive presence, though empty now. One of the longest buildings in Europe, until World War II bombs put paid to that distinction, they are the oldest multi-storey warehouses surviving in London and are listed Grade I. The alley to the side was known locally as Blood Alley because the gritty sugar seeped through its sacks and gradually flayed the shoulders of the dockers who had to carry it. The warehouses will be preserved, but their future use is still uncertain. No public access.

Sugar Warehouse Two

West India Import and Export Docks **4 E4**
E14. The import dock to the north opened first, in 1802, the export dock in 1806. Both were designed by Ralph Walker and William Jessop, both are 2,600ft (793m) long, though their widths are 510ft (155m) and 400ft (122m) respectively, and both were marvelled at in their day. The nearby sugar warehouses testify to the principal import, but rum, coffee and mahogany passed this way, too. The dock walls are listed Grade I, and the design of the new development must allow for their preservation. The docks are also the site for cranes, retained for restoration.

Dockside Cranes

The Sea Scouts' training ship, the *Lord Amory*, is moored at the eastern end of the export dock in an area called 'Dollar Bay', and their canoes and kayaks are often on the water here.

West India Pier **3 D5**
West Ferry Rd E14. The pier has been refurbished and will eventually be one of the ports of call of the planned riverbus service. At present it is used by The Daily Telegraph for its own service, ferrying workers in from the west.

Eating and Drinking
Early breakfast (*from 03.00*) at the Billingsgate Fish Market Cafés; a pizza at the Brunswick Arms (which also has restaurant food); or pub grub at Charlie Brown's or the City Pride.
See Pubs and Restaurants.

Isle of Dogs (South)

Asda Superstore **6** F2
East Ferry Rd E14. 01-987 2614. Very large supermarket with a cafeteria and a spacious car park and filling station. A bite was taken out of the Mudchute to make space for Asda, but the soil was used to create an interesting and useful new amphitheatrical feature on the Mudchute itself. *Open 09.00-20.00 Mon-Thur, 09.00-21.00 Fri, 08.30-20.00 Sat.*

The Brunel Centre **6** F2
Limeharbour E14. A waterfront development which will have offices, restaurant, wine bar, hotel, multi-storey car park, a leisure and watersports centre and a medical centre aimed in particular at aching athletes from the adjacent Docklands Arena. Scheduled for completion early 1989. No public access until then.

Burrell's Wharf **6** E4
West Ferry Rd E14. This is the site of Napier Yard where Brunel's ill-fated *Great Eastern* steamship was built 1853-7. She was five times the size of any ship then afloat. The project aroused great public interest, as did the launch, in 1857, which had to be carried out sideways. The launch went seriously wrong and the ship, originally named *Leviathan*, was left stranded for months until she was eventually launched in January 1858. Her career as a passenger ship was equally unsuccessful and she was turned into a cable-laying vessel, ending her days as a floating funfair before being broken up in 1888. The remains of the timber slipway, found in 1984, will be restored and opened to the public. Part of the old Napier Yard buildings survive, as the former Burrell Colour Works, and are to be preserved within the housing and leisure complex now being developed on the site. A self-build housing scheme is planned in the development of the area, which includes Maconochie's Wharf and Masthouse Terrace. No public access until building work completed.

Chapel House Conservation Area **6** E3
E14. The Chapel House estate of cottage-style housing, pleasantly laid out on tree-lined streets and crescents, was built by Poplar Borough Council after World War I as 'Homes for Heroes'. The name comes from the medieval stone chapel which stood in the centre of the Island until the mid-15thC. Some of the streets, such as Hesperus Crescent, Harbinger Road and Thermopylae Gate, were named after ships built at Millwall in the 1840s.

Church of Christ and St John **6** G3
Manchester Rd E14. 01-987 1915. Formerly called Christ Church. A Victorian-Gothic church of brick (originally pale cream, now clothed in London grime) with stone dressing. Designed by F. Johnstone, it was completed in 1857 and its cost (£7,000) donated by the builder William Cubitt. Some pieces of the old London Bridge were incorporated into its structure. The interior is unexpected: there can't be many churches with a wallpapered chancel, for example. The organ loft, with a row of lively-looking angels blowing trumpets, occupies the south transept of the cruciform church, giving the interior space a lopsided feel. There is an excellent organ, originally by Walker but rebuilt in the 1950s. The entrance doubles as a busy parish office with a staircase leading to a meetings room above. *Open 09.30-15.30 Mon, Wed & Fri, 09.30-12.00 Sat.* Services: *11.00 & 18.00 Sun, 12.45 & 19.30 Wed, 10.00 Sat.*

Cubitt Town **6** G3
E14. The area is named after the builder William Cubitt, son of a Norfolk carpenter. His brothers Thomas and Lewis built for the rich in Belgravia while he specialised in public buildings, bridges and railways. In the 1840s he leased 79 acres (32 ha), including a mile of river frontage, from the Countess of Glengall and built a workers' housing estate, now mostly disappeared. He also built Manchester Road and had an interest in several local factories and wharves. The Cubitt Town Library in Strattondale Street was built in 1904 and endowed by Andrew Carnegie. It has a small central tower topped by a timber cupola and weather vane.

Globe Ropewalk **6** F3
East Ferry Rd E14. The site of the Globe Rope Works which operated from 1881-1971 has been landscaped by the LDDC and transformed into an attractive tree-lined footpath which starts at Mudchute station.

Greenwich Foot Tunnel **6** G4
Saunders Ness Rd E14. The small round building with a dome is the entrance to the lift and staircase which descend 60ft (18m) to the tunnel. The latter runs 1,217ft (370m) under the Thames to emerge at Greenwich near the *Cutty Sark*. It was opened in 1902

for the hundreds of workers who crossed the river in either direction every day, and replaced the ferry which had probably existed since the Middle Ages, and which Pepys says he used in 1665. Until recently, the near-deserted tunnel was not for the frail or faint-hearted but now, with the Docklands Light Railway terminus nearby, it is becoming a popular route for tourists visiting Greenwich. Tunnel always open; lift operates *06.00-23.00 Mon-Sun. Closed Christmas and New Year. Free.*

DLR, Island Gardens Station

Harbour Exchange **6** F1
Limeharbour E14. One of the largest office developments in Docklands with 1 million square feet (93,000 square metres) of office space in eight buildings. It will have a central plaza with shops, restaurants and a pub, and a dockside promenade. Replaces a building completed only in 1984. No public access yet.

Island Gardens **6** G4
Saunders Ness Rd E14. The riverside gardens, now the centre of a conservation area, were created at the end of the 19thC on former reedbeds. It is a pleasant strip with mature trees and a breathtaking view of the Royal Naval College and Queen's House across the river at Greenwich. Canaletto sat near here in about 1750 to paint his *Greenwich Palace*. The view is shared by the lucky owners of new houses and flats at either end of the gardens, Felsted Wharf to the west, Luralda Wharf to the east. Also on the west is Johnson's Draw Dock, which is being refurbished and reopened to provide public access to the river. To the north is the George Green's Centre, a large comprehensive school and community centre built in 1976 and named after a local Victorian shipbuilder and philanthropist. *Open 07.30 to 30 mins before sunset Mon-Sun.*

Island Resource Centre **6** G3
Manchester Rd E14. 01-987 3226. The Association of Island Communities, founded in 1976 as the Isle of Dogs Action Group, has its headquarters here. It is a federation of several local groups and publishes a monthly community newspaper, *The Islander*. The centre also houses the Island History Trust's collection of more than 2,500 photographs (which has been called the 'biggest family album in Britain'): a wonderful record of the people of the Isle of Dogs over the generations, and of their homes and workplaces. The photographs have been contributed mainly by the Islanders themselves and are indexed where possible by the names of people appearing in them. There are also exhibition panels depicting the Island's history. Visitors welcome but a prior telephone call advisable. *Normally open 09.00-17.00 Mon-Fri. Open Days are held during the 1st Bank holiday weekend in May & the 1st weekend of Oct every year.*

Jubilee Crescent **6** G2
E14. Built as retirement homes for workers by local shipbuilders Green & Silley Weir in 1935. King George V and Queen Mary are portrayed in two central plaques. Originally there was a bowling green in front.

London Docklands Arena **6** F1
Limeharbour E14. A former banana shed is being transformed into Britain's major new indoor sports arena, seating 12,000. It will include running tracks and facilities for tennis, squash, badminton, table tennis, weight lifting and gymnastics. Scheduled for completion autumn 1988. No public access until then.

Millharbour **6** E1
E14. This new road is for the most part lined with low-rise buildings made of brightly coloured components and a lot of glass. Their toybox appearance has led to this area of Docklands being described as 'Legoland'. Many of these office and warehouse units are 'first wave' minimum-cost buildings and will probably be knocked down to make way for taller, more permanent blocks as land values soar. Here to stay, however, are the solid brick offices of Penthouse publisher, Northern & Shell Group (the first firm to hang up its hat, as it were, in the Enterprise Zone), the printing works of The Guardian Newspapers and, overlooking Outer Dock, those of The Daily Telegraph, another early settler.

Millwall Docks **6** E2
E14. The last of the docks to be built on the

Island, they were designed for the newly formed Millwall Dock Company by John Fowler and opened in 1868. Grain and timber were the main imports handled and there were flour-mills and sawmills on the quayside. The company's engineer Frederick E. Duckham devised the first pneumatic system for sucking grain from ship to shore. The former graving (dry) dock at the south east corner of the outer (south) dock has been filled with water and is now surrounded by the Clippers Quay housing development.

A watersports centre is planned for the west end near the old dock entrance which has also been filled in.

Millwall Cut is the narrow strip of water connecting these docks with the West India Docks. The old lock gates have been refurbished and a new lifting bridge installed.

Millwall Park **6 G3**
Stebondale St E14. A flat L-shaped park with grass and a few flower beds as well as football pitches, synthetic cricket wicket, running tracks and bowling green. Bookings 01-790 1818. *Open 07.30 to 30 mins before sunset Mon-Sun.*

The Mudchute **6 F2**
Cubitt Town E14. A 32 acre (13 ha) area of grassy hillocks and hollows encircled by a belt of saplings, it feels like a bit of transplanted countryside. A flock of sheep from the Mudchute City Farm adds to the rural atmosphere, while little pink pigs scampering up and down the hills provide entertainment for walkers. There are also good views over Docklands and Greenwich. The Muddie, as it is known affectionately by locals, is not a natural feature. It was formed out of solidified mud and silt dredged out of Millwall Docks and deposited on settling beds which grew ever higher, from the 1880s until 20 years later. The mud was held in place by retaining banks built out of industrial clinker.

In the 1960s the Port of London Authority planned to extend the docks and moved the 400 allotment-holders off the land which had become a wild place, much used by local children. In the event, the docks were never extended. Proposals to build houses on it met with strong local protest and in 1976 it was leased to a local community group. The Mudchute Association was formed to manage the area as an open space and start a city farm, and about 60 allotments were reopened.

On the Mudchute's southern border is the Newtie, an old drainage ditch where children have fished for newts for as long as anyone can remember.

The Greenwich Axis, the line which forms the basis on which Greenwich Park was laid out, lies across a corner of the Mudchute and is marked by a stone near the top of the steps leading up from East Ferry Road. The steps were deliberately built to coincide with the line, which runs direct from the statue of General Wolfe at the top of the Park, through the Queen's House and, to the north west of the Mudchute, the prominent tower of St Anne's Limehouse.

Other access points are the steps from Asda car park and from Mudchute Station, and Pier Street.

Mudchute Farm **6 G2**
Pier St E14. 01-515 5901. More like the real thing than most city farms, because it has grassland spreading over the Mudchute's 32 acres (13 ha). Local people set it up in 1977 and formed the Mudchute Association to run the farm as well as manage the Mudchute as a whole. Two full-time staff and several dedicated volunteers look after the beef cattle, ponies, sheep, goats, pigs, poultry, rabbits and bees. School groups come to observe and handle the animals and there is a riding school with a qualified teacher, with a pony club for local children.

The range of buildings includes a classroom and a teashop. A small part of the Mudchute has been made into timber-fenced fields and pens and there is even a mini sheep-dip. An orchard has been planted but the lead content of the soil, probably a legacy of the former leadworks near the bottom of East Ferry Road, was found to be still too high for the first crop of fruit to be safe to eat. The Mudchute is the venue for the annual Isle of Dogs Agricultural Show (see Events p. 112). *Open 09.00-17.00 Mon-Sun. Free.*

Newcastle Draw Dock **6 H3**
Saunders Ness Rd E14. Small coasters and barges used to draw into these riverside docks at high tide; when the tide ebbed, cargo was unloaded onto carts which were driven down on to the foreshore. This one dates from about 1850 and is a listed structure.

Railway Viaduct, Millwall Park **6 F3**
Stebondale St E14. The jaunty Docklands Light Railway now runs to and fro over this grand Victorian viaduct, which curves across the end of Millwall Park. It was built in 1872 to carry an extension of the London & Blackwall Railway down to the North Greenwich terminus which connected with

the ferry at the Island's southern tip. The old railway was closed in 1926.

St Paul's Presbyterian Church **5 D2**
West Ferry Rd E14. Sometimes known as the Episcopalian Chapel, this little Byzantine-style church with its red and blue brickwork and white stone, and rows of Romanesque blind arches, catches the eye even in its semi-derelict state. It was designed by Thomas Knightley and built in 1859 probably for Scottish shipyard workers in the area (it has always been known locally as 'the Scotch Church'). The foundation stone was laid by John Scott Russell, owner of the nearby shipyard which built Brunel's *Great Eastern*. Until recently the church was used as a workshop and store. Now Grade II listed, it will be restored and a new use found for it. No public access.

Sir John McDougall Gardens **5 D1**
West Ferry Rd E14. A small park, named after the inventor of self-raising flour who had a large granary at Millwall Dock. Rather forlorn but soon to be refurbished. It has splendid views across the river to Surrey Docks and upstream to Tower Bridge. Just to the north is Seacon Wharf, a large blue and white building with a canopy extending over the river. This is the main steel terminal on the Thames. *Open 07.30 to 30 mins before sunset Mon-Sun.*

Eating and Drinking
A simple sandwich at the Café in the Park or Island Gardens Café; a snack at Asda Shoppers' Restaurant; pub food at the Dorset Arms, the Ferry House, the George, the Kingsbridge Arms, the Telegraph or the Waterman's Arms; or a lavish meal at the Café du Commerce.
See Pubs and Restaurants.

Services

All services closed Sat & Sun unless otherwise stated.

ADULT EDUCATION

Tower Hamlets Institute of Adult Education
Head Office, Smithy St E1. 01-790 3358.

Cubitt Town Centre **6 G1**
Manchester Rd E14. 01-987 4610. Evening classes only, including car maintenance, dancing, dressmaking. *Open 19.30-21.00 Mon-Fri.*

George Green's Centre **6 G4**
George Green's School, 80 Manchester Rd E14. 01-515 4774/5154. Morning classes for parents. Varied evening programme including Vietnamese music, Cantonese classes and sports for disabled people. *Open 10.00-17.00 Mon-Fri, 19.00-20.30 Tue-Thur.*

St Matthias Centre **4 G3**
Bullivant St E14. 01-538 4424. Daytime classes mainly for the Chinese and Vietnamese community. Evening classes include tai-chi and yoga for everyone. *Open 10.00-17.00, 18.30-21.00 Mon-Fri.*

BANKS

Barclays Bank **3 D4**
Hertsmere House, Western Gateway E14. 01-538 4646. *Open 09.30-15.30 Mon-Fri.*

Barclays Bank **4 F3**
159 East India Dock Rd E14. 01-538 4574. *Open 09.30-15.30 Mon-Fri.*

National Westminster Bank **6 F4**
429 West Ferry Rd E14. 01-987 7973. *Open 09.30-15.30 Mon-Fri.*

BUILDING SOCIETIES

Abbey National **4 F3**
16 Vesey Path E14. 01-515 0522. *Open 09.00 (09.30 Tue)-17.00 Mon-Fri, 09.00-12.00 Sat.*

CHEMISTS

Allens Pharmacy **6 G1**
19 Castalia Sq E14. 01-987 1362. *Open 09.00-13.00, 14.00-18.00 Mon-Wed & Fri, 09.00-13.00 Thur, 09.00-17.00 Sat.*

Arms Chemist **4 G4**
259 Poplar High St E14. 01-987 3493. *Open 09.00-19.00 Mon, Tue, Thur & Fri, 09.00-18.30 Wed, 09.00-18.00 Sat.*

Boots **4 F3**
18/20 The Vesey Path E14. 01-987 5364. *Open 08.45-17.30 Mon-Sat.*

D.D. Chandegra **5 D1**
15 The Quarterdeck, Barkantine Estate,

West Ferry Rd E14. 01-987 4313. *Open 09.00-19.00 Mon-Wed, 09.00-13.00 Thur, 09.00-17.00 Sat.*

Cubitt Town Pharmacy **6** G3
143 Manchester Rd E14. 01-987 1487. *Open 09.00-13.00 & 14.00-18.00 Mon-Wed & Fri, 09.00-13.00 & 14.00-17.00 Thur & Sat.*

Lansbury **4** F3
173 East India Dock Rd E14. 01-987 1875. *Open 08.45-18.00 Mon-Fri, 08.45-17.30 Sat.*

CITIZENS ADVICE BUREAUX

Poplar Citizens Advice Bureau **4** F3
Woodstock Terrace E14. 01-987 6040. *Open 10.00-13.00 Mon, Tue, Thur & Fri. Closed Wed.*

COMMUNITY AND YOUTH CENTRES

Docklands Settlement **6** F3
197 East Ferry Rd E14. 01-538 4000. Junior and senior clubs, Chinese and Vietnamese evenings, pensioners' group, aerobics and Island History Trust workshop. *Open 12.15-13.15 & 18.00-22.00 Mon, 19.00-22.00 Tue, 13.00-15.00 & 18.00-22.00 Wed & Thur, 12.15-13.15 Fri.*

George Green's Centre **6** G4
Manchester Rd E14. 01-515 5154/5226. Facilities include badminton, volleyball, football, fitness, trampolining, table tennis and cricket nets. *Open 18.00-22.00 Mon-Fri, 09.00-22.00 Sat & Sun.*

Island House Church Community Centre **6** G1
4 Roserton St E14. 01-987 3679. Clubs include playgroup, karate, tennis, mother and toddler and religious group meetings. Two halls available for functions. *Open 09.30-16.00 Mon-Fri.*

Poplar Play Centre **4** F4
Poplar High St E14. 01-515 1111. Playgroup, family centre and facilities for 5-8 year-olds. *Open 08.30-18.00 Mon-Fri.*

Samuda Community Centre **6** G1
Ballin Court, Manchester Rd E14. 01-538 2341. Clubs and facilities organised by Tenants' Association. *Open 09.00-16.30 Mon-Fri (closed for lunch 13.00-14.00), 09.00-13.00 Wed.*

COUNCILLORS

Members of London Borough of Tower Hamlets. Council offices at the Town Hall, Patriot Sq E2. 01-980 4831. The councillors for the Poplar Neighbourhood are B. Blandford (Liberal), T. Connolly (Liberal), G. Deakins (Liberal), P. Fletcher (Liberal), S. Lewis (Liberal), C. Manser (Liberal), C. Rayment (Liberal), A. Delargy (Labour), A. Downes (Labour), P. Little (Labour) and N. McAree (Labour). The councillors for the Isle of Dogs Neighbourhood are A. Porter (Labour), T. Shanahan (Labour), T. Staten (Labour), C. Shawcroft (Labour) and J. Matthews (SDP). If you have any complaints, suggestions or queries write to your councillor at the Town Hall.

COURTS

Poplar Coroner's Court **4** F4
Poplar High St E14. 01-987 3614. Main office at St Pancras Coroner's Court NW1. Coroner comes to Poplar *Mon & Wed mornings*. Public admitted, but not much room.

DENTISTS

M.C. Joshi **6** G1
155 Manchester Rd E14. 01-515 7043. *Open 09.00-14.00 Mon-Sat.* Afternoon by appointment only.

D.B.G. Moss **3** D3
320a Burdett Rd E14. 01-987 4880. *Open 09.30-13.00 Mon & Thur, 09.30-13.00 & 14.00-17.30 Tue & Fri. Closed Wed.*

Padraig G. O'Reachtagain **4** G3
204a East India Dock Rd E14. 01-987 2233. *Open 09.30-17.00 Mon-Fri (to 19.30 Thur). Closed 13.00-14.00.*

C.K. Tiwary **3** D3
62 East India Dock Rd E14. 01-987 2763. *Open 09.30-17.30 Mon-Wed & Fri (closed 13.00-14.00), 09.30-12.30 Thur & Sat.*

P.A.K. Vale **3** D3
48 East India Dock Rd E14. 01-987 5953. *Open 09.30-13.00 & 14.00-18.00 Mon, Tue, Thur & Fri, 09.45-13.00 Sat. Closed Wed.*

DHSS OFFICES

Poplar DHSS Office **3** D2
13 Dod St E14. 01-987 1231. *Open 09.30-15.30 Mon-Fri.*

DOCTORS

General Practitioner Centre **4** E6
Office Suite No 1, Scott House, Waterside, Marsh Wall E14. 01-515 4586. Private patients only. *Open 09.00-17.00 Mon-Fri.* (Part of the London Independent Hospital, 1

Beaumont Sq, Stepney Green E1. 01-790 0990.)

Drs Jenkins, Keys and Meyer **4** G6
13 Kimberley House, Galbraith St E14. 01-980 3130. *Open 09.00-11.00 & 16.00-17.30 Mon-Fri (closed Thur evening). Emergencies only Sat morning.*

Dr C.V. Kotheiri **4** G4
South Poplar Health Centre, 260 Poplar High St E14. 01-987 3536. Surgery hours: *10.00-12.00 & 16.00-18.00 Mon-Fri (closed Wed evening).* Health centre *open 09.00-17.00 Mon-Fri.*

Dr V. Mahajan **6** F4
1 Julian Place E14. 01-515 4601. *Open 10.00-11.30 & 17.00-18.30 Mon-Fri (17.00-18.00 Tue & Wed). Closed Thur evening.*

Dr V. Nebhrajani **4** E3
60 East India Dock Rd E14. 01-515 5525. *Open 09.30-11.00 & 17.00-18.00 Mon & Tue, 12.00-13.00 Wed, 09.30-11.00 Thur, 12.00-13.00 Fri. 17.30-18.00 Fri for emergencies only.*

Dr S. Yogadera **6** G1
519 Manchester Rd E14. 01-987 4231. *Open 09.30-11.00 & 16.30-18.00 Mon-Fri. Closed Thur evening.*

DRY CLEANERS

Betta Press **4** G2
33 Aberfeldy St E14. 01-987 4866. *Open 09.00-17.30 Tue, Wed, Fri & Sat, 09.00-13.00 Thur. Closed Mon.*

Clothes Care **3** D3
86 West India Dock Rd E14. 01-515 0173. *Open 08.30-17.30 Mon, Tue, Wed & Fri, 08.30-13.00 Thur, 08.30-16.45 Sat.*

Reliable Dry Cleaners **6** G1
5 Castalia Sq E14. 01-987 8283. *Open 09.00-17.00 Mon, Tue, Wed & Fri, 09.00-16.30 Sat. Closed Thur.*

EMPLOYMENT AGENCIES

Anglo-Technical Recruitment **6** F1
25 Skylines, Limeharbour E14. 01-538 5151. Technical employment agency. *Open 09.00-18.00 Mon-Fri.*

Brook Street Bureau **6** F1
3-4 Limeharbour E14. 01-538 0232. Full range of employment services. *Open 09.00-17.30 Mon-Thur, 09.00-18.00 Sat.*

ESTATE AGENTS

Aylesford Grant & Partners **4** E6
50 Marsh Wall E14. 01-538 2535. Residential. *Open 09.00-17.30 Mon-Fri.*

Bairstow Eves **6** F1
5 Skylines, Limeharbour E14. 01-538 5535. Residential and commercial. *Open 09.00-18.00 Mon-Fri, 09.00-16.30 Sat, 12.00-16.30 Sun.* Commercial office *open Mon-Fri* only.

Chestertons Residential **3** D3
3 Pennyfields E14. 01-538 4921. *Open 09.00-18.00 Mon-Fri, 10.00-16.00 Sat, 10.00-13.00 Sun.*

Peter Clapshaw & Co **4** G3
237 East India Dock Rd E14. 01-515 8800. Residential. *Open 09.00-17.30 Mon-Fri, 09.30-16.00 Sat, 10.00-13.00 Sun.*

Peter Clapshaw & Co **4** E6
Ensign House, Admirals Way, Waterside, E14. 01-515 8800. Commercial. *Open 09.00-17.30 Mon-Fri.*

Collins Druce **6** F1
28 Skylines, Limeharbour E14. 01-538 1821. Residential. *Open 09.00-18.00 Mon-Fri, 10.00-17.00 Sat, 12.00-17.00 Sun.*

Edgars **6** F1
4 Skylines, Limeharbour E14. 01-538 1144. Residential. *Open 09.00-17.30 Mon-Fri.*

Parris & Quirk **6** G2
2 Amsterdam Rd E14. 01-987 4473. Residential. *Open 09.30-17.00 Mon-Fri.*

Ricketts Boreham **9** C3
341-343 Roman Rd E3. 01-980 7431 (residential), 01-981 2721 (commercial). Residential office *open 09.00-18.00 Mon-Fri, 09.00-17.00 Sat, 10.00-14.00 Sun.* Commercial office *open 09.00-18.00 Mon-Fri.*

Alan Selby & Partners **3** D5
Cascades, 2-4 West Ferry Rd E14. 01-538 5421. Residential. *Open 09.30-19.00 Mon-Fri, 09.30-17.00 Sat, 11.30-17.00 Sun.*

HAIRDRESSERS

Alan's Hairdressers **3** D3
5 West India Dock Rd E14. 01-987 2223. Unisex. *Open 09.00-17.00 Tue-Fri, 08.00-16.00 Sat. Closed Mon.*

Charlie's Barbers **4** G3
227 East India Dock Rd E14. 01-538 0725. Men only. *Open 09.00-18.00 Tue, Wed & Fri, 09.00-17.00 Thur, 07.00-16.00 Sat. Closed Mon.*

Harry **3** D3
40a East India Dock Rd E14. 01-987 3747. Men only. *Open 09.00-18.00 Mon, Tue, Thur-Sat, 09.00-13.00 Wed.*

Heads Hairdresser **4** G3
204 East India Dock Rd E14. 01-987 8327. Unisex. *Open 09.00-16.00 Tue-Fri, 08.00-16.00 Sat. Closed Mon & Sun.*

Kisscurl **4** F2
100 Burcham St E14. 01-515 5363. Unisex.

Open 09.00-17.00 Tue, Wed, Fri & Sat. Closed Mon & Thur.

S. Lyn 4 G3
251b East India Dock Rd E14. 01-515 9589. Ladies only. *Open 09.00-16.00 Tue-Fri, 07.00-13.30 Sat. Closed Mon.*

Tibor Hair Artiste 4 G2
37 Aberfeldy St E14. 01-987 2733. Unisex. *Open 09.15-17.00 Tue & Wed, 09.15-18.00 Thur, 09.15-19.00 Fri, 08.30-17.00 Sat.*

Wickers 6 G1
25 Castalia Sq E14. 01-515 3231. Unisex. *Open 09.30-17.30 Tue-Thur, 09.30-19.00 Fri, 08.30-17.00 Sat. Closed Mon.*

HEALTH CENTRES

Island Clinic 6 G1
Roserton St E14. 01-987 4988. Child health development and immunisation), family planning, well woman clinic, antenatal, parentcraft, nurses and health visitors as well as a dentist. Clinic *open 09.00-17.00 Mon-Fri (closed 12.30-13.30).*

South Poplar Health Centre 4 G4
260 Poplar High St E14. 01-515 6522. Antenatal clinic, well woman clinic, health visitor. *Open 09.00-17.00 Mon-Fri.*

LIBRARIES

Cubitt Town Library 6 G1
Strattondale St E14. 01-987 3152. Books plus cassettes. *Open 09.00-12.00 & 13.30-20.00 Mon, Tue & Thur, 09.00-12.00 & 13.30-17.00 Wed, Fri & Sat.*

Poplar Library 4 G3
Brunswick Rd E14. 01-987 3234. Books plus talking books, records, cassettes and CDs. *Open 09.00-12.30 & 13.30-17.00 Mon, 09.00-12.30 & 13.30-19.00 Thur.*

JOB CENTRES

Isle of Dogs Job Centre 6 G1
Cubitt Town Library, Strattondale St E14. 01-538 3608. *Open 09.00-13.00 & 14.00-17.00 Mon-Thur, 14.00-17.00 Fri.*

Poplar Employment Office 3 D2
113 Burdett Rd E14. 01-987 4101. *Open 09.30-15.30 Mon-Fri. Closed 12.00-14.00 Thur.*

MINI-CABS

Island Car Service 3 D4
1 West Ferry Rd E14. 01-987 3674/ 692/3000. *Open 24hrs Mon-Sun.*

Kingsley Car Hire 4 F3
Susannah St E14. 01-980 3630/538 4100. *Open 08.00-24.00 Mon-Sun.*

M. I. Car Services 4 G3
218 East India Dock Rd E14. 01-515 9090. *Open 24hrs Mon-Sun.*

Multi Station 4 F3
172a East India Dock Rd E14. 01-987 1100 or 538 3020/3022. *Open 24hrs Mon-Sun.*

Smart Cars 3 D3
224 East India Dock Rd E14. 01-987 1888. *Open 24hrs Mon-Sun.*

Smart Cars 3 D3
6 West India Dock Rd E14. 01-515 9940. *Open 24hrs Mon-Sun.*

PETROL STATIONS

Cairn Filling Station 6 F2
53 Glengall Grove E14. 01-987 2164. *Open 07.00-19.00 Mon-Fri, 08.00-18.00 Sat.*

Fina 7 C1
95-99 Barking Rd E16. 01-476 6953. *Open 24hrs Mon-Sun.*

PLACES OF WORSHIP

Many churches have to remain closed except for services. Where this is the case anyone can get in by arrangement if they phone the number given.

All Saints 4 F3
Newby Place, East India Dock Rd E14. 01-987 1795. Services: Spoken Mass *08.00 Sun*. Parish Mass *10.00 Sun*. Spoken Evening Prayer *18.00 Sun*. Mass *07.00 Mon, Tue, Wed & Fri, 20.00 Wed, 09.30 Thur, 08.00 Sat.*

Church of Christ & St John 6 G3
Manchester Rd E14. 01-987 1915. *Open 09.30-15.30 Mon, Wed & Fri, 09.30-12.00 Sat*. Services: Sung Eucharist *11.00 Sun*. Evensong *18.00 Sun*. Holy Communion *12.45 & 19.30 Wed, 10.00 Sat.*

Island House Church Community Centre 6 G1
4 Roserton St E14. 01-987 3679. United Reformed Church service *10.30-12.00 Sun*. Methodist service *18.30-19.30 Sun.*

Poplar Methodist Mission 4 E3
East India Dock Rd E14. 01-987 1994. *Open 09.00-14.00 Mon-Fri*. Services: *11.00 & 18.30 Sun*. Lunch club *12.00 Mon-Fri* for senior citizens.

POLICE STATIONS

Isle of Dogs Police Station 6 G3
160 Manchester Rd E14. 01-488 5212.

Poplar Police Station 4 F3
2 Market Way E14. 01-499 5212.

POST OFFICES

Cubitt Town **6** G1
15 Castalia Sq E14. 01-987 1080. *Open 09.00-17.30 Mon-Wed & Fri, 09.00-13.00 Thur & Sat.*

Millwall **6** E3
369 West Ferry Rd E14. 01-987 2684. *Open 09.00-13.00 & 14.00-17.30 Mon, Tue, Wed & Fri, 09.00-13.00 Thur & Sat.*

Poplar **4** F3
22 Market Sq E14. 01-987 3469. *Open 09.00 (09.30 Tue)-17.30 Mon-Fri, 09.00-13.00 Sat.*

Poplar High Street **4** G4
257 Poplar High St E14. 01-987 1031. *Open 09.00-13.00 & 14.00-17.30 Mon, Tue, Thur & Fri, 09.00-13.00 Wed & Sat.*

Quarterdeck **5** D1
Quarterdeck, Millwall E14. 01-987 2105. *Open 09.00-13.00 & 14.00-17.30 Mon, Tue, Thur & Fri, 09.00-13.00 Wed & Sat.*

PUBLIC CONVENIENCES

Hale Street **4** E3
E14. *Open 08.00-18.00 Mon-Sun.*

Manchester Road **6** G4
E14. Next to the Island Gardens DLR station. *Open 08.00-18.00 Mon-Sun.*

SCHOOLS AND COLLEGES

Cubitt Town School **6** G2
Glengall Grove E14. 01-987 3373. State school for ages 3-8.

Cubitt Town School **6** G2
Manchester Rd E14. 01-987 4362. State school for ages 8-11.

George Green's Centre **6** G4
Manchester Rd E14. 01-987 6032. Voluntary aided school for ages 11-16.

Hackney College **4** F4
Poplar High St E14. 01-987 4205. Short and full-time courses for ages 16+. *Open 09.00-17.00 Mon-Fri.*

Harbinger School **6** E3
Cahir St E14. 01-987 1924. State school for ages 3-11.

Mayflower School **4** E3
Upper North St E14. 01-987 2782. State school for ages 3-11.

St Edmund's School **6** E3
297 West Ferry Rd E14. 01-987 2546. Roman Catholic school for ages 3-11.

St Luke's School **6** H3
Saunders Ness Rd E14. 01-987 1753. Church of England school for ages 3-11

St Mary & St Joseph's School **4** E3
Wade's Place E14. 01-987 3066. Roman Catholic school for ages 3-11.

St Philip Howard School **4** E3
Upper North St (Off East India Dock Rd) E14 01-987 7028. Roman Catholic school for ages 11-18.

Seven Mills School **5** D1
Malabar St E14. 01-987 2350. State school for ages 3-11.

SHOPPING CENTRES

Asda Superstore **6** F
151 East Ferry Rd E14. 01-987 2614. Complex includes shoe shop, hairdresser and video shop. *Open 09.00-20.00 Mon-Thur 09.00-21.00 Fri, 08.30-20.00 Sat.*

Local Shopping Areas
These include Limeharbour and Poplar High Street. Many more shopping facilities are planned and are due to open this year at Glengall Bridge, Crossharbour, South Quay Plaza, Marsh Wall and the Heron Quays Development.

SOLICITORS

Alexander Johnston **4** E
Scott House, Admiral's Way, Marsh Wall E14. 01-538 5621. Deals mainly in property matters. *Open 09.30-17.30 Mon-Fri.*

Alexander Johnston **4** F
202 East India Dock Rd E14. 01-987 5611 Deals mainly in litigation. *Open 09.30-17.30 Mon-Fri.*

Denton Hall Burgin & Warrens **6** E
3 Millharbour E14. 01-515 7676. Deals mainly in property matters. *Open 09.30-17.30 Mon-Fri.*

ROYAL DOCKS

The Royal Docks area is in the early stages of its redevelopment programme, a place of present demolition and future plans, in which the best of the old will be preserved and much of the new is still on the drawing board.

There is intense activity here as the infrastructure is laid down and construction begins. Everything is in a state of flux – the dockside cranes and grain hoppers are to be saved but resited, and most of the important Museum of Docklands lies stored in a warehouse here while it waits to know the address of its permanent home.

There are striking contrasts. The futuristic British Telecom Teleport is a near neighbour of the steam railway museum in old North Woolwich Station; the 19thC Woolwich foot tunnel beneath the Thames is not much more than a dock away from the brand new City Airport; the dereliction around the three huge expanses of water – the Royal Victoria, Royal Albert and King George V Docks – is counterbalanced by popular watersports on all three.

Television and film producers have already noticed the dramatic possibilities of a landscape haunted equally by ghosts of the past and of the future. Abandoned warehouses, modern structures, and the grim wreckage of old Beckton gasworks have been used as locations by Stanley Kubrick among others.

When they were built, the Royals were the largest enclosed docks in the world, impounding 230 acres (93 ha) of water between them. The Victoria, the oldest, begun in the mid-1850s, was served by the newly extended Great Eastern Railway. The newest, the King George V, was opened in 1921. The importance of these Docks during World War II, when they served as a naval base as well as a vital food port, made them a key target for German bombers, but they survived, and indeed flourished until the early 70s when the resiting of the docks downriver at Tilbury was responsible for their final demise.

Although the whole area comes under one Council, Newham, it divides easily into three parts. To the north is residential and light industrial Beckton, named after Simon Adams Beck, who was Governor of the Gas-Light and Coke Company when the gasworks were built in 1867. Before the coming of the railway this area was marshy wasteland which had to be drained before the houses and small factories could be built. Further drainage was necessary before the intense residential and retail building programme of the 80s could begin, and most of the 4,000 new homes in Beckton rest on sunken piles.

South of Beckton lies North Woolwich, across the river from Woolwich proper, with the Royal Albert and King George V Docks cradling the new airport between them. West of Woolwich is Silvertown, called after S.W. Silver & Co whose explosives manufacturing works were established here in the 1850s.

The monumental size of the docks themselves, and the extent of the available land surrounding them, means there is immense scope for development and when the proposed new road links and river crossing, and the planned extension of the Docklands Light Railway, become operational, their immense potential can be even more thoroughly exploited.

Beckton

Beckton Alps **10** E3
Alpine Way E6. 01-511 0351/2. The popular dry ski slope has been constructed on the side of a minor mountain, formed over many years by the dumping of detritus from the old gasworks. Could be your only chance to ski on industrial waste – securely sealed beneath the surface of the slope.

Well worth taking the winding trail from Whitings Way to the top, not only to watch the skiers but also to enjoy stunning views out over Docklands and far beyond. Bar, restaurant and other facilities were being constructed as this book went to press. (See Sport and Recreation p. 107 for more details.)

Skiing at Beckton Alps

Beckton District Centre **9** D4
Tollgate Rd E6. The centre has an Asda Superstore, with generous parking space and opening hours, and its own Shoppers' Restaurant. Several independent shops rent units in the covered mall which adjoins it, and there is also a pub and a service station. Just across the roundabout, on Manor Way, is a large Texas Homecare store. *Asda store open 09.00-20.00 Mon-Thur, 09.00-21.00 Fri, 08.30-20.00 Sat.*

Beckton District Park **9** B4
Tollgate Rd E6. 01-552 0939 (Parks Booking Office). Playing fields and park with eleven football pitches, two cricket pitches and a pitch and putt course. The section of the park on the north side of Tollgate Road has a boating lake, an island haven for ducks and geese, and a café. This section of the park *closes at dusk*.

Beckton Gas Works **10** G4
East Beckton E6. Once Europe's largest gasworks, now a mighty glowering ruin rising out of bleak wasteland. No public access – the site, though not the works, is still operational and North Thames Gas have their new district offices nearby. Imminent demolition seems likely.

Chrissy's Garden Centre **8** G1
1 Tollgate Rd E6. 01-474 8183. Miniature garden centre which has steadily blossomed as Beckton has become more heavily populated. As well as plants and planters it sells some fruit and vegetables, pet foods and a limited range of health foods. *Open 08.30-17.00 Mon-Sat, 09.30-about 16.00 Sun.*

New Beckton Park **9** D5
Savage Gdns E6. 01-552 0939 (Parks Booking Office). Playing fields and public park with four football pitches, one cricket pitch, bowling greens, tennis courts, a five-a-side play area and also a children's play area with swings and roundabouts.

Newham City Farm **8** H2
Stansfield Rd E6. 01-476 1170. Small, attractive city farm with a 'toy farmyard' look to its purpose-built sties and stables and its chunky fencing. Plans to be open to the public during 1988.

Eating and Drinking
Asda Shoppers' Restaurant or the Tollgate Tavern.
See Pubs and Restaurants.

North Woolwich

Albert Dock Basin **12** G2
Royal Albert Dock E16. The dock basin, originally built as an entrance to the Royal Albert Dock, once had a quarantine station to cope with the imported livestock. It was used as a pleasure boat marina in the 1970s, and is shortly to be developed as a marina for the berthing of private yachts.

British Telecom Teleport **11** D3
Pier Rd E16. The impressive array of large dish aerials of this satellite earth station became operational in February 1984. Linked to an expanding fibreoptic network, they receive and transmit cable television and facilitate such modern business boons as teleconferencing.

Central Buffet **11** D1
North Quay, Royal Albert Dock E16. A Grade II listed building, with the look of a large cricket pavilion. It was designed in

1883 by Vigers and Wagstaffe, who were also responsible for the Dock Manager's Office, next door, also listed Grade II. Both will be preserved, although their future use is uncertain. No public access.

Gallions Hotel **12 G1**
Gallions Rd E16. Derelict hotel built by the London and St Katharine Dock Company in 1881-3 to cater for passengers travelling by the P & O line. In its time its lights must have been visible from the river because Dick in Kipling's *The Light that Failed* asked, 'Is it Tilbury and a tender, or Gallions and the Docks?' Today it is rather reminiscent of the motel in *Psycho*. As a Grade II listed building it will be preserved and may be refurbished as part of the new marina development. No public access.

King George V Dock **12 E2**
E16. This 62 acre (25 ha) expanse of water, with jetties and south-side quays, is the newest of the Royal Group of Docks, begun by the Port of London Authority in 1912, delayed by World War I, and finally opened in 1921. P & O liners came in here from Gallions Reach and aerial photographs of August 1939 show the 35,655-ton *Mauretania* making a neat entry with minimal space each side. Up for development, just like its neighbours, it already has a Waterski Club.

London City Airport

London City Airport **11 C2**
E16. 01-476 5555. The small, and surprisingly quiet, Dash 7 aeroplanes of Brymon Airways and Eurocity Express link London's newest airport with others in the UK, Europe and the Channel Islands. The 2,500ft (763m) runway lies like the deck of an aircraft carrier between the Royal Albert and the King George V Docks. When the airport buildings are complete they will include a restaurant and bar, both open to non-passengers and a viewing area. (See Getting To and Around Docklands p. 113.)

North Woolwich Old Station Museum **12 E3**
Pier Rd E16. 01-474 7244. The small but very appealing railway museum is housed in the original mid-19thC North Woolwich Station building, which has been carefully restored, in Great Eastern Railway colours, for the purpose. (The new and operational North Woolwich Station is conveniently placed alongside.) The booking hall and waiting rooms have displays of tickets, documents, photographs and objects and the ticket office is furnished as it was when fully functional in the 1930s. Rolling stock and a preserved Robert Stephenson & Hawthorn 0-6-OST stand at the platforms outside. On Sundays a working locomotive gets up steam.

Future plans include more exhibition space, a cafeteria and a car park. *Open 10.00-17.00 Mon-Sat, 14.00-17.00 Sun & Bank hols. Free.*

Proposed East London River Crossing **12 H1**
The proposal, known as ELRIC, is for a new Thames bridge, to be linked by a brand new highway to the M11, thus opening up the Docklands from the other side and relieving congestion on its through roads from the west.

Royal Albert Dock **11 D1**
E16. The huge expanse of water – 86 acres (35 ha) – is currently used for rowing and other watersports, and the docksides are to be extensively redeveloped. The Royal Albert was built by the London and St Katharine Dock Company, to extend the capacity of the Victoria Dock, to which it is linked by a lock. Opened in 1880 by the Duke of Connaught, it was the first dock to be fully lit by electricity, and had a mechanised berth to speed up banana distribution. As well as merchant ships carrying grain and frozen foodstuffs, it docked P & O liners, for whose passengers the nearby Gallions Hotel was a reassuring landmark.

Royal Victoria Gardens **12 F3**
Albert Rd E16. 01-474 6984. A pleasant and well-kept park with mature trees and a raised promenade on the flood barrier which offers excellent views of the river. The former name, Royal Pavilion Gardens, is echoed by the adjoining pub. First opened in 1851, the year of the Great Exhibition, as a Victorian pleasure garden, it became disreputable towards the end of the 19thC and was closed. It was refurbished, retitled and reopened in 1890 by the London County Council. Nowadays, under Newham Council, it has a bowling green, tennis courts, children's play area and small refreshment counter.

Waterski Club **11 D2**
King George V Dock E16. 01-511 2000. The large area of water lends itself perfectly to watersports and the club is flourishing. *Open 10.00-dusk Mon-Sun. Closed 21 Dec-21 Mar. Charge.* (For more detail see the entry in Sport and Recreation p. 108.)

Woolwich Foot Tunnel **12 E3**
Pier Rd E16. The attractive red brick and cast-iron dome covers the lift shaft to the 1,655ft-long tunnel (505m) which was opened in 1912 as a short cut between residential Woolwich and the working Docks.

Woolwich Free Ferry **12 E4**
Pier Rd E16. 01-854 9615. The famous free ferry has been carrying passengers and vehicles since 1889, though paddle and steam power gave way to diesel in 1963. It is maintained by Greenwich Council and, in theory, operates a regular daily service. In fact, it is always wise to telephone first to check if it is running. Ferry crossing takes approximately 10-15 minutes and there is a continuous service between the stated times. *Operational 06.00-22.00 Mon-Sat, 08.00-21.30 Sun.*

Woolwich Pier **12 E4**
Pier Rd E16. The old floating pier that gave the road its name is now more or less derelict and the Woolwich Free Ferry operates from a new terminal nearby.

Eating and Drinking
Pub grub at Churchill's and the Royal Pavilion or more variety at the City Brasserie in the Airport complex.
See Pubs and Restaurants.

Silvertown

The Connaught Tavern **11 A1**
Connaught Rd E16. This handsome red brick building with tall chimneys was one of the large hotel/public houses put up by the dock company. It dates from 1881 and is Grade II listed. The architects were Vigers and Wagstaffe, who also designed Gallions Hotel and the Central Buffet. Because it stands in isolation amidst a proposed new road complex, the LDDC may dismantle the Connaught and transfer it bodily to a more suitable site, but they still have to find some use for it. On the remains of an old tree, known as the Stump, which stood near the Connaught's entrance until 1985, generations of dockers' leaders used to stand to address mass meetings. No public access.

Grain Mills **8 G4**
Royal Victoria Dock South Side E16. The range of massive granaries and flour mills which rise at the water's edge along the south side of the dock were built, in reinforced concrete, in the 1930s. The gleaming white CWS (Co-operative Wholesale Society) mill at the east end has been acquired by the LDDC. Transformation into a huge luxury hotel has been mooted, but its future is uncertain. West of the entrance to the Pontoon Dock there are three more buildings, all of monumental grandeur. The two outer mills were Rank's and are now owned by the LDDC. The middle one, Spillers Millenium Mills, is the only one still working – for the time being anyway – and is not LDDC-owned. The pneumatic grain elevators on the quayside which used to suck the grain out of the ships' holds are being preserved by the LDDC. No public access.

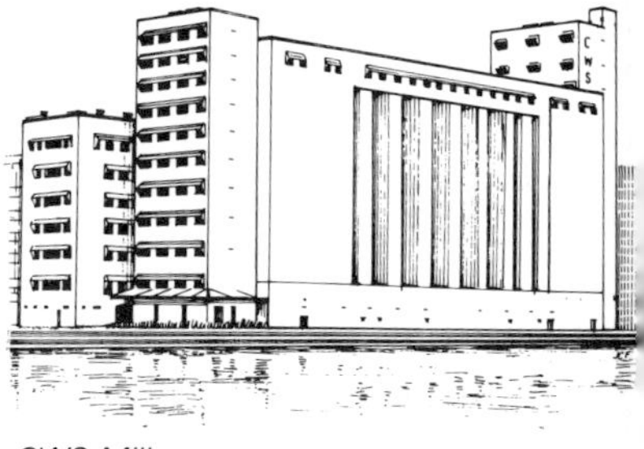

CWS Mill

'K'-'S' Warehouses **8 E4**
Royal Victoria Dock North Side E16. This range of warehouses is being preserved, although their future use has yet to be decided. They were the first generation of warehouses on the dock, built in the late 1850s as bonded tobacco warehouses. 'K' at the eastern end is Grade II listed. The dock's north side will be the site of a large scale development which will incorporate the warehouses. One proposal is for a 25,000-seat conference and exhibition centre, complete with hotel, offices, shops,

restaurants and residential units, to be called the London Dome. No public access.

Lyle Park **8 E6**
Bradfield Rd, off North Woolwich Rd E16. 01-472 1430. A haven of peace amidst ugly industrial buildings, marred only by the unsavoury odours from a nearby animal by-products plant, when the wind is in the wrong direction. The park was provided by Lyle & Sons for their workers and is now carefully tended by Newham Parks Department. There are lawns, trees and flowerbeds, and a terrace overlooking the river. Park-keeper on site. Tennis courts and putting green. *Open 08.00-dusk Mon-Sat, 09.00-dusk Sun.*

Pontoon Dock and 'D' Silo **8 G5**
Royal Victoria Dock South Side E16. Built in 1855-60 and famous in its day for its revolutionary system in which ships were lifted out of the water by hydraulic jacks and placed on pontoons which were then shunted into the dock's 'fingers' – narrow strips of water stretching outwards like the fingers on a hand – for repair work to be done. All the fingers have now been filled in. To the south west is 'D' Silo, which has an octagonal cupola. A new use for the silo has yet to be thought up by the LDDC which now owns it. No public access.

Public Urinal **11 A1**
Connaught Rd, E16. One of the few Victorian cast-iron examples surviving in London. Its original users would be amazed to know that this ornate circular specimen is Grade II listed. The LDDC will almost certainly resite it. No public access.

Royal Docks Area Office **8 G4**
Gate 8, Royal Victoria Dock North Side E16. 01-476 3000. Headquarters of the LDDC Area Team for the Royal Docks. The building is heated and air-conditioned by a heat pump system submerged in the dock. The same technology will probably be used for offices and residential units to be developed round the docks. Occasional exhibitions relating to development proposals are held here. Telephone for details.

Royal Victoria Dock **8 F4**
E16. The 1¼-mile-long dock was the first of the 'Royals' to be built, and the first-ever dock to be purpose-built for steamships. Opened by Prince Albert in 1855, it was a great financial success for its owners. Bulk grain, tobacco and timber were the main cargoes handled, with frozen meat and other foodstuffs coming in by the turn of the century. Ships entered through the tidal basin at the western end. The dock cranes, which look like huge prehistoric birds standing at the water's edge, are being preserved by the LDDC but are likely to be resited. The Victoria is coming back to life, with its 87 acres (35 ha) of water now used for windsurfing, wetbiking, sailing, canoeing and rowing. The UK Power Boat Championships have been held here since 1982.

Windsurfing

St Mark's Church **11 B3**
North Woolwich Rd E16. A colourful Victorian church which stands out from its industrial surroundings, with its yellow, red and black brick, stonework and gabled tower topped by a squat spire. It was built in 1861-2 with funds raised through an appeal in *The Times* and designed by S.S. Teulon. A fire in 1980 destroyed its hammerbeam roof but this has now been replaced with a replica, using timber from piles lifted from the river bed. When current restoration work is complete the redundant church will become the Museum of Victorian Life, run by the Passmore Edwards Museum. The Museum has been gathering and organising material which will illustrate life in the area from early Victorian times up to World War I. Until the museum is fully open, probably in 1990, the Trust is hoping to organise guided visits. Information from Passmore Edwards Museum 01-519 4296.

Silvertown Tramway **8 F5**
North Woolwich Rd E16. Half-a-mile of fenced-in footpath and cycleway lined with newly planted trees, running parallel with the North Woolwich Road. It was once the track for trains which carried freight to and from factories by the river. At present it runs rather uninvitingly alongside an area of insalubrious industrial wasteland. However,

it is intended by the LDDC as an example of what is to come and will eventually be part of a whole network of attractively landscaped paths and tracks.

Tate & Lyle Building **7 D5**
Plaistow Wharf, North Woolwich Rd E16. A huge, imposing 1930s building in Portland stone, saved from drabness by the familiar Golden Syrup emblem carved high on the north western façade. The recumbent lion with attendant swarm of bees can be seen from Silvertown Way (Britain's first flyover, opened in 1934). The legend 'Out of the strong came forth sweetness' comes from one of Samson's riddles in *Judges* 14:14. Nobody knows why Abram Lyle (inventor of Golden Syrup in 1883) chose it as a slogan. The building is now used for storage and packing and for making Golden Syrup. Lyle & Sons started sugar refining at Plaistow Wharf in 1881 and Tate & Co, at the nearby Thames Refinery, Factory Road, in 1878. The two firms amalgamated in 1921. No public access.

Thames Barrier **8 H6**
One of London's more recent landmarks, which looks like a row of enormous upended silver boats. It is in fact a spectacular feat of engineering built to protect London from dangerously high tides which were increasingly threatening to flood the capital. London and south east England are slowly sinking, according to records kept over the last 180 years. The barrier became operational in 1982, having taken eight years to build, at a cost of £435 million. It was designed by Rendel Palmer & Tritton and built by a consortium of Costain, Tarmac and HBM of the Netherlands. When needed, the barrier's gates, normally lying flat on the river bed, rise to an upright position. This takes 15 minutes. A large area between North Woolwich Road and the barrier is to be reserved for an open space with an arboretum. There are good views of the barrier from various points in the Royal Docks area, but for a closer look, and access to the Thames Barrier Visitor Centre, make the journey to Woolwich, south of the river.

'W' Warehouse **8 E4**
Royal Victoria Dock North Side E16. Grade II listed tobacco warehouse built around 1863. The Museum of London is using it as a store, restoration workshop and visitor centre until a suitable permanent home is found for its planned Museum in Docklands. Its collection covers commercial and industrial activities on the Thames since Roman times, and the history of London's crafts and industries in general. Until the museum is fully open, probably in 1991, the public can have a preview by taking a Museum of London coach tour of Docklands, which includes a visit to 'W' Warehouse; or visit on one of the occasional open days. Information from Museum in Docklands Project, Poplar Business Park E14. 01-515 1162.

Eating and Drinking
Try a pub lunch at the Essex Arms or an elegant Chinese meal at the Beijing.
See Pubs and Restaurants.

Thames Barrier Visitor Centre **11 A4**
Unity Way, Eastmoor St SE18.
01-854 1373. To get a close-up view of the Thames Barrier and to find out how it works, go to the Visitor Centre south of the river. There's an exhibition, a filmshow on the Barrier's construction, an audio-visual presentation about the history of London and the river, a souvenir shop, snack bar and restaurant. For a really close view, take the 25-minute Barrier Cruise from the Barrier Pier beside the Visitor Centre. *Open 10.30-17.00 Mon-Fri, 10.30-17.30 Sat, Sun & Bank hols. (Closed Christmas & New Year.) Charge.*

Access: BR from Charing Cross or London Bridge; bus 177 from Waterloo; boat from Embankment or Tower Bridge to Greenwich Pier, then shuttle bus; or boat from Westminster or Tower Bridge to Barrier Pier.

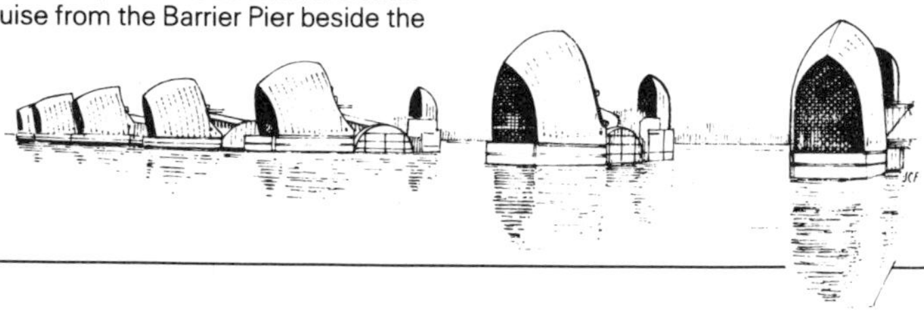

Services

All services closed Sat & Sun unless otherwise stated.

ADULT EDUCATION

London Borough of Newham
Head Office, East Ham Centre, High St South E6. 01-472 1480. Full range of courses from accounts to word processing plus full-time 'A' level courses. Centre *open 09.00-21.30 Mon-Fri.*

Canning Town Centre **7** C1
105 Barking Rd E16. 01-476 2059. Offers a range of non-technical courses including painting for pleasure, dressmaking and craftwork. *Open 10.00-16.00 & 19.00-22.00 Mon-Fri.*

BANKS

National Westminster **11** B3
13 Albert Rd E16. 01-476 1846. *Open 09.30-15.30 Mon-Fri.*

National Westminster **9** D4
Unit 15 Asda Centre, Tollgate Rd E6. 01-511 0951. *Open 09.30-15.30 Mon-Fri.*

BUILDING SOCIETIES

Woolwich Equitable **9** D4
Asda Centre, Tollgate Rd E6. 01-511 0311. *Open 09.00 (09.30 Thur)-17.00 Mon-Fri, 09.00-12.00 Sat.*

BUREAUX DE CHANGE

Travelex Plc **11** C2
London City Airport, George V Docks E16. Offers foreign exchange facilities and will cash personal cheques on a commission basis. *Open 06.30-21.00 Mon-Fri, 06.30-14.30 Sat, 15.00-19.00 Sun.*

CHEMISTS

Beckton Pharmacy **9** D4
Asda Complex, 11 Mary Rose Mall, Frobisher Rd E6. 01-476 0243. *Open 09.00-20.00 Mon-Thur, 09.00-21.00 Fri, 08.30-20.00 Sat.*

Chapharm **8** G3
9 Cundy Rd E16. 01-474 3527. *Open 09.00-18.00 Mon, Tue, Wed & Fri, 09.00-13.00 Thur, 09.00-17.00 Sat.*

East Beckton Health Centre **9** D4
Tollgate Rd E16. 01-474 5656. *Open 08.30-18.00 Mon-Fri, 08.30-12.00 Sat.*

Elmfield Drugs **12** E3
5 Woodman Pde, Pier Rd E16. 01-476 1202. *Open 09.00-18.00 Mon-Wed & Fri, 09.00-13.00 Thur, 09.00-17.00 Sat.*

Elmfield Drugs **8** F3
17-19 Freemasons Rd E16. 01-476 2254. *Open 09.00-18.30 Mon-Fri, 09.00-17.00 Sat.*

CITIZENS ADVICE BUREAUX

Beckton Mobile Citizens Advice Bureau
Open 10.30-12.30 Tue Strait Rd E6 & *10.30-12.30 Wed* Manwood St E6.

COMMUNITY AND YOUTH CENTRES

St John's Community Centre **11** D3
Albert Rd E16. 01-474 8951. Facilities for all ages. Include playgroup, Brownies, junior, intermediate and senior youth club, over 50s and over 60s club, lunch club, literacy classes, badminton, keep fit, fishing club. Also hold regular DHSS surgeries. There is a hall available for private functions at weekends and a meeting room for hire. Centre *open 09.00-22.00 Mon-Fri & Sun morning* for services – see St John's church.

West Beckton Children's Community Centre **8** H2
Lawson Close E16. 01-511 3222. Day nursery, parent and toddler group, toy library, keep fit, after school club and Saturday club for ages 5-8. *Open 08.00-18.00 Mon-Fri, 10.00-13.00 Sat.*

COUNCILLORS

Members of London Borough of Newham. Council offices at the Town Hall, East Ham E6. 01-472 1430. The councillors for the Custom House and Silvertown Neighbourhood are Bill Chapman (Labour), Julie Garfield (Labour) and Judy Jorsburg (Labour). The councillors for the Southward Neighbourhood are Eddie Corbett (Labour), Tom Jenkinson (Labour) and Alec Kellaway (SDP). The councillors for the Ordnance Neighbourhood are Charles Flemwell (Labour) and Ann King (Labour). If you have any complaints, suggestions or queries write to your councillor at the Town Hall.

DENTISTS

M.R. Patel **11** C3
Kennard Street Health Centre, Kennard St E16. 01-511 8600. *Open 09.00-12.00 Tue & Thur.*

DHSS OFFICES

Canning Town DHSS **8** E1
199 Freemasons Rd E16. 01-476 3667. *Open 09.30-15.30 Mon-Fri.*
Plaistow DHSS
790 Barking Rd E13. 01-552 5421/8. *Open 09.30-15.30 Mon-Fri.*

DOCTORS

Dr Doshi Navinchandra **12** E3
7 Pier Pde, North Woolwich E16. 01-474 9717. Phone for surgery times.
Dr K.H. Sutton **9** D5
34 Parry Av E6. 01-474 5656. *Open 09.00-11.00 & 16.00-18.00 Mon-Fri, 09.00-11.00 Sat.*

ESTATE AGENTS

Bryants **9** D4
1 East Beckton District Centre, Tollgate Rd E6. 01-474 8866. Residential only. *Open 09.00-20.00 Mon-Thur, 09.00-18.00 Fri & Sat, 10.00-17.00 Sun.*
Docklands Property Centre **7** C2
99 Silvertown Way E16. 01-474 1000. Commercial properties. *Open 09.00-18.00 Mon-Fri, 10.00-17.00 Sat & Sun.*
Anthony Gover
120 High St South E6. 01-470 3758. Mainly residential. *Open 09.30-20.00 Mon-Sat. Closed Sun.* Also at 3-5 Dock St E1. 01-480 6815.

HAIRDRESSERS

Andre's **8** F3
5 Freemasons Rd E16. 01-476 5032. Unisex. *Open 09.00-15.30 Tue, Wed, Fri & Sat, 09.00-13.00 Thur. Closed Mon.*
Gemini **7** C1
60 Hermit Rd E16. 01-476 6744. Unisex. *Open 09.00-17.00 Mon, 09.00-18.00 Wed & Thur, 09.00-19.00 Fri, 08.00-17.00 Sat. Closed Tue.*
Guys 'n' Dolls **10** E5
6 Manor Way E6. 01-511 8316. Unisex. *Open 09.30-18.00 Mon-Fri, 09.00-18.00 Sat.*
Hair Razor Salon **12** E3
3 Albert Rd E16. 01-476 8942. Unisex. *Open 09.30-15.30 Wed, 09.30-17.30 Fri, 09.00-15.00 Sat. Closed Mon, Tue & Thur.*
Heads We Do **12** E3
8 Pier Pde E16. 01-476 6297. Unisex. *Open 09.00-17.00 Mon-Fri, 08.30-13.00 Sat.*
Talking Heads **8** F3
11 Freemasons Rd E16. 01-474 6967. Unisex. *Open 09.00-18.00 Mon, Tue & Thur, 09.00-19.00 Fri, 08.30-18.00 Sat. Closed Wed.*
Toppy's at Command Performance **9** D4
Asda Superstore, Frobisher Rd E6. 01-511 7411. Unisex. *Open 09.00-20.00 Mon-Thur, 09.00-21.00 Fri, 08.30-20.00 Sat.*

HEALTH CENTRES

East Beckton Health Centre **9** D4
Tollgate Rd E6. 01-474 5656. Services include chiropody, dental treatment, health visitor and pharmacist. *Open 08.30-18.00 Mon-Fri, 08.30-12.00 Sat.*
Kennard Street Health Centre **11** C3
1 Kennard St E16. 01-476 6200. Services include childcare clinic, immunisation clinic, dental treatment and paediatrician. *Open 09.00-18.00 Mon-Fri*
Margaret Scott Clinic **7** D3
Appleby Rd E16. 01-474 5666. Health centre with psychiatric day hospital attached. Services include dentist, child health clinic, health visitors, family planning clinic, speech therapist and chiropodist. No GPs. Phone for details. *Open 09.00-17.00 Mon-Fri.*
West Beckton Health Centre **8** H2
90 Lawson Close E16. 01-476 2636. Services include GPs, family planning clinic, baby clinic, social worker and speech therapist. *Open 08.30-18.00 Mon, Wed & Fri, 08.30-17.00 Tue.*

HOSPITALS

Albert Dock **8** H3
Alnwick Rd E16. 01-476 2234. Hospital for the elderly and the mentally ill.

LIBRARIES

Custom House Library **8** G2
Prince Regent Lane E16. 01-476 1565. Books only. *Open 09.30-19.00 Mon, Tue, Thur & Fri, 09.30-17.00 Wed & Sat.*
North Woolwich Library **12** E3
Pier Rd E16. 01-476 2163. Books only. *Open 09.00-17.00 Mon-Sat (to 19.00 Thur).*

MINI-CABS

Car-Tours **12** E3
3 Woodman Pde, Woodman St E16. 01-474 3837/511 8604. *Open 08.00-01.00 Mon-Thur, 08.00-02.00 Fri & Sat, 08.00-01.00 Sun.*

PETROL STATIONS

Fleet Service Station **7** C2
53-65 Silvertown Way E16. 01-476 4276. *Open 06.00-18.00 Mon-Fri, 08.00-12.00 Sat.*
North Woolwich Self-Service Centre **11** A3
279 North Woolwich Rd E16. 01-476 2769. *Open 07.00-19.00 Mon-Fri, 07.00-13.30 Sat.*
Silvertown Way Service Station **7** C3
51 Brunel Rd E16. 01-474 5746. *Open 24hrs Mon-Sun.*

PLACES OF WORSHIP

St John's Church **11** D3
Albert Rd E16. 01-474 8951/476 2388. Community centre attached. Services: Catholic Mass *09.30 Sun*, 08.30 Wed. Eucharist *11.00 Sun*. St Mary Edward's Roman Catholic church has amalgamated with St John's following extensive storm damage to their church in October 1987.

POLICE STATIONS

North Woolwich Police Station **12** E3
2 Albert Rd E16. 01-593 8232. North Woolwich Police Station covers Silvertown and mid-Beckton. The new developments in West Beckton are covered by Plaistow Police Station, 444 Barking Rd E13. 01-593 8232.

POST OFFICES

Beckton **9** D4
11 Mary Rose Mall, Frobisher Rd E6. 01-476 0243. *Open 09.00-13.00 & 14.00-17.30 Mon, Tue, Thur & Fri, 09.00-13.00 Wed & Sat.*
Canning Town Branch Office **7** C2
22 Barking Rd E16. 01-476 2326. *Open 09.00-17.30 Mon-Fri, 09.00-13.00 Sat.*
Canning Town Sub Post Office **8** F3
25 Freemasons Rd E16. 01-476 1748. *Open 09.00-13.00 & 14.00-17.30 Mon-Wed & Fri, 09.00-13.00 Thur & Sat.*
Cundy Road **8** G3
11 Cundy Rd E16. 01-476 1148. *Open 09.00-17.00 Mon-Wed & Fri, 09.00-13.00 Thur & Sat.*
North Woolwich **12** E3
1 Pier Pde, Pier Rd E16. 01-476 1916. *Open 09.00-13.00 & 14.00-17.00 Mon-Wed & Fri, 09.00-13.00 Thur & Sat.*
Silvertown **11** B2
5 Albert Rd E16. 01-476 2359. *Open 09.00-13.00 & 14.00-17.00 Mon-Wed & Fri, 09.00-13.00 Thur, 09.00-12.30 Sat.*

PUBLIC CONVENIENCES

Albert Road **11** D3
E16. (Opposite Fernhill St.) Men only. *Open 24hrs Mon-Sun.*
Asda Centre **9** D4
E6. (Junction of Manor Way & Tollgate Rd.) *Open 07.00-20.00 Mon-Sat, 09.00-19.00 Sun.*
Newham Way **8** F1
E16. (Opposite Canning Town recreation ground.) *Open 07.00-20.00 Mon-Sat, 09.00-19.00 Sun.*
Pier Road **12** E3
E16. *Open 07.00-20.00 Mon-Sat, 09.00-19.00 Sun.*

SCHOOLS AND COLLEGES

Beckton School **8** H1
Tollgate Rd E16. 01-474 6326. State school for children (ages 2-19) with severe learning difficulties.
Calverton School **8** H3
King George Av E16. 01-476 3076. State school for ages 3-11.
Cumberland Comprehensive School
Prince Regent Lane E13. 01-474 0231. State school for ages 11-18.
Drew School **11** C2
Drew Rd E16. 01-476 1727. State school for ages 3-11.
Edith Kerrison School **8** F2
Sophia Rd E16. 01-476 1735. State school for ages 3-5.
Ellen Wilkinson School **9** B4
Tollgate Rd E16. 01-476 3000. State school for ages 3-11. Will be a social and recreational centre out of school hours.
Rosetta School **8** F2
Sophia Rd E16. 01-476 5308. State school for children 5-11.
St Joachim's School **8** F3
Shipman Rd E16. 01-476 1658. Roman Catholic school for ages 5-11.
Scott Wilkie Primary School **8** H2
Hoskins Close E16. 01-474 4138. State school for ages 3-11.

Storey School **12** F3
Woodman St E16. 01-476 2595. State school for ages 3-11.

West Silvertown School **8** F5
Evelyn Rd E16. 01-476 1814. State school for ages 3-11. Lansbury school for children (ages 3-11) with learning difficulties is on the same site.

Winsor School **10** E4
Manor Way E6. 01-476 2323. State school for ages 3-11.

SHOE REPAIRS

Jetbros Heel Bar **8** F2
39 Freemasons Rd E16. 01-476 1649. *Open 09.00-17.30 Mon-Wed, Fri & Sat, 09.00-13.00 Thur.*

SHOPPING CENTRES

Beckton District Centre **9** D4
Tollgate Rd E6. Includes Asda Superstore and shopping mall which contains a solicitor, estate agent, shoe shop, health food shop, pharmacist, bank, building society, hairdresser, boutique, jeweller and an optician. Asda Superstore *open 09.00-20.00 Mon-Thur, 09.00-21.00 Fri, 08.30-20.00 Sat.*

Local Shopping Areas
These include Pier Parade, North Woolwich; Barnwood Court and Prince Regent Lane.

London Industrial Park **10** F4
Alpine Way E16. A number of retail warehousing units including Texas Homecare and Grandstand Sport and Leisure shop.

SOLICITORS

E. Edwards Son & Noice **9** D4
Asda Centre, Tollgate Rd E6. General practice. *Open 09.15-17.00 Mon-Fri (closed 13.00-14.00).*

PUBS AND RESTAURANTS

This is an area traditionally rich in pubs, ranging from famous old inns, well-established on the tourist circuit, such as the Prospect of Whitby and the Town of Ramsgate, to basic local boozers whose reputation doesn't extend much further than the next street. Restaurants used not to be so much in evidence, apart from the collection of excellent and authentic – if occasionally somewhat basic – Chinese establishments around Limehouse. However, redevelopment and the consequent arrival of a whole new potential clientele, is rapidly changing the eating and drinking scene. Several pubs have already smartened themselves up and extended their food repertoire and more will doubtless follow suit; new restaurants have quickly become established; pioneers have introduced early examples of those two essentials to yuppie happiness, the wine bar and the brasserie; and numerous places of refreshment, of various types and persuasions, are planned in most of the major new developments.

A selection of the best follows, but further exploration is likely to be rewarding.

NB: *Opening times* Restaurant opening times are given at the end of each entry – note that 'closing' time in a restaurant usually indicates the latest time at which an order will be taken, generous 'eating up time' is allowed thereafter. Unless otherwise stated, pubs *open 11.00-14.30 and 17.30-23.00 Mon-Sat; 12.00-14.00 and 19.00-22.30 Sun. Note that many pubs in the area close at 14.30 at lunchtime and there is unlikely to be much food available after 14.00.*

In the following selection of pubs and restaurants the credit cards they accept are indicated as follows: A = Access, Ax = American Express, Dc = Diners Club, V = Visa (Barclaycard etc).

Price for a three-course meal for one inclusive of VAT and service but excluding wine is shown thus: **£** – up to £7.00; **££** from £7.00-15.00; **£££** – from £15.00-20.00; **£££**+–£20 and over. If it is advisable to reserve for lunch (*L*) or dinner (*D*) this has been noted – (*Reserve LD*).

Anchor Tap **1** C3
28 Horselydown Lane SE1. 01-403 4637. *Courage*. John Courage's first pub stands within a peanut's throw of the old Courage Anchor Brewhouse. The Brewhouse is now a smart residential development; the pub is still serving real ale and food (anything from a ham salad to a rump steak) at every session, seven days a week. Believed to be haunted by the spirit of a previous landlord in the cellar, but lively enough upstairs. *Open normal licensing hours*. No credit cards. **£**

The Angel **2** E4
101 Bermondsey Wall East SE16. 01-237 3608. *Courage*. Historic 15thC inn with balcony, partly supported on piles so that it can extend out over the river. Dark wood, wrought-iron lamps, traditionally a watering hole to both Samuel Pepys and Captain Cook. Bar snacks at every session – and the smart à la carte restaurant upstairs serves English cuisine with a bias towards fish – try the famous Greenwich fish pie. *Pub stays open to 15.00 Mon-Sat*. No credit cards. **£** *Restaurant open 12.00-15.30 & 18.30-23.00 Mon-Fri, 18.30-23.00 Sat, 12.00-14.00 & 18.30-22.30 Sun*. (*Reserve LD*). A.Ax.Dc.V. **£££**

Asda Shoppers' Restaurant **6** F2
Asda Superstore, East Ferry Rd E14. 01-987 2614. Self-service cafeteria,

sensibly designed for shoppers who can wheel in loaded trolleys and park them by the tables without creating an obstruction. Breakfasts, sandwiches, snacks ranging from quiche and salad to fish and chips; gateaux and a children's menu. *Open 09.00-20.00 Mon-Thur, 09.00-21.00 Fri, 08.30-20.00 Sat. Closed Sun.* No credit cards. **£**

Asda Shoppers' Restaurant **9 D4**
Asda Superstore, Beckton District Centre, Tollgate Rd E6. 01-476 4800. See above. *Open 09.00-20.00 Mon-Sat. Closed Sun.* No credit cards. **£**

Balls Bros Wine Bar **1 B3**
Hay's Galleria, Tooley St SE1. 01-407 4301. Balls Bros are a firm of wine shippers and merchants who run one of the oldest wine bar chains in London. Sound selection of about 70 wines, a snack counter on the ground floor serving pâtés, pies and salads, and a reliable fish restaurant upstairs. *Open 11.30-15.00 & 17.30-21.00 Mon-Fri, may open Sat in season. Closed Sun.* (*Reserve LD*). A.Ax.Dc.V. **£** or **££**

Beefeater by the Tower of London **1 D2**
Ivory House, St Katharine's Way E1. 01-408 1001. A 'theatre restaurant' in the cellars of the Ivory House. Five-course medieval banquets are served nightly (eat with your fingers in true medieval manner!); jugglers and magicians perform between courses; Henry VIII in full costume proposes the toasts; there are wenches, much roistering and some participation. It is essential to book – and note that the highish price includes everything, even unlimited wine and beer. *Open 20.00-23.30 Mon-Sun (unless there's a private function).* (*Reserve*). A.Ax.Dc.V. **£££+**

Beijing **7 C1**
59-61 Barking Rd E16. 01-476 3624. Elegant and deservedly popular Chinese restaurant serving Cantonese and Pekingese food – with so many interesting speciality dishes it would be misleading to highlight any one. *Open 12.00-14.00 & 18.00-23.00 Mon-Thur, 12.00-14.00 & 18.00-24.00 Fri & Sat, 18.00-24.00 Sun. Closed L Sun.* (*Reserve LD*). A.Ax.Dc.V. **££**

Billingsgate Cafés **4 F4**
Billingsgate Fish Market, West India Dock E14. 01-987 1118. The two cafés are both open to the general public as well as to the market porters. Ray's Café serves full breakfasts and bacon sandwiches. Chris's Café is currently being 'done up' but is likely to offer the same sort of fare. *Open 03.00-12.00 (though you won't get much after 10.00) Tue-Sat only.* No credit cards. **£**

Blacksmith's Arms **2 H2**
257 Rotherhithe St SE16. 01-237 1349. *Fullers.* Pleasant wood-panelled pub with blacksmith's tools on the walls and a large games room at the back. The sofas, little tables and fireplace give a teashop air to one side of the big horseshoe bar. Hot and cold snacks are served on weekday lunchtimes. The upstairs restaurant, The Smithy, serves English food – start with tartlet of quail's eggs or King Richard's leek and mushroom soup, go on to steak and kidney pie or venison, finish with Kentish apple tart. Short, safe wine list. *Pub open normal licensing hours.* No credit cards. **£** *Restaurant open 12.00-14.00 Mon-Fri, 19.00-22.30 Wed-Sat, 12.00-14.30 Sun.* (*Reserve LD*). A.V. **££**

Booty's Riverside Bar **3 B3**
92A Narrow St E14. 01-987 8343. *Free House.* Once a pub called the Waterman's Arms, this was probably the first in Docklands to see the potential and turn itself into a wine bar. Reasonable selection of 50 wines, some cask beer, food at every session – that mythical ploughman can be sure of getting his lunch here, but there are home-made pies and other snacks as well. Wise to book at lunchtime, when it's full of business folk. Nice river views if you go right through to the back. *Stays open till 15.00 at lunchtime Mon-Fri, open 19.00-23.00 only Sat. Closed Sun.* (*Reserve L*). Ax.Dc.V. **£**

Brunswick Arms **4 G4**
78 Blackwall Way E14. 01-515 3068. *Watneys.* Pretty and friendly – incorporating Maybe's Wine and Pizza Bar which means a better wine list than in the average pub, and various sizes of pizza made before your eyes. There are also other interesting snacks, and hefty meals, all at reasonable prices. Looks small, with its raised patio and parlour-like front bar, but it extends back through a central lounge bar to a games room. Clientele a cheerful mix of ages and job descriptions. Traditional Sunday lunch must be booked in advance; pizzas can be taken out; private parties catered for. *Open normal licensing hours Mon-Sat. Sun, reservation only.* No credit cards. **£-££**

Byron's Licensed Restaurant **1 C3**
224 Tower Bridge Rd SE1. 01-403 4704. Pink and green and pretty with little green tables, a bar to one side, and a wide window which opens on to the street for the sale of ice creams and drinks in summer. Serves full breakfasts, coffee and snacks, and hot meals. The menu has

plenty of pasta dishes, but also steaks, burgers and scampi. *Open 08.00-21.30 Mon-Sun.* No credit cards. **£-££**

Café du Commerce **6** F1
Business Efficiency Centre, 3 Limeharbour E14. 01-538 2030. Very busy, highly glossy venue in which to breakfast on champagne, smoked salmon and scrambled eggs, and croissants – newspapers provided. By lunchtime a full à la carte and a set menu are in force featuring such delights as foie de veau, timbale, fresh Scotch salmon, jugged hare with honey and cinnamon, and guinea fowl. In the afternoon the extensive bars are open for wines, champagne, cocktails, spirits, but the food is limited to charcuterie, cheese, and steak sandwiches. The Folly House in the same complex, which has just opened, has an even larger menu and will feed you lavishly throughout the evening to the soft sounds of a string quartet. *Café du Commerce open 08.00-17.00 Mon-Fri only. The Folly House open 08.00-24.00 Mon-Sun. (Reserve LD).* A.Ax.Dc.V. **££-£££+**

Café in the Park **6** G3
Millwall Park (Douglas Place entrance) E14. 01-987 7273. A handy pit stop for hot snacks and cold drinks – or cold snacks and hot drinks. Unlicensed. *Open 09.00-14.30 Mon-Fri, 09.00-11.45 Sat. Closed Sun.* No credit cards. **£**

Café Pelican **1** B3
Hay's Galleria, Tooley St SE1. French-style brasserie which plans to open in early summer 1988. The operation will be similar to their branch in St Martin's Lane – which is happy to be telephoned for information on 01-379 0309.

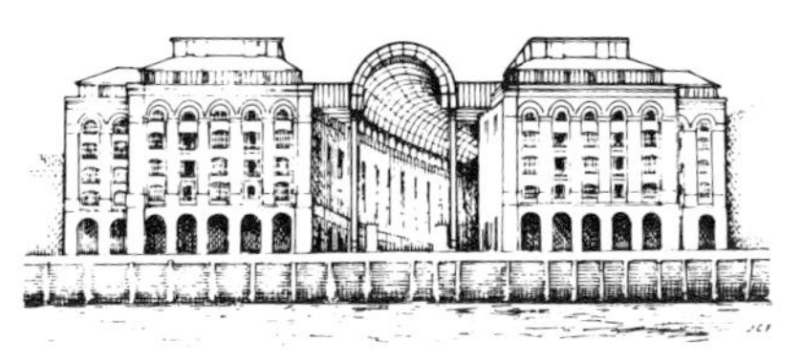

Hay's Galleria

The Caxton **2** E2
50 The Highway E1. 01-480 5599. *Watneys.* Comfortable pub, with a garden, where you can get hot meals on weekday lunchtimes and light snacks on weekday evenings. Newspaper orientated decor – the *Chicago Daily Tribune* and the *News Chronicle* feature on the walls – seems to have attracted staff from News International. Occasional live music in the evening. *Open normal licensing hours.* No credit cards. **£**

Charlie Brown's **3** D3
114-116 West India Dock Rd E14. 01-987 6889. *Charrington.* Charlie Brown was a well-known East End father-figure, money lender and agony uncle who had a magnificent East End funeral in 1932. His pub is now Irish-run and rather gruff – but if you feel the need for a curry, a Guinness and possibly some live music it might be worth a visit. *Open normal licensing hours.* No credit cards. **£**

Churchill's **12** F3
206 Albert Rd E16. 01-511 1803. *Free House.* Modern estate pub with loud taped music, bench seating outside and hot and cold snacks at every session. Plans to introduce 'theme food' but hasn't quite hit on the theme yet. Crowded with the nearby workforce at lunchtimes and popular with residents in the evening. Regular disco on a Friday evening. *Open normal licensing hours.* No credit cards. **£**

City Brasserie **11** D2
London City Airport, Gate 20, King George V Dock, Connaught Rd E16. 01-474 3065. The airport brasserie looks over the dock and the runway with a view not only of aeroplanes taking off and landing but also of the exertions of the Waterski Club. Open to the general public as well as passengers, it offers light or hearty breakfasts and à la carte luncheons – filled baguettes, croissants baked on the premises, croque monsieur, salads and a reasonable wine list. Can also cater for private functions. *Open 07.00-21.00 Mon-Fri, 07.00-14.00 Sat, 14.00-19.00 Sun (but there are plans to extend the hours considerably).* A.Ax.Dc.V. **£-££**

City Pride **3** D5
1 West Ferry Rd E14. 01-987 3516. *Watneys.* Large, recently refurbished pub that used to be called the City Arms and to face in the opposite direction. Externally has the appearance of a vaguely colonial cricket pavilion with balcony: all white and green, set in a huge beer garden that overlooks Heron Quays across the road. Inside it is kitsch-rich with loud music and framed witticisms. Favoured by young business people. Usual hot and cold bar food every session except Sunday. *Open normal licensing hours.* No credit cards. **£**

Dickens Inn **1** D2
St Katharine Docks E1. 01-488 2208. *Free House.* Fine views of the yacht marina and Tower Bridge from this artfully converted warehouse which was dismantled and

reassembled here, and is now one of the most popular pubs in London. Exposed beams, antique furniture, a brass-topped bar and sawdust on the floor add atmosphere. Pub grub in the Tavern Room on the ground floor; traditional English and classical French dishes in the first-floor Pickwick Room; fish in various forms and sauces in the top-floor Dickens Room. *Tavern open normal licensing hours. Restaurants open 12.00-15.00 & 18.30-22.30 Mon-Sun.* (*Reserve LD*). A.Ax.Dc.V. **££**

Dorset Arms **6 G2**
379 Manchester Rd E14. 01-987 3397. *Watneys*. Smart, modern interior in an old building, with a grassy garden at the side, and also a paved barbecue area decorated with old dockside artefacts. Despite its refurbishment it has great charm and the feel of a family local where old men shed their shoes and dogs wait for dropped crisps. Food at every session and the menu is more imaginative than usual – burgers and grills are there but they do interesting things with fish, too. *Open normal licensing hours*. No credit cards. **£**

Essex Arms **7 C3**
Victoria Dock Rd E16. 01-476 2726. *Courage*. A bit of an oasis in a Docklands desert – family pub offering good hot lunches on weekdays and with the added bonus of a small garden. Very much a local at weekends, with darts and pool played regularly, and a disco on Saturday evening. *Open normal licensing hours*. No credit cards. **£**

Ferry House **6 F4**
26 Ferry St E14. 01-987 5141. *Courage*. Small, friendly, busy – it seems more likely that it was built on the site of the old ferry house than that this was the ferry house itself. Light lunchtime snacks on weekdays. *Open normal licensing hours*. No credit cards. **£**

Five Bells & Bladebone **3 C3**
27 Three Colt St E14. 01-987 2329. *Ind Coope*. The 'five bells' used to be rung in the nearby docks to mark the time of 14.30. The 'bladebone' may have been added because the pub was built on the site of an abattoir or because, when the abattoir was operational, the bones were sold off cheaply after the better cuts had travelled up west. Theme of the pub is boats, old tea clippers and Docklands tools and artefacts. Bar snacks at lunchtimes. *Open normal licensing hours*. No credit cards. **£**

The George **6 F2**
114 Glengall Grove E14. 01-987 2954. *Watneys*. Two-bar pub with a pretty beer garden – a relative newcomer to the area, built in the 1930s. The usual bar snacks, well-filled rolls, and Ruddles to drink. One of the 'Marketing Support Docklands Tours' regularly calls in here on its evening jaunt. Opposite, where the filling station now stands, were 'the stones', the cobbles where dockers hoping for work stood, waiting to be called-on. *Open normal licensing hours*. No credit cards. **£**

Good Friends **3 C3**
139-141 Salmon Lane E14. 01-987 5541. Strictly speaking, this is outside the area, just to the north of Commercial Road, but worth including as one of the best of the 'Friends' group of Cantonese restaurants. Large, simple, reliable – try spring rolls, roast duck, stuffed chicken, or anything made with fish, fresh from nearby Billingsgate. Unlicensed, bring your own wine. *Open 12.00-15.00 & 18.00-24.00 Mon-Sun.* (*Reserve LD*). A.Ax.Dc.V. **££**

The Grapes **3 C4**
76 Narrow St E14. 01-987 4396. *Taylor Walker*. Atmospheric riverside pub, with good Thames views from the veranda. Said to be the original of the Six Jolly Fellowship Porters in Dickens' *Our Mutual Friend*. Excellent bar snacks and an upstairs fish restaurant of high renown, serving fish soups, oysters in season, Dover sole and several puddings. *Pub open normal licensing hours (till 15.00) lunchtime*. No credit cards. **£** *Restaurant open 12.00-14.30 Mon-Fri, 18.00-22.00 Mon-Sat. Closed Sun.* (*Reserve LD*). A.V. **£££+**

The Gun **4 G5**
27 Coldharbour E14. 01-987 1692. *Taylor Walker*. Engaging old pub with a slight list, standing at the corner of a demure residential street like a discreet drunk. Three bars, and a large balcony overhanging the water from which to contemplate the Blackwall Power Station environs. There are rumours of an assignation between Admiral Lord Nelson and Lady Hamilton upstairs, but who can say . . . Good bar lunches but no food in the evenings or at weekends. *Open normal licensing hours*. No credit cards. **£**

Harry's Java Brasserie **2 F3**
78-80 Wapping Lane E1. 01-481 4282. Attractive and unusual restaurant on two floors of a small warehouse – surprisingly pretty and cosy-looking despite exotic marble floors and gilded pillars. There are basketwork chairs, good linen, lights gleaming from the overhead beams, an extremely well-stocked bar, an interesting In-

donesian menu upstairs, and a French *prix fixe* menu downstairs. Will probably extend the opening hours to include breakfasts when the surrounding developments are complete and demand justifies it. Also has car parking space – very handy in narrow Wapping Lane. *Open 12.00-23.30 Mon-Sun.* (*Reserve LD*). A.Ax.Dc.V. **£££**

Horniman at Hay's **1** B3
Hay's Galleria, Tooley St SE1. 01-407 3611. Huge brasserie-style pub with extravagant pillared and gilded interior and a vaguely Hollywood-Egyptian slant to the decor. It is open all day every day for breakfasts, lunches, dinners, snacks, afternoon tea, ice creams – and drinks when the fully licensed bar is open. There are seats outside beside the river with good views of the north bank, Tower Bridge and HMS *Belfast*. Staff are young and amiable – service was exceedingly slow, but may have speeded up by now. *Open 08.00-23.00 Mon-Sat, 09.30-22.00 Sun.* A.Ax.Dc.V. **£-££**

The House They Left Behind **3** C4
27 Ropemaker's Fields, Narrow St E14. 01-538 5102. *Watneys*. Thoroughly friendly and welcoming, its long narrow bar decorated with prints and riveting newspaper cuttings and policed by an affable ginger mouser. Builders drink at the front, *Telegraph* staff in the middle; there is an eating area at the back. Cheerful chef produces home-made pies, burgers, sandwiches and good coffee at every session, seven days a week. There are real ales and a sensible wine list as well as the usual spirits. Friday lunchtime and Saturday night a jazz pianist entertains – and guitar owners have been known to give an impromptu recital. *Open normal licensing hours.* A.Ax.Dc.V. **£**

Island Gardens Café **6** G4
Island Gardens, Saunders Ness Rd E14. No phone. Simple park caff, serving snacks, sandwiches and hot and cold drinks. Unlicensed. *Open 07.00-20.00 (dusk in winter) Mon-Sun.* No credit cards. **£**

The Ivories **1** D2
43 East Smithfield E1. 01-481 2152. The name is dual purpose – the establishment is opposite the Ivory House entrance to St Katharine Docks, and it is a piano bar. In its voluptuous pink interior a gathering of yuppies and East Enders enjoys cocktails, wine and music – usually piano music, though there is often a band at weekends. A bar rather than a restaurant, it will nevertheless feed you a hamburger, steak sandwich or seafood special. Aims to make itself 'the hottest place in town'. *Open 12.30-15.00 & 18.30-11.00 Mon-Thur, 12.30-15.00 & 18.30-24.30 Fri, 18.30-24.30 Sat. Closed Sat lunch & Sun.* No credit cards. **£-££**

Kingsbridge Arms **5** D1
154-156 West Ferry Rd E14. No phone. *Whitbread*. Genial, slightly dusty local where *Telegraph* staff, among others, congregate to drink Wethereds and draught Guinness. Snacks at lunchtime on weekdays only. *Open normal licensing hours. Closed Sat lunchtime.* No credit cards. **£**

Ma Averil's Riverview Café **2** G2
King Edward Memorial Park E1. No phone. Simple and unpretentious, serving sandwiches, snacks and hot and cold drinks. Unlicensed. *Open 08.00-dusk (19.00 in summer) Mon-Sun.* No credit cards. **£**

Mala Restaurant **1** D2
St Katharine Docks E1. 01-480 6356. Smart restaurant by the marina serving Tandoori and other Indian dishes – try king prawn masala or murg jelfarezi. Take-away service, too. *Open 12.00-15.00 & 18.00-22.30 Mon-Sun.* (*Reserve LD*). A.Ax.Dc.V. **££**

The Mayflower **2** G4
117 Rotherhithe St SE16. 01-237 4088. *Charrington*. Famous, partially rebuilt Tudor inn overlooking the river – originally called the Shippe, it changed its name when the *Mayflower*, which sailed from this part of the river, reached America. Drink on the wooden veranda outside while the Thames tides slosh in and out beneath. Bar snacks are available at lunchtimes on weekdays. Wise to book for the restaurant upstairs, which has an international menu – Dover sole, chicken chasseur, lamb curry. *Pub open normal licensing hours.* No credit cards. **£** *Restaurant open 12.30-15.30 & 19.30-21.30 Tue-Fri, 19.30-21.30 Sat. Closed Sat lunchtime, Sun & Mon.* (*Reserve LD*). A.Ax.Dc.V. **££**

New Friends Chinese Restaurant **3** D3
53 West India Dock Rd E14. 01-987 1139. Not much more than 20 yards from Limehouse Police Station stands this one-roomed, fully licensed Cantonese restaurant, as friendly as its name, with seating for 50-70 people (though they freely admit that 70 is a 'bit squeezy'). Large menu includes such favourites as roast duck, sweet and sour pork, crackling pork, or deep-fried chicken Cantonese style. *Open 12.00-23.00 Sun-Wed, 12.00-23.30 Thur-Sat.* (*Reserve LD*). A.Ax.Dc.V. **££**

Old Friends Chinese Restaurant **3** B3
659 Commercial Rd E14. 01-790 5028. Large, fully licensed Chinese restaurant and

bar, which is now independent from the 'Friends' group, but keeps the name. Both Cantonese and Pekingese dishes are served here. Parties who book in advance can sit down to whole suckling pig – for the rest there is a choice of some 120 specialities including Peking duck, aromatic duck, prawn Cantonese style and spicy beef. *Open 12.00-23.00 Sun-Thur, 12.00-23.30 Fri & Sat.* (*Reserve LD*). A.Ax.Dc.V. **££**

Old Justice **2 E4**
94 Bermondsey Wall East SE16. 01-237 3452. *Charrington.* A well-hidden riverside pub with views along to Tower Bridge; a traditional family local which doesn't go in for food in a big way but will make you a sandwich anytime. Paul McCartney filmed part of his video *Lonely Nights* here and his fans sometimes visit. *Open normal licensing hours.* No credit cards. **£**

Old Star **2 F3**
14 Watts St E1. 01-481 1934. *Taylor Walker.* Quiet street corner local which is about to be refurbished as 'Turner's Old Star' because the painter held regular assignations here. Bar snacks and full meals lunchtime and evening. *Open normal licensing hours.* No credit cards. **££**

The Peking **3 D3**
92 West India Dock Rd E14. 01-987 3418. Authentic, unlicensed Chinese restaurant in the old Chinese mission house (no corkage charge). Retains its honest charm despite the fact that it has been discovered by newly located media types (though no one visits the lavatories twice). *Open 12.00-24.00 Mon-Sun.* (*Reserve LD*). A.V. **££**

Prince of Orange **2 H6**
118 Lower Rd SE16. 01-237 9181. *Truman.* Well known as an excellent jazz pub, it has recently been refurbished. No meals at lunchtime (except Sunday), but sells pizzas in the evening. *Open normal licensing hours.* No credit cards. **£**

Prospect of Whitby **2 G2**
57 Wapping Wall E1. 01-481 1095. *Watneys.* Historic Docklands tavern with famous associations – Samuel Pepys and Rex Whistler drank here, and so did Judge Jeffreys, not to mention such numbers of thieves and smugglers that it came to be known as the 'Devil's Tavern'. Restaurant terrace overlooks the Thames – it's wise to reserve a table to enjoy the international cuisine and seasonal specialities. Live music nightly in the downstairs bar. Very popular with tourists. *Pub open normal licensing hours.* No credit cards. **£** *Restaurant open 12.00-15.00 & 18.00-21.30 Mon-Sun. Closed Sat lunch.* (*Reserve LD*). A.Ax.Dc.V. **£££**

Quayside Restaurant **1 C2**
World Trade Centre, St Katharine Docks E1. 01-481 0972. The World Trader's Luncheon Club opens to the public as a restaurant in the evenings and for lunch on a Sunday. Very smart and efficient, with luxury-class food; spinach and bacon salad, lobster, sole, beef, mushroom and Stilton pie, rich puds, good cheeseboard and extensive wine list. *Open 18.30-23.00 Mon-Sat, 12.00-14.30 Sun.* (*Reserve LD*). A.Ax.Dc.V. **£££+**

Rogue's Kitchen **2 G4**
St Marychurch St SE16. 01-237 7452. Family owned restaurant offering unusual Louisiana Creole food and Mexican dishes. Try Jambalaya seafood, steak in hot chilli sauce, apple pie. Unprepossessing exterior but attractively chummy inside, cluttered with old photos and nick-nacks. *Open 18.00-22.30 Wed-Sat only. Lunches for groups by arrangement.* (*Reserve LD*). No credit cards. **££**

Royal Pavilion **12 E3**
2 Pier Rd E16. 01-476 2455. *Courage.* This large, attractive pub, right on the riverside, was just reopening at the time of going to press. The new licensee plans to run it as a traditional East End family pub with a separate restaurant area serving simple home-cooked meals at every session, seven days a week; live music at weekends. Other advantages are the large car park, the riverview terrace and the partially enclosed patio area where you can drink partially outside if the weather is partially nice. *Open normal licensing hours.* No credit cards. **£**

The Ship **2 G4**
St Marychurch St SE16. 01-237 4103. *Youngs.* Pleasant family local in the appealing Rotherhithe village. There's a beer garden at the back and hot and cold bar snacks at lunchtimes on weekdays. *Open normal licensing hours.* No credit cards. **£**

Ship Yorke **5 A2**
15 Redriff Rd SE16. No phone. *Watneys.* Large one-bar pub with pretty hanging baskets outside and a large secluded patio. Real fire to comfort you in winter and good substantial bar snacks at all times. *Open normal licensing hours.* No credit cards. **£**

SS Yarmouth **1 D2**
St Katharine Docks E1. No phone. Not so much in dry dock as high and dry on the dock. Self-service counter inside dispenses sandwiches, filled baps, cream cakes, hot drinks and ice creams to take away or to eat

on the deck, high above the marina. Billed as a 'steam museum' which means you can put 10p in a slot and watch the steam engine turn over a couple of times. Unlicensed. *Open 08.30-around 17.00 (depending on demand) Mon-Sat*. No credit cards. **£**

The Telegraph **5 D2**
194 West Ferry Rd E14. 01-987 3684. *Watneys*. The old Magnet and Dewdrop has renamed itself – after a ship it says, and certainly there are brass ships' lamps and a sextant inside. Hard to believe, though, that it isn't trying to ensnare nearby *Telegraph* staff with its quasi-wine bar ambience, its telephones available at the tables, and its waitress service for the home-made, and quite varied, pub food. And a very congenial snare it is, too. At the moment food is only available during weekday lunchtimes, but there are plans to extend the operation to every session. *Open normal licensing hours*. A.Ax. **£**

Tides **11 A4**
Thames Barrier Visitor Centre, Unity Way, Eastmoor St SE18. 01-316 4438. Out of the area, on the south side of the river, with stunning views of the Barrier itself. Downstairs there is a snack bar and kiosk, upstairs a licensed restaurant specialising in fish dishes, but with fresh pies, quiches and salads as well. *Open 10.30-17.30 Mon-Sun (with plans to extend the opening hours into the evening)*. No credit cards. **£-££**

Tollgate Tavern **9 D4**
Beckton District Centre, Tollgate Rd E6. 01-476 3716. *Whitbread*. Modern pub with traditional ales, darts and bar lunches – what doesn't come with salad comes with chips. Clientele an easy mix of shoppers and construction workers; decor a cheery mix of brash and genteel with pictures of old dockland and fairy lights in the plastic weeping figs. *Open normal licensing hours*. No credit cards. **£**

Tower Thistle Hotel **1 C2**
St Katharine's Way E1. 01-481 2575. Large and luxuriously appointed modern hotel – much prettier inside than out. The three restaurants, and the Thames Bar with its balcony and Tower Bridge views, are all open to non-residents. **The Carvery**, which has views over St Katharine's Yacht Marina, presents a choice of roast meats and vegetables, with conventional starters and puddings to round out the meal. *Open 06.30-09.30 (for English or Continental breakfast), 12.00-14.30 & 18.00-22.00 Mon-Fri, 18.00-22.30 Sat, 12.15-15.00 Sun*. (*Reserve LD*). A.Ax.Dc.V. **££ The Picnic Basket**, which overlooks the Thames and Tower Bridge, is a blend of brasserie and coffee shop which provides an English or Continental breakfast, a quick snack, light meal or something more satisfying. *Open 07.30-24.00 Mon-Sun*. A.Ax.Dc.V. **£-££ The Princes Room Restaurant**, with its Tower Bridge views and lavishly refurbished interior which boasts a marble dance floor, has a cocktail bar and an à la carte English and Continental menu. It also serves breakfast to those who can rise to such sumptuousness early in the day. *Open 06.30-10.30, 12.30-14.30 & 19.00-22.30 Mon-Sat (closed Sat L). Dinner dances on Fri & Sat*. (*Reserve LD*). A.Ax.Dc.V. **£££**+

Town of Ramsgate

Town of Ramsgate **2 E3**
62 Wapping High St E1. 01-488 2685. *Charrington*. 17thC tavern with a glamorously grisly past. Wapping Old Stairs, alongside, lead down to the post where pirates were chained to be drowned by successive incoming tides, and were the scene of the capture of Colonel Blood who was making off with the Crown Jewels at the time. The 'hanging Judge', Jeffreys, was apprehended within the pub itself, and secret tunnels are said to lead to the Tower of London. Timbered and comfortable with a good range of bar meals at every session and a nice atmosphere. *Open normal licensing hours*. No credit cards. **£**

The Vineyard **1 C2**
International House, St Katharine's Way E1. 01-480 6680. One of the Davy's chain of City wine bars, with a strongly masculine Victorian image – dusty barrels, old prints, sawdust covered floors. Six good house wines and a range of twenty-four more ex-

pensive ones, backed by a choice of ports and sherries and a cold buffet – ham off the bone, roast beef, fresh salmon and gentlemanly sandwiches. *Open 11.00-15.00 & 17.30-20.30 Mon-Fri. Closed Sat & Sun.* A.Ax.Dc.V. **£-££**

Waterman's Arms

Waterman's Arms **6 G3**
1 Glenarnock Av E14. 01-538 0712. *Taylor Walker*. Very large, with comfy sofas, the Arms of the Watermen framed on the wall, and some nice river pictures. Drink Burton's ale and eat food in the chicken and chips or ploughman's lunch range, at every session, seven days a week. Full-size pool table and, sometimes, live music at weekends. *Open normal licensing hours*. No credit cards. **£**

White Swan and Cuckoo **2 F3**
Wapping Lane E1. No phone. *Taylor Walker*. Large wood-floored, wood-panelled bar with Tiffany lamps, pictures of Thames barges on the walls and books on the mantlepiece. Comfortably crowded with local residents, business people and the occasional priest. Hot and cold buffet at one side of the bar serves food at lunchtimes on weekdays. *Open normal licensing hours*. No credit cards. **£**

Young Friends Chinese Restaurant **3 D3**
11 Pennyfields E14. 01-987 4276. One of the popular and reliable 'Friends' group of licensed restaurants serving Cantonese and Pekingese dishes. Favourites with regular customers are aromatic duck or Peking duck, prawns Cantonese style and crispy fried shredded beef. *Open 12.00-24.00 Mon-Sun*. A.Ax.V. **££**

Party Bookings and Business Entertaining

None of the following is open to casual diners, all serve as floating function rooms for a party that is memorably different – and 'very Docklands'! Capacity is about 15 if seated, 45 for a buffet. They have catered for small weddings, business parties and conferences, formal balls and dances, and book launches, among other events.

Aak Salaam **4 E5**
01-538 0911. A 1920s Dutch barge, usually to be found moored at Heron Quays on the Isle of Dogs.

Leven is Strijd **4 E5**
01-987 4002. A Dutch sailing barge, whose name translates 'life is a struggle', permanently moored off Canary Wharf near Limehouse Studios.

Res Nova **4 F5**
01-538 2030. Late 19thC Dutch clipper barge, moored in West India Docks. Elegant and intimate venue for anything from a dinner party for eight up to a business conference. Owned and run by the Café du Commerce.

Scone **4 E5**
01-515 8826. Thames sailing barge, c1919, moored at Marsh Wall, between Heron Quays and Canary Wharf.

SPORT AND RECREATION

In some cases, individual sports – angling, sailing or swimming for example – have their own clubs or specialist centres and these are listed below under the name of the sport itself. But note also the section Parks with Sports Facilities, where you will find football pitches and tennis courts among other things; Sports Centres where tennis, badminton and gymnastics are among the sports catered for; and Watersports Centres where more than one energetic method of getting wet is available.

Angling

This traditional Docklands activity is suffering a little as new developments grow around the docksides. Access to the water is becoming increasingly difficult and there are noticeably fewer fish than there used to be but you can still enjoy fishing if you know where to go and coarse fishing for bream, dace, roach, perch and rudd continues.

Isle of Dogs
Contact Jack Shelton (secretary), Millwall Angling Consortium, 27 Rosemary Close, South Ockenden, Essex RM15 6JJ for information on the individual societies who can issue permits (sae appreciated).

Royal Docks
Contact the London Anglers' Association, Forest Road Hall, Harvey Park Rd E17. 01-520 7477. Membership brings the right to fish an area of the Royal Victoria and the Royal Albert Docks.

Surrey Docks
Contact the Southwark Fishing Preservation Society via Allan Hutchison on 01-691 4769, evenings only. The society holds fishing rights in the area and membership grants you a seasonal fishing pass. Day tickets are also available, apply to Drury Fishing Tackle, 194 Jamaica Rd SE16, 01-237 7702 (**2 E5**).

Riding

Newham Riding Club **11 B2**
92A Camel Rd E16. 01-476 1706. The riding school has been operating in this unlikely spot since the mid-1960s. It is a registered charity financed through fund-raising events and grants from Newham Council and the LDDC, and the charges are kept low to enable local people to learn to ride. There are 14 horses and ponies and 3 instructors. Lessons – for adults and children – take place in the indoor school, with occasional trips to a nearby open space. A Riding for the Disabled scheme is one of the club's main activities and has its own instructor. *Open 08.00-19.00 Mon-Thur, 08.00-16.00 Fri-Sun, lessons 17.00-19.00 Mon-Thur, 09.30-12.30 Sat, 09.30-11.30 Sun.*

Rowing

Poplar, Blackwall & District Rowing Club **6 G4**
Ferry St E14. 01-987 3071. (*Best times to telephone are 17.30-21.00 Tue & Thur.*) Conveniently situated near the Island Gardens Terminus of the Docklands Light Railway. The club – a registered charity – is very welcoming to newcomers, who may 'test row' for a month or so to see if they want to join, and is also highly competitive,

practising on the Thames or Royal Albert Dock and attending regattas all over the south east. They have club boats, from sculls up to eights, and a clubhouse with changing rooms and hot showers, a weights room, a tank for simulated rowing, and a bar and function room. (Please phone for information.) *Open 07.00-23.00 Mon-Sun. Membership fee.*

Royal Albert Dock **11** D1
Contact No: Royal Victoria Dock Project, 01-511 2326. At an early stage of its development as the guide went to press – local clubs currently use the dock for training, leisure and events but as time goes on there will be a more formal structure with charges and also more facilities. Please phone for details.

Sailing

Isle of Dogs Sailing Club **4** G5
Dollar Bay, West India Dock E14. Secretary: Mike Coughlin on 01-987 6097. Sailing and windsurfing for adults, from 18 upwards, with beginners' courses. Sailboards, canoes, rowing boats and a mixture of dinghies (including 5 Wanderers and 2 Wayfarers) are available for members' use. Temporary membership can be taken out if you just want a tuition course. The portacabin club facilities are minimal, but there are plans to move to Millwall in summer 1988 where there is to be a pukka clubhouse and access to the river as well. Contact the above number for an update.

St Katharine's Yacht Club **1** D2
12 Ivory Quay E1. 01-481 8286. Smart but friendly club for boat owners – members tend to be business people and locals. (If your yacht needs a home phone 01-488 2400 for information on moorings.) Dockside facilities include showers and toilets; the clubhouse, with its patio and wide views of the marina, has a bar, lounge, and a restaurant area with a full grill menu backed by ploughman's lunches, seafood platters and salads. There is often a jazz pianist in the evenings and parties are held for special events such as Christmas, Hallowe'en etc. Strictly members only.

Skiing

Beckton Alps **10** E3
Corner Alpine Way/Whitings Way E6. 01-511 0351. The dry ski slope is open to all, though members can enjoy extended hours, special rates and extra facilities. Tuition is available – there's a six-hour course for a set price. Hire of skis is included in all prices – you can take your own but the surface is tough on snow skis. The caravan and portacabins which serve as the administrative centre are to be replaced, just after we go to press, with a brand new

building housing a bar, restaurant, ski shop, workshop, changing rooms, fitness room, sauna, solarium and jacuzzi. *Open 09.00-22.30 Mon-Sat, 09.00-18.00 (to 22.00 for members) Sun. Charge.*

Swimming

Island Baths **6** E1
Tiller Rd E14. 01-987 5211. There is one 27yd (25m) pool, changing rooms, showers and a buffet for soft drinks, tea and beans on toast. There are also regular keep-fit sessions: enquire for times. Launderette, open at the same times as the baths, has large and small machines, dryers and large ironers. On weekdays the baths are used by schools; *on Saturday between 10.00 and 12.00* there is a public 'watersplash' for children, with inflatables competing for pool space with the kids. *Open 12.30-13.30 Mon-Fri, adults only.*

Then 15.30-17.00 Mon & Wed, 15.30-18.00 Tue, 15.30-20.00 Thur & Fri, 15.30-19.00 Sat. Closed Sun. Charge.

On the same premises is the Arts Centre, 01-987 7925. This is a community arts centre running workshops in pottery, photography, video, drama and screen printing; they also run 'outreach' workshops around the borough and sometimes put on events and exhibitions. Telephone or call in for details. *Open 10.00-18.00 Mon, Wed & Fri, 10.00-21.00 Tue & Thur.*

St George's Baths **2** F2
The Highway E1. 01-709 9714. There is a large pool, 36yd (33m) long; a small training pool; a keep-fit room with equipment and instructor; changing rooms and showers; and a small buffet for soft drinks, crisps or egg on toast. There is also a public launderette at one end of the building with large and small machines, dryers and large ironers. *Open for an adults only pre-office swim 08.00-09.00 Mon-Fri. Then 09.00-17.45 Mon & Thur, 09.00-18.00 Tue & Sat, 09.00-20.00 Wed & Fri, 08.00-11.45 Sun. Launderette open 07.30-19.30 Mon-Fri, 07.30-18.30 Sat, 08.00-11.45 Sun. Charge.*

Water Skiing

Royal Docks Waterski Club **11** D2
King George V Dock E16. 01-511 2000. The club has two power boats and over a mile of water at its disposal. The course runs parallel with the runway of the new London City Airport. Day membership is available for up to four days, after which annual membership should be taken out. Special courses for beginners and all necessary equipment available for hire. Good changing facilities. *Open 10.00-dusk Mon-Sun. Closed 21 Dec-21 Mar. Charge.*

Wetbiking

London Wetbike Club **8** E4
Unit 1, Gate 3, Royal Victoria Dock, Silvertown Way E16. 01-511 5000/7000. This is the only club in the UK where beginners can have a taste of this still new sport. Open to non-members, who should telephone to book for their first lesson: half an hour on a simulator (and expect to fall off several times), half an hour on the real thing, then you're away. A rescue boat and instructor are always to hand. Wetbikes, wetsuits and lifejackets can be hired. There is a lower age limit of 16 but cheap pillion rides are on offer for younger children. *Open 10.00 to dusk Mon-Sun. Closed Tue mid-Nov–end Mar.*

Windsurfing

Peter Chilvers Windsurfing Centre **7** D4
Gate 6, Royal Victoria Dock, Tidal Basin Rd, off Silvertown Way E16. 01-474 2500. A private venture owned by the man who claims to have invented the windsurf board. Non-members should book for a Royal Yachting Association-approved course, which lasts a whole day. Boards and wetsuits for hire and for sale. *Open 10.30 to dusk Tue-Sun. Closed Mon.*

Windsurfing

Parks with Sports Facilities

Note that the opening times of these parks vary throughout the year, but the general rule is dawn to dusk.

Beckton Park
There is a huge area of park and playing fields which comes under the main heading of Beckton Park. The individual parks within it are King George V Park, King George Av E6, 01-474 4960. North Beckton District Park, Tollgate Rd E6, 01-511 1501. South Beckton District Park, Strait Rd E6, 01-476 3020. New Beckton Park, Savage Gdns E6, 01-476 5114.
Bowling: greens at New Beckton Park.
Cricket: sixteen cricket pitches in South Beckton District Park and one in New Beckton Park.
Football: two pitches in King George V Park; eleven pitches in South Beckton District Park; four pitches in New Beckton Park.
Pitch and Putt: one 9-hole course at South Beckton District Park.
Tennis: two hard courts in New Beckton Park.
All these parks have changing facilities.

King Edward VII Memorial Park **2** H2
The Highway E1. Pitch booking on 01-790 9365.
Bowling: one green.
Football: one Redgra football pitch with floodlights.
Netball: one hard court.
Tennis: two hard courts.

King George's Fields **2** G5
Lower Rd SE16. Pitch booking on 01-703 3499.
Football: one five-a-side pitch.
Netball: one court.
Tennis: one hard court.

Lyle Park **8** E6
Bradfield Rd, off North Woolwich Rd E16. 01-476 0753. Small local park.
Football: one pitch.
Putting: one green.
Tennis: two hard courts.
Changing facilities and showers.

Mellish Playing Fields and Pavilion **3** A5
Salter Rd SE16. Pitch bookings 01-703 3499.
Cricket: one pitch.
Football: three grass pitches, one with floodlighting.
Running: one track.
There is also a social room, catering facilities, car and coach park, changing rooms and showers.

Millwall Park **6** G3
Manchester Rd E14. Booking on 01-538 4571.
Bowling: greens.
Cricket: one artificial wicket.
Football: one Redgra pitch with floodlighting, three full-sized grass pitches and one junior pitch.
Changing facilities and showers.

Poplar Recreation Ground **4** F3
Hale St E14. Booking on 01-538 4571. Small local park beside St Matthias church.
Netball: two courts.
Putting: one green.
Tennis: two hard courts.
No changing facilities.

Ropemaker's Fields **3** B3
Narrow St E14. Booking on 01-790 9365. Small open space.
Tennis: two hard courts.
No changing facilities.

Royal Victoria Gardens **12** F3
Albert Rd E16. 01-476 3760. Local park with modest sports facilities.
Bowling: greens.
Tennis: two hard courts.
Changing facilities and refreshments.

St Paul's All Weather Games Area **3** B4
Beaton's Walk SE16. 01-703 3499. The title refers to the all-weather tarmac surface – it doesn't mean there's a roof!
Football: one pitch with floodlighting, one five-a-side pitch.
Hockey: one pitch.
Tennis: two hard courts.
Changing facilities.
Open 08.00-dusk Mon-Sun.

Southwark Park **2** G6
Hawkstone Rd SE15. 01-703 3499. Large and well-equipped park and sports ground.
Bowling: greens.
Cricket: one pitch.
Football: one Astroturf with floodlighting; seven grass pitches; four Redgra pitches; two junior pitches.

Netball: four courts.
Putting: one green.
Running: track with floodlighting so you can run after dark in winter.
Swimming: outdoor pool, *open Jun-Sep, 10.00-17.30 Mon-Sun.*
Tennis: four hard courts.
Full changing room and shower facilities.

Sports Centres

All these have indoor sports facilities; some have outdoor sports facilities as well.

George Green's Sports Centre **6 G4**
80 Manchester Rd E14. 01-515 5154. The school uses the facilities during the day, but in the evenings and at weekends they are open to the public.

There are courts, equipment and instructors for badminton, basketball, five-a-side football, martial arts, netball and volleyball. There is also a trampoline and two outdoor courts which can be used for netball, tennis or football training. The centre runs a sports club for disabled people and offers full changing facilities, showers and a cafeteria. *Open 18.00-22.00 Mon-Fri, 10.00-18.00 Sat & Sun.*

Rotherhithe Leisure Centre **2 G5**
Lower St SE16. 01-237 3296. Reopened in March 1988 after refurbishment. It has a full-sized swimming pool, a training pool and a small hall with facilities for tennis, table tennis and badminton. Changing facilities and showers too. Centre works on a two-week timetable. Week one *open 10.30-15.00 Mon, 08.00-15.00 Tue, 13.30-18.30 Wed, 13.30-19.30 Thur, 09.00-15.15 Fri. Closed Sat & Sun.* Week two *open as above Tue-Fri, 10.30-15.30 Sat, 08.00-12.00 Sun. Closed Mon.*

Wapping Sports Centre **2 E3**
Tench St E1. 01-488 9421. Large and well-equipped with facilities for badminton, basketball, five-a-side football, handball, volleyball, tennis (indoor and outdoor courts), table tennis, and the brand new sport of short tennis (played on a smaller than standard court). There are also trampolines, an aerobics hall, a gymnasium and a weight-training room, and courses and classes in keep fit, karate and similar pursuits.

The outdoor tennis court has floodlighting, but the football pitch is suffering from subsidence and it will be some time before it can be used again.

There are changing rooms and showers, a bar for soft drinks and snacks, a lounge area and an art exhibition hall where local artists display their work.

The whole complex can be hired for functions and conferences – Sogat met here during the dispute with News International – and there is seating for 400 delegates. *Open 09.00-22.00, Mon-Fri, 09.00-18.00 Sat, 09.00-19.00 Sun.*

Watersports Centres

Royal Victoria Dock Project **8 E4**
Shed 1, Gate 3, Southside, Royal Victoria Dock, Silvertown Way E16. 01-511 2326. A community-based scheme aimed at providing opportunities for locals to take part in sailing, canoeing, rowing, off-shore cruising and windsurfing, at reasonable rates. It will encourage clubs to be formed, which will then operate independently. Courses are all approved by the Royal Yachting Association or British Canoeing Union. *Open 09.00-17.00 Mon-Sun.*

Shadwell Basin Project, **2 G2**
East London Marine Venture
Shadwell Pier Head E1. 01-481 4210. A registered charity, launched in 1976 to provide adventure activities for young people. Adults may use the facilities at specially allocated times (*18.00-21.00 Tue, 10.30-17.00 Sat*), in return for some voluntary help. Angling, canoeing, sailing and windsurfing have been going since the start – recently they have acquired Peacock Boats from Bangladesh and Dragon Boats from Hong Kong and plan to race them. *Open 09.00-dusk Mon-Sun. Please phone for details.*

Surrey Docks Watersports Centre **5 B2**
Gate 6, Greenland Dock, Redriff Rd SE16. 01-237 4009. Currently for schools and youth groups only, but plans to expand. Holds courses in sailing, rowing, canoeing and windsurfing – equipment for hire, changing rooms, showers and a café. *Open 09.00-dusk Mon-Sun. Please phone for details.*

EVENTS

There are numerous events in Docklands, some organised by the three councils of Newham, Southwark and Tower Hamlets, some by sporting clubs or associations, some by arts groups and some by local communities. A few are regular annual events, one or two are impromptu, many are variable in date. Any event of reasonable size will advertise itself – usually by means of posters or handbills distributed locally.

For information on imminent sporting events contact Sportsline on 01-222 8000 between *10.00 and 18.00 Mon-Sun*; for general information on a variety of Docklands events contact Marketing Support Partnership on 01-538 0022 during office hours. Another good source of information is the *Evening Standard*, published *Mon-Fri*, or the local newspapers.

LOCAL PAPERS

East London Advertiser published every Friday, the main local paper for Tower Hamlets.

Docklands News free weekly paper produced by the LDDC and available from their offices and also local banks, Asda Superstores and other such places.

Docklands Recorder published every Thursday.

The Islander published by the Association of Island Communities, every 6-8 weeks. Free. Delivered throughout the Island, or pick up a copy from the Island Resource Centre, Manchester Rd E14.

Newham Recorder published every Friday – the Royal Docks are in the Borough of Newham.

South London Press published Tuesday and Friday, includes the Surrey Docks area in its coverage.

Sparrow free local council newspaper delivered throughout the Borough of Southwark (which includes Surrey Docks) – copies can be collected at Southwark Town Hall, Peckham Rd SE5.

The following are among the major regular events.

Daily

Ceremony of the Keys **1C2**
Tower of London, Tower Hill EC3. 01-709 0765. Every evening the Chief Warder of the Yeoman Warders of the Tower steps out towards the Byward Tower carrying a lantern and wearing a long red cloak and Tudor bonnet. Escorted by four soldiers from the Brigade of Guards, he locks the West Gates, the Middle Tower and Byward Tower at *21.40 Mon-Sun* in one of the oldest continuous military ceremonies in the world. Apply in writing for tickets to the Governor of the Tower, enclosing an sae, well in advance.

Tower of London

Annual

MARCH/APRIL

The East End Festival (TEEF)
Information from Tower Hamlets Arts and Entertainments on 01-790 1818. Three weeks of lively entertainment and arts related events which take place in community centres throughout Tower Hamlets, always including the George Green's Centre and the Wapping Sports Centre among its venues.

JUNE

Isle of Dogs Carnival
Information on 01-987 3226. A one-day event of long standing. Floats, bands, a Carnival Queen and a procession right around the Island. *Last Sat in Jun.*

JULY

Limehouse Festival
Well publicised locally. A community festival featuring music, dance, exhibitions, events and stalls, which runs for two or three days. *Usually during Jul.*

Doggetts Coat and Badge Race
London Bridge to Chelsea Bridge. Information from Worshipful Company of Fishmongers 01-626 3531. A rowing race for Thames Watermen, sometimes called the 'Watermen's Derby'. Initiated by Thomas Doggett, theatre manager, to commemorate the accession to the throne of George I. Doggett himself made the original provision, in his will, for the winner's coat to be made up and a silver badge attached. *Late Jul.*

Isle of Dogs Agricultural Show
Information from Mudchute Farm 01-515 5901. An extremely popular one-day event – where cattle, goats, dogs, pets, cakes and junior showjumpers carry off prizes and rosettes. Beer tent, side shows, produce stalls, much good humour. *Late Jul/early Aug.*

AUGUST

Annual UK Powerboat Grand Prix
Royal Victoria Dock E16. Information from London Motor Boat Club 01-578 2440 or Marketing Support Partnership 01-538 0022. Noisy, exciting, with national TV and press coverage. *Aug Bank hol.*

Clipper Week
On the Thames in the Greenwich area. Information from the London Borough of Greenwich 01-854 8888x2274/5. A week of river events – rowing and sailing races, sub-aqua competitions, regattas, culminating in the Thames Barge Race from Gravesend to Greenwich. *Towards the end of Aug.*

SEPTEMBER

The Newham People's Festival
Information from London Borough of Newham 01-472 1430x23040. A full week of arts and entertainment in various venues, including some within the Docklands area, culminating in a carnival procession.

GETTING TO AND AROUND DOCKLANDS

See Transport in Docklands map p. 13.

Once a problem, the transport situation has been greatly improved by the opening of the Docklands Light Railway (DLR) and the arrival of the Docklands Clipper single decker bus. The City Airport has made the area, and the City, easily accessible from Europe and other British airports. The Riverbus service, due to commence operations in summer 1988, offers a most attractive and suitable approach. Future plans include a revision of the bus routes and an extension to the DLR. Meanwhile, this is how to get about:

By Air

London City Airport **11** C2
Gate 20, King George V Dock, Connaught Rd E16.
General flight information: 01-474 5555.
Brymon Airways Reservations: 01-476 5000.
Eurocity Express Reservations: 01-511 4200.
London City Brasserie: 01-474 3065.
Officially opened by Her Majesty the Queen on 5 November 1987 the new STOLport (Short Take Off and Landing) is right in the heart of the Royal Docks, its runway lying like the deck of an aircraft carrier between the King George V Dock and the Royal Albert Dock. Although aimed principally at European business people, it also hopes to attract tourists. The small, quiet, 50-seater, De Havilland Dash 7 aircraft of Brymon Airways and Eurocity Express are already taking passengers to and from Paris, Brussels and Plymouth. Destinations to be added to the schedules include Amsterdam, Rotterdam, Düsseldorf, Manchester, Newquay, Jersey and Guernsey.

Airport facilities include short and long-term car parking; car hire; duty free shop; bank and bureau de change; florist and newsagent-cum-confectioner; licensed bars and the London City Brasserie which serves breakfast, lunch and dinner from Monday to Saturday (breakfast and lunch only on Saturday) and dinner on Sunday evening. *Open 07.00-21.00 Mon-Fri, 07.00-14.00 Sat, 14.00-19.00 Sun.* (See Pubs and Restaurants for more details.)

The Business Centre (01-476 3999) which offers secretarial services and offices for short-term hire, plus telex, fax and telephone facilities, should be *open 07.30-20.30 Mon-Fri from early in 1988.*

For those who prefer not to leave the ground, there is a viewing area, and the brasserie, bars and shops (apart from the duty-free) are open to all.

London City Airport

Greenline Coach
A new Greenline Coach Service, No **787**, operates between Victoria Station and the City Airport with stops at Embankment, Blackfriars, Cannon Street Station, Aldgate and All Saints DLR Station. For further information telephone 01-668 7261.

By Docklands Light Railway

Travel enquiries on 01-222 1234. The cost of extending the London Underground system further into Docklands would have been prohibitive. The Docklands Light Railway – a subsidiary of London Regional Transport – was the most efficient option, and the cheapest despite the advanced technology it employs.

The red, white and blue computer-operated trains which glide around Docklands high on their viaducts have great charm and offer stupendous views. After some teething troubles the service now runs regularly, at ten minute intervals, *between 05.30 and 00.30 Mon-Sun*. Though there is no driver each train carries a Train Captain, to check tickets and offer information, who is in two-way radio contact with the control room supervisor of the Operations and Maintenance Centre. Lifts, and platforms at the appropriate height, ensure ready wheelchair access.

The Route At present there are seven-and-a-half miles of track and two routes. Tower Gateway links with the Isle of Dogs, with stations at Shadwell, Limehouse, Westferry, West India Quay, (Canary Wharf to be opened when development complete), Heron Quay, South Quay, Crossharbour, Mudchute and Island Gardens. The other route (the northern spur) extends to Stratford with stations at Bow Church, Devons Road, All Saints, Poplar, West India Quay, (Canary Wharf to open when development complete), Heron Quay, South Quay, Crossharbour, Mudchute and Island Gardens.

There are plans to extend the system westwards to Bank Station, to make a more efficient link with the City, and eastwards to the Royal Docks, London City Airport and Beckton.

Fares These are comparable with fares on the London Underground and all stations will fall into Zones 1, 2 or 3A as defined by LRT – at the moment, pretty well the whole thing is in Zone 2.

Tickets Travelcards and Capitalcards are both valid, and if travelling from outside the area, using the Underground and the DLR, you can buy a through ticket. Alternatively, buy a single ticket (undated) at the DLR station of departure; or buy a pack of tickets (undated) at local shops (usually a newsagent). Because these single and pack tickets are undated they have to be 'validated' immediately before the journey – that is, they must be pushed into the cashcard-style opening in the blue 'totem pole' on the station. This will date and return the ticket. (If using a pack, be sure only to validate one ticket per trip.)

Island Gardens Shop The terminus at Island Gardens is a magnet for tourists because Greenwich, across the river, not only looks beautiful from here but can be reached by way of the foot tunnel. A good place, then, for the DLR Shop with its posters, postcards, souvenirs and guides. *Open 11.00-16.00 Mon-Fri, 11.00-17.00 Sat & Sun.*

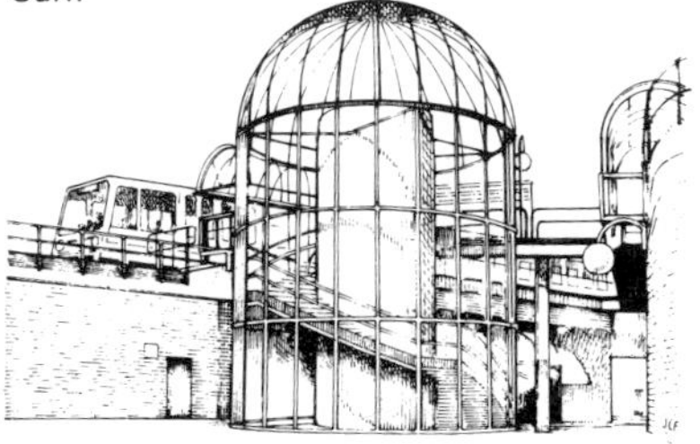

DLR, Island Gardens Station

The Docklands Light Railway
The route followed by the steel rails, which carry the lightweight trains, was carefully planned to make use of existing 19thC railway tracks and viaducts, linked by modern structures and with ultra modern new stations at each stop except Stratford, where an existing platform has been redeveloped. The system took three years to build: at present it has 11 cars, each one 30.6yds (28m) long, weighing 39 tons when empty, with a passenger capacity of 210, a maximum speed of 50 mph and an average running speed of 18½ mph. The route covers 7.5 miles with planned extensions of roughly 5.6 miles; the total cost of the initial system was £77 million.

By Underground

This does not penetrate far into Docklands, but does reach Shadwell, Wapping and Surrey Docks.

The District Line serves Tower Hill and crosses north of Docklands to Mile End and Bow. (The **277** bus and the **D1** both stop at Mile End.) The station at Plaistow, though a couple of miles from the London City Airport, has its own taxi rank.

The Metropolitan Line's East London section links Whitechapel and New Cross/ New Cross Gate via Shadwell, Wapping, Rotherhithe and Surrey Docks.

The Northern Line has a station at London Bridge – from here you can pick up buses **47** and **70** to Surrey Docks.

For further information telephone 01-222 1234.

By Bus

The following are the most useful routes.

1 Runs between Trafalgar Square and Bromley; stops include Strand, Waterloo Bridge, Elephant & Castle, Bermondsey and Surrey Docks.

5 Runs between Waterloo Station and Becontree Heath; stops include Shoreditch, Liverpool Street Station, Aldgate East, Commercial Road (New Road), Limehouse Station, Poplar (Blackwall Tunnel) and Canning Town.

15 Runs between Ladbroke Grove and East Ham; stops include Tower Hill, Aldgate, Commercial Road, Poplar and Canning Town. It also serves Marble Arch, Oxford Circus, Piccadilly and Trafalgar Square – a handy link between East End and West End.

40 Runs between Herne Hill Station and Poplar; stops include Borough Station, London Bridge, Monument, Aldgate, Commercial Road and Limehouse.

47 Runs between Downham and Shoreditch Church; stops include Surrey Docks Station, Rotherhithe, Bermondsey, Tooley Street (Tower Bridge Road) and London Bridge Station.

70 Runs between Victoria and Peckham; stops include Westminster, Waterloo, London Bridge and Surrey Docks. (*Mon-Fri daytime only*.)

70A Runs between Waterloo and Peckham; stops include London Bridge and Surrey Docks. (*Eves & weekends only*.)

106 Runs between Finsbury Park and Isle of Dogs (Asda Superstore, District Centre); stops include Mile End Station, Limehouse, East India Dock Road, Poplar (Blackwall Tunnel), Prestons Road and East Ferry Road.

188 Runs between Euston Station and Greenwich Church; stops include Russell Square, Holborn, Aldwych, Waterloo, Elephant & Castle, Bermondsey, Surrey Docks.

277 Runs between Smithfield and Poplar via the Isle of Dogs; stops include Mile End Station, Limehouse, Millwall Dock and Cubitt Town.

278 Runs between Limehouse and North Woolwich; stops include Bow Bridge, Forest Gate, Victoria and Albert Docks, Connaught Road and Albert Road.

D1 The Docklands Clipper, a single decker which runs during the daytime (*Mon-Sat only*) linking Mile End Station with Cubitt Town and stops at Burdett Road, Limehouse, Canary Wharf, Mastmaker Road, Lighterman's Road, Millharbour, Daily Telegraph, Marsh Wall, Limeharbour, Isle of Dogs (Asda Superstore, District Centre) and Manchester Road.

LRT produces free bus guides, complete with route maps, including a Night Bus (Night Owls) Guide. For further information on how to get there by bus, telephone 01-222 1234.

By British Rail

South of the river, trains link London Bridge Station with South Bermondsey. Information on 01-928 5100.

North of the river, the North London Line, which runs a regular daily service from Richmond in Surrey to North Woolwich, has stations at Stratford, West Ham, Canning Town, Custom House, Silvertown and North Woolwich. Information on 01-283 7171.

By Riverbus

Thamesline Riverbus
Information on 01-987 0311. The Riverbus service is scheduled to begin operations in early summer 1988. It will run 6 water-jet propelled catamarans, each one with a seating capacity of 60-70 and a cruising speed of approximately 23 knots. The service will run from Chelsea to Greenwich and back, with 7 pier stops in between. At the time of going to press the pier stops were still under discussion, but the likely candidates are Charing Cross Pier (definite), Festival Pier, London Bridge City, Swan Lane, Tower to Wapping area (pier as yet unspecified), West India Pier (definite), and Greenwich Pier. Boats will run at 12-15 minute intervals between *07.00-22.00 Mon-Sun*. Prices yet to be determined (season ticket facilities likely), one boat may be available for charter.

By Taxi

The famous London black taxis are reliable but are not yet a common sight in Docklands. There is a taxi rank at London City Airport, or telephone Radio Taxicabs, 01-272 0272, Owner Driver's Radio Taxi Service, 01-268 4848 or Computercabs 01-286 0286.

If opting for a mini-cab choose a firm based in the area – the likelihood is that the driver will know the way and which roads are reasonably clear and which currently blocked by construction traffic, possibly causing delays.

Mile End Cabs
Mile End Tube Station E1. 01-980 1433.

Smart Cars **3** D3
6 West India Dock Rd E14. 01-987 1888.

Station Cars **4** F3
172A East India Dock Rd E14. 01-538 3020/3022.

By Car

The principal route through Docklands north of the river is the busy A13 which enters the area from the west via Stepney and links with the M25 London orbital route to the east of Newham. To the south, Tooley Street – which becomes Jamaica Road and then Lower Road – by-passes Surrey Docks while the parallel Salter Road and Rotherhithe Street loop around the promontory formed by Rotherhithe.

The planning and building of new roads is already in hand. These will include a relief road between South Woodford and Barking, which will link the M11 to the A13. There are also hopes of a new road bridge across the Thames at Woolwich – the so-called East London River Crossing (ELRIC) – but a lengthy public inquiry has not yet made its views on this known. The Docklands Northern Relief road is already underway – it will run south of, and parallel to, the A13. For those who need to hire a car, two major firms have branches at London City Airport.

Godfrey Davis: 01-511 1149
Hertz: 01-511 2746.

Tours

A guided tour is an excellent way to get the feel of the place before exploring on your own.

COACH AND CAR TOURS

Docklands Tours **1** C2
Depart from Tower Hill Underground Station. Details and booking on 01-252 0742 or 01-515 0960. The tour guides are local – one from Bermondsey and one from the Isle of Dogs – and insert local news and views into their historical commentary. They already operate regular coach tours north of the river – by summer 1988 they hope to have a tour south of the river extending as far as the Thames Barrier. Booking essential. *Charge. Length of tour approx 2½ hrs.*

Marketing Support Partnership **1** C2
Depart from Tower Hill Underground Station. Details and booking on 01-538 0022 or 01-515 3000x3515. Organises two or three different coach tours, north of the river, with commentary and a stop at the LDDC Visitor Centre for coffee and to see the audio-visual presentation. Also do a pricier 'limousine tour' in a private car with a local driver; commentary highly entertaining mix of unashamed gossip and solid fact, and the route is more flexible. Booking essential. *Charge. Length of tour approx 2½ hrs.*

Museum in Docklands Tour
Depart from Museum of London, London Wall EC2. Details and booking on 01-515 1162. The Museum in Docklands Team organises regular coach tours, with commentary, of the area north of the river. The high point is a visit to 'W' Warehouse in the Royal Docks to see some of the exhibits owned by the museum – machinery, craftsmen's tools, fascinating items relating to the import of wine and tobacco – the only chance to see the exhibition until the museum acquires and prepares its own premises. (Portaloo and soft drink dispenser, but take your own sandwiches.) Booking essential. *Charge. Length of tour approx 3 hrs.*

RIVER TRIPS

As yet, there are no river trips centring on the Docklands area, but those which go from Westminster or the Tower out to Greenwich or the Thames Flood Barrier do pass through Docklands. Some have running commentaries which will expound on the death of the old docks and their new role. The London Visitor Centre offers a recorded River Boat Information Service on 01-730 4812.

Campion Launches **6** G5
01-305 0300. Runs daily trips from Greenwich Pier to the Thames Barrier. Variable times.

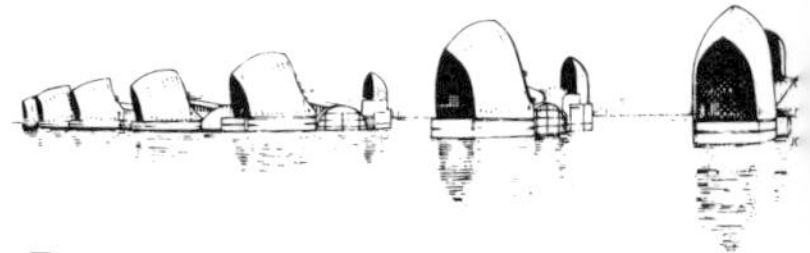

Thames Barrier

Catamaran Cruisers
01-839 3572. Runs trips from Charing Cross Pier to the Tower and Greenwich at 45-minute intervals between *10.30 and 15.45 Mon-Sun*. Also runs luncheon and disco cruises – enquire for times and booking.

London Launches
01-930 3373. Runs trips from Westminster Pier to the Thames Barrier at *11.15 and 13.30 Mon-Sun*.

Tidal Cruises
01-928 9009 or 01-839 2164. Runs luncheon and disco cruises. Enquire for times and booking.

Tower Pier Launches **1** B2
01-488 0344. Runs trips between the Tower and Westminster and between the Tower and Greenwich at 50-minute intervals between *10.50 and 16.00 Mon-Sun*.

Westminster Passenger Services Association
01-930 4097. Runs trips to the Tower and Greenwich from Westminster and Charing Cross Piers at 30-minute intervals between *10.30 and 16.00 Mon-Sun*.

LONDON DOCKLANDS GUIDE

INDEX

INDEX